More praise for *What's Yo*

"A scrupulous and absorbing survey. . . . Language, as [Dennis] Baron eloquently shows, works as a dynamic democracy, not as rule by experts. The sticklers may not like 'they' (singular) but they (plural) will eventually have to bow to the inevitable."

—Joe Moran, *New York Times Book Review*

"Grammar has rarely produced as much public acrimony as in the battle over pronouns being waged around the world. . . . Many fulminating commentators spy political correctness running amok yet again. Into the breach comes a useful corrective in the form of Dennis Baron's well-timed new book, *What's Your Pronoun?*"   —*Economist*

"Learned and entertaining."   —Oliver Kamm, *Times* (UK)

"A delightful account of the search for . . . 'the missing word': a third-person singular, gender-neutral pronoun."

—Amia Srinivasan, *London Review of Books*

"A meticulous, consummate dissection of the pronoun wars in which [Baron] outlines how the conversations and arguments being made against flexibility (and pronoun innovations) are not new ones. . . . Offers hope for the pronoun battle the LGBTQ community finds itself waging with those who would deny many the right to be acknowledged in the manner in which they identify."

—Otamere Guobadia, *Attitude*

"Based on decades of research, Baron's masterly work documents the historical and continued importance of personal pronouns. Those interested in gender politics or English grammar, or who feel that 'he' and 'she' are inadequate, would benefit greatly from perusing this book."   —*Library Journal*, starred review

"Controversies over gender-neutral pronouns, in which language becomes the surrogate for addressing deep social questions, have been going on for centuries. *What's Your Pronoun?* is the most authoritative treatment to date of these issues, and should be required reading for anyone interested in the linguistic expression of gender."
        —Geoff Nunberg, UC Berkeley, and commentator on *Fresh Air*

"Dennis Baron has spent years researching the quest for a gender-neutral third-person singular pronoun in English. Lively, accessible, and full of fascinating details, *What's Your Pronoun?* will appeal to anyone with an interest in linguistic and cultural history."
        —Deborah Cameron, Worcester College, University of Oxford

"An entertaining and thoroughly documented account of two centuries' worth of attempts to solve the problem of the English language's 'missing word.' . . . [Baron] digs deeply into the legal and cultural implications of pronoun usage. . . . [His] 'annotated historical lexicon' of more than 250 gender-neutral pronouns [is] a gold mine for readers who delight in the strangeness of language, as well as a clear demonstration of the thorniness of the issue."   —*Publishers Weekly*

"Catnip for the grammarian, especially the culturally and politically conscious variety."   —*Booklist*

"A thorough history of pronoun debates. . . . The author's playful tone imbues the text with friendly sensitivity, and readers will appreciate his decades of research and meticulous attention to documents and sources. The result is a book that reflects the transformational capacity of language. A lively book for language lovers, those confused about uses of they/them, and anyone curious about writing while gendered."   —*Kirkus Reviews*

"A gem of a book. Captivating and filled with insight, *What's Your Pronoun?* entertains, enlightens, and pulls us joyfully into rethinking our ideas about what's new and old in language."
—Shirley Brice Heath, Stanford University

"Pronouns seem a bit of a mess of late in American English, and Dennis Baron shows us the plain sense in what may seem chaotic. The final chapter, which lists the attempts over the centuries to come up with a new gender-neutral pronoun—anyone for *hesh*?—is worth the price of the ticket."
—John McWhorter, Columbia University, and host of *Slate*'s language podcast *Lexicon Valley*

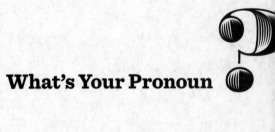

What's Your Pronoun

Also by Dennis Baron

What's Your

Pronoun

Beyond He & She

Dennis Baron

LIVERIGHT PUBLISHING CORPORATION

A Division of W. W. Norton & Company

Independent Publishers Since 1923

For information about permission to reproduce selections from this book, write to
Permissions, Liveright Publishing Corporation, a division of W. W. Norton & Company, Inc.,
500 Fifth Avenue, New York, NY 10110

For information about special discounts for bulk purchases, please contact
W. W. Norton Special Sales at specialsales@wwnorton.com or 800-233-4830

Manufacturing by LSC Communications, Harrisonburg
Book design by Abbate Design
Production manager: Anna Oler

ISBN 978-1-63149-871-8 pbk.

Liveright Publishing Corporation, 500 Fifth Avenue, New York, N.Y. 10110
www.wwnorton.com

W. W. Norton & Company Ltd., 15 Carlisle Street, London W1D 3BS

1 2 3 4 5 6 7 8 9 0

for Iryce

Contents

What's Your Pronoun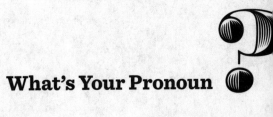

Introduction

P*ronouns are suddenly sexy.* They're in the air, on the news, all over social media, generating discussion pro and con. Or at least one pronoun is: the third-person singular gender-neutral pronoun. Yes, the pronoun *without* sex is suddenly sexy. People are asking each other, "What's your pronoun?"—it's the new "Hello, my name is _____." And sometimes they don't even wait to be asked. They introduce themselves with "I'm Alex. My pronouns are *they, them, their.*" Or "*Ze, hir, hirs.*" Or they put it in their profile:

> **Dr. Andrew Foles** @drandrewcomic
> I'm a linguist and a comic book
> editor @comicsuniv. I also have
> experience herding sheep. He/him.

Pronouns are even on TV. In 2019, in a scene from the long-running BBC police procedural *Silent Witness*, Nick, a suspect in a series of murders at a transgender support center, asks an investigator, "What gender pronouns are you going to use for me in your report?" The investigator responds, "What would you like me to use?" And Nick replies, "She, please." The investigator honors that request.[1]

● ● ●

"What's your pronoun?" is an invitation to declare, to honor, or to reject, not just a pronoun, but a gender identity. And it's a question about a part of speech. Repeat: a question about a part of speech.

A new report by the Pew Research Center confirms that most Americans have heard of gender-neutral pronouns and 18 percent know someone who uses them.[2] It used to be nerdy to discuss parts of speech outside of grammar class. Now it's cool. When the talk turns to "What's your pronoun?" suddenly everybody has an opinion, not just about pronouns, but about *that* pronoun. English has masculine and feminine and neuter pronouns, but it is missing a pronoun for someone whose gender is unknown, unclear, nonbinary, or "other." For centuries, grammarians recommended generic *he* in such cases. But generic *he* turns out to be not so generic: too often *he* means "only men."

That's why some people claim we need a new pronoun. And there's no shortage of people eager to supply the missing word by coining pronouns like *zie* or *tey*. The grammar sticklers are always sure that English speakers don't need any new pronouns, they've gotten along just fine with generic *he*, thank you very much. Fortunately, and apologies if you are one of them, the sticklers are becoming hard to find. And a growing number of people are realizing that we've had the missing word all along: it's singular *they*.

At a recent dinner with friends, a Turkish electrical engineer and an American biologist suddenly veered into a debate over two gender-neutral pronouns. Turkish pronouns have no gender, the engineer explained, so why does English need gender? The biologist said singular *they* allowed him to trash another colleague's work without mentioning their gender. The engineer objected that *they* was plural, so why use it for one person? He had a better idea: "Just

My pronouns are ⚲ and ⚢.

pick a pronoun—pick *she* why don't you—and use it for everyone. Why can't you English speakers manage to do that?"

What's Your Pronoun? is a book about why we English speakers can't manage to do that. Maybe someone tells you their pronouns are *zie* and *hir,* and you wonder, *Where is that coming from?* Or maybe you know that it comes from a way of looking at gender as a sliding scale and not a simple binary. Or that gender, like language, is a social construct, not a scientific constant. Or maybe you believe that gender is a biblical truth or the result of that X and Y chromosome thing. Or maybe the whole gender debate just isn't on your radar. But if you want to know the stories behind these coined pronouns, or the rise and fall of generic *he,* or the changing status of singular *they,* this book will tell you those stories.

You yourself may have tried to answer the question "What's my pronoun?" If you've already picked one, this book will tell you where it came from, and maybe where it's going. If you don't already have a pronoun, this book will help you find one. Maybe you don't want to be put on the spot about your own gender identity and you wish the whole pronoun thing would just go away. Then this book will tell you about the nonbinary pronouns that provide some breathing room because they sidestep the issue of gender altogether. And even if you think it's a question whose answer is obvious, this book will help you understand what the fuss about pronouns and gender is all about.

And here's the bonus: You will have read an entire book about a part of speech. And you just might find it informative, useful—and even fun.

● ● ●

Today's sudden interest in personal pronouns is tied directly to the recent focus on gender inclusivity, nonbinary gender, and gender nonconformity. If you google *gender* and *pronoun,* you'll find lots of reports about colleges asking students to declare their pronoun along with their major. Or a story about students resisting such requests, as one did by declaring that his pronoun was *his majesty*.[3] Or students upset that suddenly they have to announce this decision to total strangers when they're not even sure how, or what, to say about their gender identity to their friends and family.[4] Or stories about public figures like Caitlyn Jenner and Chelsea Manning who've changed their pronouns along with their names to match their gender identity. Or prisoners suing for the right to switch their pronoun along with their cell block to better fit who they are, not who their birth certificate says they are. Or parents requiring teachers and friends to refer to their child as *they* or just by the child's name, so that the child can develop their own sense of gender, free from outside influence.[5]

You'll also find people openly mocking gender-neutral pronouns. For instance, when United Airlines decided to add the gender-neutral title *Mx.* to their booking options, saying that people could now fly the way they identify, their Twitter announcement was greeted by a flood of responses along the lines of "I identify as a carry-on bag and will now fly for free."[6]

Attacking pronouns, whether sarcastically or seriously, hasn't stopped the search for a gender-neutral pronoun. For more than two hundred years—long before *transgender* (1974), *cisgender* (1997), and *gender-fluid* (1987) entered our vocabularies—a small but vocal number of writers, editors, and grammarians, mostly men, have lamented the fact that English has no third-person singular, gender-neutral pronoun to refer to both a man and a woman, or to either a man or a woman, or to conceal gender, or to prevent gender from causing a distraction. Recognizing that gender is political as well as grammatical, they've sought a pronoun—some call it "the missing word"—that includes the traditional binary genders, or all genders, and doesn't leave anyone out.

What's Your Pronoun? explores this hunt for the missing word. Those seeking a better way to include all the genders, whether they think of gender as a traditional male/female binary or something more nuanced and complex, have answered the pronoun question in multiple ways. They've coined a new word, like *heer* or *tey*. They've repurposed a current word, like *it* or *one*. They've borrowed a word from another language, like *le* from French, or *hse* from Mandarin. Or they've acknowledged that *they*, like *you*, could be both singular and plural. To be sure, there have been defenders of the status quo who've simply invoked generic *he*, long approved by grammarians who insisted that such use of *he* includes *she*. Some nineteenth-century feminists capitalized on this inclusive *he* by arguing that, if *he* means "she," then surely the voting laws, which always referred to voters as *he*, meant that women could vote. Unfortunately, judges and legislators—all of them men—disagreed. "Of course *he* is generic," they mansplained, "but not for voting."

It wasn't just voting. There have been too many occasions where generic *he* didn't seem generic. For example, one Minnesota public health law, proposed in 1903, decreed, "No person shall kiss another person unless *he* can prove that *he* is free from contagious or infectious diseases."[7] Does *he* in the bill include women who kiss? Or parents kissing children? Or children kissing grandparents? Or politicians kissing babies? Or trans persons? The word *transgender* didn't exist in 1903, but gender dysphoria did. Would people identifying as gender-nonconforming today be bound by that Minnesota *he?*

He is just a pronoun, just a part of speech. But put a pronoun in a law, as some well-meaning Minnesota legislator tried to do, and suddenly, you've got yourself a problem, whether that law is about kissing or about voting. Because the problem's not just about who's kissing who. In 1916, when Jeanette Rankin, of Montana, became the first woman elected to the US House of Representatives, the *Minneapolis Star Tribune* ran this headline challenging the grammatical rule that says the masculine pronoun can refer to women: "Can 'She' Be 'He', a Congressman, and Be Woman?"[8] Pronouns aren't just a part of speech. Pronouns are political.

In 1922, Edith Wilmans became the first woman elected to the Texas State Legislature, prompting a prediction by the *San Antonio Express* that she would not be allowed to serve, because Texas law referred to state legislators as *he.* The *San Antonio Evening News* shrugged off this objection, at the same time reminding readers that the masculine pronoun doesn't just keep women out of the statehouse: "The same pronoun stands between many women and their liberty."[9]

The men who made and enforced the laws insisted the *he* in a statute included women when it came to imposing penalties, as in the Minnesota kissing bill, which would have fined offenders between $1 and $5 (about $30–$150 today). But these same men used the pronoun *he* to exclude women who tried to assert their right to vote or to hold elected office. Or, as the *San Antonio News* wryly observed, when women tried to assert any rights at all.

Confronting generic *he*

Pronoun gender is a hot topic today, but it's hardly a new topic. From the first English grammars in the seventeenth century to the language commentators of the later twentieth, writers who tackled the question of pronoun gender dealt with generic *he* in a number of ways:

➤ Simply decreeing that *he* was generic and assuming that anything else was just plain wrong.

➤ Sensing resistance to generic *he*, but still insisting that *he* was both inclusive and grammatically correct, so no problem, right?

➤ Acknowledging discomfort with generic *he*, but finding no alternative, and feeling compelled to indicate that *he* included *she*—still no problem, right?

➤ Rejecting generic *he* as ambiguous or sexist and using singular *they* instead, defending it as both natural and common, sometimes adding that if *you* could be singular and plural, why not *they* as well?

➤ Rejecting both generic *he* and singular *they* in favor of an invented pronoun, perhaps asking some expert to coin one in order to avoid error and ambiguity.

In addition, any of the above might be accompanied by a condemnation of the compound *he or she*, along with *him or her* and *his or her*, options that are technically grammatical but universally disliked—too long, too awkward, too binary.

A new pronoun would fix all that

Starting in the eighteenth century, a few adventurous souls thought that the best way to deal with the missing word would be to invent one. More than 200 of these pronouns were invented, most of them before the 1970s, and many of them before 1900. There were crackpots coining pronouns, to be sure, but most of the neologists—the new word makers—were writers, educators, or professionals who knew a bit about language and who thought they could improve on a bad situation. Most of the word coiners were men, though a few women got into the act. Some of the word coiners were concerned with gender parity, some with grammatical correctness, and a few of them with both. Some of their proposals were met with mockery and derision, but a few were taken seriously enough to be adopted by small numbers of enthusiasts. Two gender-neutral pronouns, *thon* and *heer,* even made it into major dictionaries, though they were later dropped for lack of use. But most of these pronouns made a small splash and then were lost to history.

The early word coiners were typically concerned with correctness. In their view, the current options were simply wrong. Generic *he* used a masculine pronoun for a woman as well as for a man, violating the rule that pronouns should agree with their antecedents in gender as well as number. Singular *they* used a plural pronoun for a singular noun, violating the number agreement part of that rule. A new pronoun would fix all that.

The pronoun almost everyone already used

The first word coiners didn't care so much about gender politics. That came later. But as women's rights and suffrage grew prominent both in the United States and England after the 1840s, pronouns were discussed by feminists and antifeminists alike. They were discussed by legislators. By grammarians. By editors. And by ordinary people around the dinner table. An article in the *Springfield Republican* in 1896 claimed that these ordinary folk had already found the solution to the missing word. Instead of the generic *he* mandated by grammarians, it was *they:* "At least two men out of three and four women out of five use 'they' already, with sublime contempt for rule."[10] Of course these statistics were a fanciful guess. There was no way in 1896 to tell how many men or women used singular *they,* or any other pronoun. But the *Republican* didn't need hard data to know what was obvious to even the most casual of observers, that almost everyone used singular *they* in speech, and many careful writers used it as well. The *Republican* had an answer to the pronoun question: singular *they.*

●●●

In Chapter 1, "The Missing Word," we'll look at all the options for a gender-neutral or nonbinary pronoun and see why there are only three serious contenders: generic *he,* singular *they,* or a new, coined pronoun. Chapters 2, 3, and 5 explore each of these in historical detail, while Chapter 4 takes on some of the present-day political and legal manifestations of gender pronouns.

In *Chapter 2,* "The Politics of He," we see that the generic masculine was never truly generic: far too many times, *he* meant "only men." As British and American women began to assert their political and economic rights in the nineteenth century, both feminists and antifeminists enlisted the pronoun *he* to support their cause. American suffragists like Susan B. Anthony observed that, when the criminal laws referred to lawbreakers as *he* or *him,* no one doubted that these laws also applied to women. And so both logic and consistency demanded that, when the voting laws referred to voters as *he,* that meant women could vote as well as men. Or so you would think. As you'll see in this chapter, it didn't turn out to be that simple.

Chapter 3, "The Words That Failed," recounts the long history of coined pronouns—*thon, hir, zie,* and many more—that were proposed as a solution to the less-than-adequate generic *he.* These words failed because they look strange on the page; it isn't always clear how to pronounce them; and they have to be explained. Plus, there are too many coined pronouns to choose from, and no one pronoun stands out as the obvious candidate to serve as "the missing word." Today's nonbinary pronouns are attracting more users than ever—so calling coined pronouns "the words that failed" may seem premature. But so far as their long-term success goes, it's still too early to rewrite the grammar books.

According to Merriam-Webster's online dictionary, to "queer" something is to view it in a new light, particularly "from a perspective that rejects traditional categories of gender and sexuality." *Chapter 4*, "Queering the Pronoun," extends the discussion of pronoun politics to the legal and cultural status of pronouns referring to nonbinary, transgender, and gender-nonconforming persons. Although pronouns may seem a minor concern compared with, say, physical safety and mental stability, prisoners have gone to court, with varying degrees of success, to demand to be referred to by their chosen pronoun, and employees have filed complaints against employers when supervisors and coworkers intentionally use inappropriate pronouns and create a hostile work environment. Trans and gender-nonconforming students also charge their schools with gender discrimination for not upholding their right to designate their pronoun. Laws and regulations in these areas remain unsettled, varying from jurisdiction to jurisdiction, office to office, and school to school. And yet in the United States, more and more national, state, and local governments, along with businesses and schools, are now recognizing pronoun choice as one of the rights of trans and gender-nonconforming persons.

Chapter 5, "The Missing Word Is *They*," explores the use of *they* as a gender-neutral singular from when it first appeared in English writing in the fourteenth century, through the eighteenth and nineteenth centuries, when it was roundly condemned as ungrammatical, to its growing acceptance in the present day. By the late nineteenth century, a few language experts pushed back against conservative "grammarians," arguing that officially approving singular *they* would not only acknowledge the fact that pretty much everyone used it, but it would also confirm the success of the feminists by freeing women from the tyranny of generic *he*. But acceptance of singular *they* came slowly. As we'll see, some uses of singular *they* did get a stamp of approval, and today's language authorities accept singular *they* in more and more contexts.

What's Your Pronoun? concludes with "A Chronology of Gender-Neutral and Nonbinary Pronouns," an annotated historical lexicon of coined, borrowed, and repurposed words intended to serve as gender-neutral or nonbinary pronouns. If you yourself have been wondering "What's your pronoun?" you'll find plenty of pronouns here to choose from.

A note on what to call these pronouns

Throughout this book I use the terms "gender-neutral" and "nonbinary" pronouns. Linguists have settled on these labels for generic *he*, singular *they*, and the pronouns crafted specifically to fill the pronoun gap in English, the semantic space unoccupied by *he* and *she*. Older texts refer to "common-gender" pronouns, a grammatical term that is no longer common. But there are other synonyms that have been used as well in the past, terms almost as varied as the pronouns. These include, in alphabetical order, bisex, bisexual, cogendrous, common-sex, dual gender, duo-personal, epicene, gender pronoun, gender-free pronoun, hermaphroditic, indefinite gender, impersonal pronoun, indirect pronoun, masculor feminine pronoun, sex-free pronoun, sexless pronoun, transsexual pronoun, and unisex pronoun.

Sometimes I call pronouns like *E*, *ze* and *hir* "invented" or "coined" words, sometimes "new pronouns," sometimes even "neopronouns," which sounds very technical. Unfortunately, none of these descriptors is strictly accurate. Calling words "invented" makes them sound artificial. But word coining is a natural process, one that's essential for any language to survive. In fact all words were invented at some point, both the old staples like *he*, *she*, and *they*, whose origins are shrouded in the mists of time, and more-recent creations, like *xe*, *ip*, and *heer*, which we can trace to a specific wordsmith, or at least to a specific time and place where they were launched into the world. At some point someone, identity unknown, made up *he*, *she*, and *they*. As more and more people began to use these pronouns, they became part of the standard language. But they existed alongside competing dialect terms, and it's possible that someone even coined alternatives to *he*, *she*, and *they* that didn't make the cut and vanished without a trace. We'll never know.

In contrast, we know that Francis Brewster coined *E*, *es*, and *em* in 1841, and Charles Crozat Converse announced *thon* and *thons* in 1884, though he may have invented his common-gender pronouns as early as 1858. Neither set of pronouns became standard, though neither has entirely disappeared, either.

Calling pronouns like *ze* and *hir* "new pronouns" or "neopronouns" is misleading too, because these words are relatively old. They may be enjoying a renaissance today, but *ze* appears in 1864, introduced by someone known only by the initials J. W. L., and *hir* first popped up a century ago, invented, or at least introduced to readers in California, by the editor of the *Sacramento Bee* on August 14, 1920. How's that for specific?

Calling these words "gender pronouns"—another way to describe them—includes both the traditional binary pronouns and the non-gendered ones like *ip* and *thon*. Calling them "gender-neutral" down-plays their uses as nonbinary, and calling them "nonbinary" masks their nineteenth-century origins as a means of including both men and women, with no apparent thought at the time, for anyone who didn't fit neatly into those two categories. Calling them "trans pronouns" ignores the fact that many trans persons use the binary pronoun reflecting who they are.

In the end, I've used a number of these unsatisfactory synonyms, referring to these pronouns as invented, coined, new, and neo-, as well as gender-neutral and nonbinary, because there's no one word that accurately names them all or covers every aspect of their creation and use. Maybe someone will coin a proper word for them. But it's OK if no better term emerges: there have always been many ways to say something in English, and variation and change are natural, normal, and inevitable for any language. Since all words are invented words, if you don't see a pronoun here that meets your needs, by all means, make one up.

A note on gender terminology

English grammatical gender seems straightforward, with categories like masculine, feminine, and neuter assigned to its pronouns and some of its nouns. But not all languages sort gender the same way, and in the end grammatical gender is less about biology than about the linguistic technicalities of word classes and inflections. In addition, human gender is both complex and controversial, with biological, psychological, and social components that are the objects of professional study and the frequent subjects of popular discussion. Gender is also a popular topic of comedy, where it's not always treated in the best of taste. As with any sensitive and complex topic, the terminology of gender changes as ideas about gender change. Older terms strike the modern ear as naïve, insensitive, sometimes downright insulting. And new terms may be greeted with resistance. My study of the history of pronoun gender, and the way that ideas about grammar reflect ideas about human gender and sexuality, cites a great deal of original source material. Although I try to use terminology that is neutral, when quoting both historical and contemporary sources it has sometimes been necessary to include words and ideas that readers may find derogatory or insulting. I may not agree with all the sources that I cite, but I can't ignore their role in this history. Since terminology will continue to evolve along with our understanding of the subject, what seems neutral today might not remain so.

A note on the sources

I began my hunt for coined gender-neutral English pronouns forty years ago by paging through crumbling nineteenth-century newspapers buried in out-of-the-way archives or preserved on hard-to-read microfilm—if those newspapers were considered important enough to preserve at all. I found other pronouns buried in volumes of nineteenth-century journals shelved in dim library basements. None of these sources were indexed, so looking for pronouns involved guessing at likely dates or thumbing through magazines on the off chance that someone might mention a coinage. One find led to another, or sometimes to a dead end. That kind of search seems primitive today, but even so, I managed to uncover more than eighty of these pronouns.

Over the past year, I've supplemented that long-ago research by taking advantage of the vast number of early newspapers and journals that have been digitized and put online, most of them accessible through my university library portal, or through the Chronicling America website of the Library of Congress. Other newspaper archives that I rely on are subscription-only. With the right key words and persistent clicking, I've now created a collection of more than 200 coined pronouns, each one documented by publication, date, and page so you can find them too. My pronoun collection now goes back to the 1780s, and as the databases expand, it's likely that we can push that search for the missing word back even earlier. I've included every documentable early coinage that I've found, and all the recent documentable pronouns where the coiner is identified.

What about pronouns in other languages?

The question of gender-neutral and nonbinary pronouns is not unique to English, but the debate over such pronouns over the past couple of centuries has focused on English. A couple of gender-neutral pronouns have been proposed for French. Swedish has had some limited success in fostering the use of the gender-nonspecific pronoun, *hen*. And there have been some attempts to address perceived sexism in Spanish nouns and articles. I'll give some examples of this later in the book. But it's really been speakers of English who have zeroed in on questions of gender in the pronoun system, and that's why almost every example in this book involves English. This isn't because English is more sexist than other languages, or because speakers of English are somehow more concerned than anyone else in the world with gender parity. It's mostly an accident of how English treats gendered words. So here's a *very brief* account of grammatical gender.

Not all languages treat gender the same way. For example, all the nouns in French and Spanish and Italian are either masculine or feminine; German nouns have three grammatical genders, masculine, feminine, or neuter. This has nothing to do with how speakers of these languages treat men and women, at least not directly. Grammatical gender, which doesn't typically align with biological gender, is a way of classifying words that behave similarly in terms of agreement. (*Gender* literally means "kind" or "type" or "classification"—it's related to words like *genre* and *general*—and has no necessary connection to real-world biology.) In French, for example, articles and adjectives must match the gender of the nouns they refer to. Recent attempts to make French more gender-blind or gender-inclusive have focused on the language's nouns rather than on its pronouns. Some languages, like Basque and Turkish, do not distinguish grammatical gender at all, and so the question of gender pronouns doesn't come up—and that, by the way, has nothing to do with whether or not speakers of Basque or Turkish are sexist.

English treats grammatical gender differently from French or Turkish. While Old English nouns had three genders, masculine, feminine, or neuter, just like modern German, by the Middle English period English nouns had lost their grammatical gender, as had English articles and adjectives. However, some nouns referring to people and animals did retain what we call "natural" gender. Thus English has pairs of nouns like *lord* and *lady, king* and *queen,* or *lion* and *lioness.* But Modern English nouns like *book* or *albatross* or *person* express neither grammatical nor biological gender: they're gender-neutral or gender-inclusive. Most of the English personal pronouns are gender-inclusive too: *I, you,* and *they* don't refer to gender. There's one exception: the third-person singular pronouns retain distinct forms for masculine, feminine, and neuter: *he, she,* and *it.* But even though a word may seem to include women along with men, it may be used to exclude them, and that is what sparked the quest for the third-person singular pronoun that was as gender-blind, as gender-inclusive, as the first- and second-person pronouns.

The Missing Word

In September 2017, Chloe Bressack, a transgender teacher in Florida, announced that their pronoun was *they*. Here's part of the letter that Bressack wrote to explain the new nonbinary language policy to the parents of their fifth graders:

> One thing you should know about me is that I use gender neutral terms. My prefix is Mx. (pronounced Mix) and my pronouns are "they, them, their" instead of "he, his, she, hers." I know it takes some practice for it to feel natural, but in my experience students catch on pretty quickly. We're not going for perfection, just making an effort.
>
> —CHLOE BRESSACK, Letter to parents (2017)

Bressack added, "My priority is for all of my students to be comfortable in my classroom, and have a space where they can be themselves while learning." But some of the parents who received that letter immediately pulled their fifth graders out of Bressack's class and complained to the principal. In response, Bressack was transferred from Canopy Oaks Elementary to Tallahassee's Adult and Community Education center.[1]

The "gender-neutral teacher" story immediately went viral—both *USA Today* and *Newsweek* called Bressack "the gender-neutral teacher" instead of *they* or *Mx. Bressack*—and Bressack's pronoun letter prompted a discussion of gender rights both in the press and around the dinner table. Not surprisingly, former Arkansas governor and sometime presidential candidate Mike Huckabee, who supports the traditional gender binaries of male and female, told the *Washington Times,* "I would yank my kid out of [that] classroom, I really would."[2] (Huckabee has three grown children, one of whom happens to be Sarah Huckabee Sanders, who at the time of the "gender-neutral teacher" controversy was press secretary in the Trump administration.)

Not everyone thought that Chloe Bressack was wrong. A number of Canopy Oaks parents took Bressack's side, pointing out that in 2015 the Leon County school district, which covers Tallahassee schools, had strongly supported the rights of transgender students to use bathrooms and locker rooms reflecting their gender identity. This followed an incident in which a student who self-identified as "gender neutral" and used the pronoun *they* wore a dress to middle school on their birthday and was ordered to change or go home. Controversy over the incident led the county to adopt a policy supportive of gender-nonconforming students, a policy that included relaxed dress regulations and the right of the students to designate their pronouns.[3] In a gender-sensitivity training session, teachers and staff were told:

Names and Pronouns

Every student has the right to be addressed by a name and pronoun that corresponds to the student's gender identity.

A court-ordered name or gender change is not required, and the student need not change his or her official records.

It is recommended that teachers privately ask transgender and gender-nonconforming students how they would like to be addressed in class, in correspondence to the home, or at conferences with the student's guardian.[4]

—Leon County Schools

Bressack's supporters wanted to know why the school board didn't extend those same protections to teachers.

Other concerned citizens weighed in on the pronoun problem. Eric Miller, a local lawyer, wrote to the Tallahassee paper complaining that teachers have no right to impose their gender views on unsuspecting students. Worse still, in Miller's view, they have no right to teach impressionable fifth graders that singular *they* is good English. But instead of recommending the traditional *he or she*, à la Huckabee, Miller wanted Mx. Bressack to adopt the nonbinary pronoun *ze*, which "would create less confusion for the students."[5]

Gender-neutral *ze* was coined as early as 1864. Though it got little attention at the time, *ze* resurfaced in 1888, in 1891 (as *zie*), in 1972, and again in 1992. It's not clear where Miller came across *ze*, but ze neglected to explain why a made-up pronoun would be less confusing to fifth graders than singular *they*, a familiar word that students, teachers, school administrators, former governors, and lawyers use every day. In fact, pretty much everyone uses singular *they*. They use it not necessarily to be politically correct, but just because it sounds natural.

Ze came up in another recent pronoun gender controversy as well. In 2015, the University of Tennessee's Office for Diversity and Inclusion recommended that, instead of simply assuming students are either male or female, teachers might ask them, "What's your pronoun?"[6] It's the sort of question that's regularly heard on college campuses, where challenges to traditional gender binaries are frequently discussed. As early as 2008, Dartmouth College was asking students to designate their gender identity and their preferred third-person pronoun on its housing application.[7] Tennessee's Diversity Office offered *ze* and *xe,* along with singular *they,* as alternatives to the more conventional *he* and *she.* Back in the 1970s, Tennessee had briefly tried promoting the set of pronouns advocated by the feminists Casey Miller and Kate Swift, *tey, tem,* and *ter,* but they never caught on.[8] Like that earlier experiment, the pronouns in the 2015 initiative weren't mandatory, just suggestions aimed at inclusiveness. But the Tennessee story prompted a conservative backlash from the state's right-leaning lawmakers, who saw the school as a bastion of political correctness run amok. The university quickly disavowed the pronoun proposal and wiped any trace of it from campus websites. Not satisfied, a furious state legislature cut the Office of Diversity and Inclusion from the next state budget. And for good measure, Tennessee passed a law banning the use of taxpayer dollars to support gender-neutral pronouns—despite the fact that no one knows how much a pronoun actually costs.

When Harvard joined the "What's your pronoun?" movement in 2015, it was national news, even though only about one percent of Harvard students chose a pronoun other than *he* or *she.*[9] In 2018, the University of Minnesota offered students the chance to designate their gender, to select an alternative name, and to choose a pronoun

		Subject	Object	Pronoun	Pronunciation
Gender Binary		she	her	hers	as it looks
		he	him	his	as it looks
Gender Neutral		they*	them*	theirs*	as it looks
		ze	hir	hirs	zhee, here, heres
		ze	zir	zirs	zhee, zhere, zheres
		xe	xem	xyrs	zhee, zhem, zheres
		*used as singular			

Pronouns suggested by the University of Tennessee Office of Diversity and Inclusion were quickly deleted from university websites, though not before they were captured by web archivers. (*Inside Higher Education*, used by permission.)

preference from among *he, she, they, ze,* and "none." The university also circulated a draft of a new gender-inclusivity policy stating that failure to honor a person's choice of gender, name, and pronoun *may* result in penalties up to and including expulsion for students or termination for employees. Although advocates for inclusion saw this as a step forward, campus free-speech advocates warned that the proposal was both vague and overly punitive, as well as ultimately unenforceable under First Amendment speech protections.[10]

Hardly a back-to-school season goes by now without a report of some school letting students choose their pronouns, and some group warning that these gender-neutral words herald the death of English, the decline of the family, and the end of civilization as we know it. And yet both the English language and families with children persist. What makes this controversy so prominent and intractable, deemed worthy of a fuss by students, parents, schools and universities, the press, community groups, and even some of our elected officials? The question is not a new one, and its answer remains elusive. As one writer said over a century ago:

> Did it ever occur to anyone that there is a word missing from the English language? There is one, a very important one, too. The word wanted is a personal pronoun, third person singular number, common gender; the singular of they. . . . The person that invents a word to fill the vacancy will receive the benediction of other nations as well as this.[11]
> —ANONYMOUS, *Newton Daily Republican* (1892)

For more than 200 years, writers have sought this missing English word. English has no pronoun that refers to "either a man or a woman," no word to use when gender is unknown, or irrelevant, or when it needs to be hidden. The language has a complete set of masculines: *he, his, him.* And feminines: *she, her, hers.* It even has a pair of neuters: *it* and *its.* And the plurals *they, their, them,* which refer to any and all genders, including things that have no gender. But there's no singular third-person gender-neutral pronoun. None. Which seems strange, because there are so many times when we need one.

For example, how do you fill in the blank in a sentence like this?

Everyone forgets _____ passwords.

There are eight options, but none of them seem just right:

1. Everyone forgets *his* passwords.
2. Everyone forgets *their* passwords.
3. Everyone forgets *his or her* passwords.
4. Everyone forgets *her* passwords.
5. Everyone forgets *its* passwords.
6. Everyone forgets *everyone's* passwords.
7. Everyone forgets *one's* passwords.
8. Everyone forgets *thons* passwords.

Let's look at these options in turn, starting with the generic *he*.

Generic *he*

1. Everyone forgets *his* passwords.

Centuries ago, grammarians like William Lily, who believed that men were better than women, and women better than animals and things, extended this hierarchy to the realm of language, crafting an influential rule called "the worthiness of the genders" for Latin grammar:

> The masculine gender is more worthy than the feminine, and the feminine more worthy than the neuter.[12]
> —WILLIAM LILY, *A Short Introduction of Grammar* (1549)

By royal decree, the precepts of Lily's grammar were taught in Latin class in every school in England. Later textbooks reiterated Lily's command that the worthiness doctrine must apply whenever a Latin adjective occurs with a series of nouns of different genders.[13]

The worthiness doctrine first appeared in Latin textbooks because, before the late sixteenth century, English wasn't considered a language worthy enough to have a grammar. In those days, studying grammar, a basic part of every school curriculum, meant studying Latin. Since formal education at the time tended to exclude girls, most of these Latin students were boys, and most of them took the relative worthiness of the genders in stride. But once England began to be more of a presence in the world, both economically and politically, the prestige of the English language began to rise. When English grammars finally started to appear in the seventeenth and eighteenth centuries, they were modeled on the earlier Latin textbooks, even though English and Latin are different in important ways. Among these differences, Modern English nouns, unlike those in Latin, don't typically express gender; English adjectives don't have distinct gender forms; and in English, adjectives don't typically have to match the gender of their nouns.

But English third-person singular pronouns do have gender, and English grammarians—both men and women—simply transferred the Latin worthiness doctrine to the one instance in English where the question of gender agreement comes up: which personal pronoun should be used with indefinites like *each, everyone,* and *somebody,* words that could refer to either gender? Here's Anne Fisher's version of the new rule that the masculine pronoun *he* may refer to an unspecified person of either gender, taken from her *New English Grammar* (1753), one of the most popular eighteenth-century schoolbooks: "The *Masculine Person* answers to the *general Name,* which comprehends both *Male* and *Female*; as, *Any Person who knows what he says.*" (Fisher uses *name* for the part of speech more commonly called a noun.[14])

The eighteenth-century usage critic Robert Baker extended the worthiness doctrine to argue—incorrectly—that English started out with only one pronoun, *he,* a word so worthy that it encompassed all the genders: "Our Ancestors, in the Infancy of the Language, had but one Word for . . . *he, she* and *they.*" But Baker thought that having a single pronoun was a recipe for ambiguity, as if Beowulf and his thanes sat around the mead hall scratching their heads and wondering, "Are you talking about *him* or *her* or *them?*" So Baker imagined that, in order to make the language more precise, "a feminine pronoun became necessary."[15] The only thing missing from Baker's story is a deity fashioning the feminine pronoun from a part of the masculine.

When it came to generic masculines, there were always a few people who worried that generic *he* just didn't work, that in a statement like "Everyone forgets his passwords" women are not included among the men. There were far too many instances where the masculine pronoun was exclusive, where despite its pretense of generic status, *he* could never really stand for *she* as well. A word like *everyone* included women. That was obvious. But what about *every lawyer?* or *every president?* When a regulation says that "A lawyer must pass the bar exam before he can practice law," does that mean only men can be lawyers? In 1886, the Maryland Supreme Court said yes, that's exactly what it means.

And what about when the US Constitution says, "In case of the removal of the President from office, or of *his* death, resignation, or inability to discharge the powers and duties of the said office, the same shall devolve on the Vice President"?[16] People who didn't think women could be president pointed to constitutional *he* and *his* to support their case, asking, "Does the Constitution say *she* anywhere? No, it does not." But supporters of women's rights argued right back that when the Fifth Amendment says, "nor shall any person . . . be compelled in any criminal case to be a witness against *himself*," that means women have the right to remain silent, not just men. The US Supreme Court regards the Constitution as consistent: a word that means one thing in one part of the founding document must mean exactly the same thing when it appears in another part. It makes no sense for the Fifth Amendment to apply only to men, and so the pronoun *he* in Article II, which speaks of the duties of the president, must mean *she* as well.

It turned out that the masculine pronoun was just as ambiguous in the law as it was in ordinary speech: to be sure, it referred to mixed groups—as in "Everyone forgets his passwords"—but sometimes, until 1916, when Jeanette Rankin broke the gender barrier to become the first woman elected to the House of Representatives, it meant only boys' clubs like Congress and the White House.

Critics of generic *he* found such uncertainty problematic. For some nineteenth-century grammar purists, there was another problem with generic *he:* the pronoun declared to be inclusive by the old grammarians was *ungrammatical* when it was used inclusively. That's because pronouns are supposed to agree with the words they stand for both in number and in gender. Although *he* is singular, it's also masculine, and so it can't agree in gender with *everyone,* a gender-neutral pronoun that refers to women as well as men. So far as pronoun agreement is concerned, the generic masculine doesn't follow the pronoun agreement rule, and that makes generic *he* not just morally wrong, but also *grammatically* wrong, which for a grammarian is an even greater sin.

But that was a minority view. Most usage experts, like most lawmakers, had no trouble dealing with the paradox of *he.* Violating a little grammatical rule was no great price to pay in order to keep the masculine pronoun at the top of the gender hierarchy. And it was no great price to pay in order to keep men atop the legal hierarchy either. So generic *he* prevailed in the rule books and in English and American lawbooks, until the 1970s, when English speakers started seriously rooting out sexist language. Since then, generic *he* has become the exception, not the rule.

Singular *they*

That leads us to option 2 in the quest for the missing word: singular *they,* the pronoun of choice for most speakers of English (most of whom don't get in trouble for using it at work, as Chloe Bressack did):

2. Everyone forgets *their* passwords.
The indefinite *everyone* is technically singular (though it implies more than one person), while *they, their,* and *them* are technically plurals, so *everyone . . . their* fails the number agreement part of the pronoun agreement rule. Interestingly, although many usage critics have found singular *they* ungrammatical, many nineteenth-century

journalists saw it as a triumph of popular speech over stuffy, elitist English. This was seconded by a number of language experts, who acknowledged that singular *they* had always prevailed in speech and had a long, respectable history in writing.

For example, in 1896 the linguist E. F. Andrews called the form "a well-established colloquialism," and she cited its use by the "best" authors.[17] Supporters also pointed to singular *you* as proof that a plural pronoun could serve as singular without violating any rules (*you*, originally plural, replaced singular *thou* during the seventeenth century). The philosopher Alexander Bain argued that singular *they* was perfectly grammatical when referring to a mixed group of men and women, much more reasonable than using generic *he* for a woman.[18] More recently, the science fiction writer Ursula K. Le Guin rejected the ban on singular *they* as a "fake rule" promulgated by "grammar bullies."[19] And a number of writers even insisted that singular *they* was better than coordinate *he or she*.

All to say that singular *they* has always been one way of filling in the blank in sentences like *Everyone forgets _____ passwords*. It has become the default for many English speakers, not just in informal speech, but in formal, edited writing as well. Chloe Bressack prefers *they*, as do many of us. And it is increasingly accepted, even preferred, by dictionaries, grammars, and style and usage guides. But more about *they* in Chapter 5.

His or *her*

The only strictly grammatical way to fill in the blank (at least according to traditionalists) is the one that everybody hates:

3. Everyone forgets *his or her* passwords.
Even though *his or her* is meant to be both gender inclusive and singular in number, nobody likes it. From the start, grammarians, lan-

guage commentators, and casual observers denounced *his or her* as a cumbersome and wordy circumlocution. In 1866, a writer in the *Leavenworth Times* condemned this option as both grating and "disagreeably grammatical."[20] And in 1892 another writer, also in Kansas, faulted *his or her* because that meant adding two extra words, which in that "busy era" was "a matter of considerable importance."[21] Yet the much-hated phrase still crops up now and then, as in a label from Vivat spring water, whose slogan translates the Latin name of the product as "May he or she live long."

As for schoolroom grammars, students frequently tell me that their writing teachers tell them that the new rule is "Always use *he or she*." But even the most obedient students avoid *he or she* when the teacher isn't looking, presumably because they, too, find it disagreeably grammatical. I'm guessing that teachers also avoid *he or she* when their students aren't looking. Today we can add another objection to *he or she*: it's totally binary.

Generic *she*

This option is even less popular:

4. Everyone forgets *her* passwords.
Sometimes found in twentieth-century feminist writing as an antidote to the generic *he*, generic *she* proved too political for the average speaker or writer. Writing dismissively in 1989 about the "she rule" common "here in politically correct land [Boston]," *New Republic* columnist Andrew Sullivan called generic *she* "silly" and asked readers to come up with alternate suggestions.[22] But even as early as 1974, the well-known pediatrician Benjamin Spock announced that he would atone for his earlier use of generic *he* both

for indefinite pronouns and for singular nouns like *baby* or *child* by switching to *she* in his popular *Dr. Spock's Baby and Child Care*, the bible of mid-twentieth-century American parents that is still in print today.[23]

And the generic *she* continues to pop up every now and then. Here's Supreme Court Justice John Paul Stevens in his 2001 opinion in *Palazzolo v. Rhode Island*: "If the application of such a restriction to a property owner would cause her a 'direct and substantial injury,' . . . I have no doubt that she has standing to challenge the restriction's validity whether she acquired title to the property before or after the regulation was adopted."[24] The pronoun here is generic and does not refer to petitioner Anthony Palazzolo, who is male, though it is meant to include him. Stevens once explained that it seemed appropriate "sometimes to use a masculine and sometimes a feminine pronoun when referring to a hypothetical representative of a class that includes both."[25] And the generic *she* isn't just for male writers who want to show how sensitive they are. Justice Ruth Bader Ginsburg, a consistently progressive voice on the Supreme Court, has been known to alternate generic *she* with generic *he*, as in this example from a 2008 opinion:

> A nonparty is bound by a judgment if she "assume(d) control" over the litigation in which that judgment was rendered. Because such a person has had "the opportunity to present proofs and argument," he has already "had his day in court" even though he was not a formal party to the litigation.[26]
>
> —RUTH BADER GINSBURG, *Taylor v. Sturgell* (2008)

But switching between *he* and *she* drives editors mad and just confuses readers. In Ginsburg's example, the two pronouns seem to refer to two different people, when in fact both refer to the same person.

It

This option is rare to nonexistent:

5. Everyone forgets *its* passwords.

Once a common pronoun for infants—George Eliot used *it* for the baby Eppie in her 1861 novel *Silas Marner*—*it* is rarely used to refer to infants or children today.[27] As for adults, *it* has been deployed since the sixteenth century as a way to insult, dehumanize, or mock a person. In 1792, the Scottish philosopher James Anderson observed that using the pronoun *it* to refer to a person denoted "a high degree of contempt."[28] Article XIII of Kentucky's 1850 Constitution used *it* to dehumanize slaves: "The right of property is before and higher than any constitutional sanction; and the right of the owner of a slave to such slave and *its* increase, is the same, and as inviolable as the right of the owner of any property whatever."[29] In a racist editorial, the *New York Evening Post* defended this use of the pronoun *its:* "It is objected to this that slaves are male and female, and cannot have the neuter pronoun *it* applied to them. But the objectors have forgotten to estimate the effect of color upon gender."[30]

It has been deployed in anti-Semitic rants as well as racist ones. From time to time, nineteenth- and twentieth-century Christian commentators wondered whether it would be more appropriate to use a gender-neutral pronoun instead of *he* to refer to God. But in an 1862 over-the-top outburst, Robert Gerry, writing in the atheist journal *Boston Investigator,* declared that Jews were ignorant, violent, and "the most despicable miscreants the earth ever bore up," and that he would call their "idol" *it*.[31]

It has also been used satirically. In 1930, the mystery writer Dorothy Sayers used *it* to gently satirize a violinist at a party playing avant-garde music the reader is meant to disapprove of:

At the piano, which stood just inside the door, a young man with bushy red hair was playing something of a Czecho-Slovakian flavour, to a violin obligato by an extremely loose-jointed person of indeterminate sex in a Fair-Isle jumper. . . . The violinist put down its instrument and stood up, revealing itself, by its legs, to be female.[32]

—DOROTHY SAYERS, *Strong Poison* (1930)

In rare cases, *it* is used neutrally to conceal gender, as in this example from a 1944 mystery novel:

In the big entrance hall, lit only by a single bulb in the roof, the night porter dozed uncomfortably in his box, and so failed to see either the person who flitted silently up the big staircase to Peter Graham's room, or what that person was carrying on *its* return.[33]

—EDMUND CRISPIN, *The Case of the Gilded Fly* (1944)

The author of this book about an Oxford don who solves murders in his spare time was a stickler for grammatical correctness, and here he seems intent on avoiding singular *they*.

Avoiding the pronoun altogether

Another option is to avoid pronouns and simply repeat the noun:

6. Everyone forgets *everyone's* passwords.

You won't find this often, but sometimes it's used in contracts and other official documents. For example, California amended its constitution in 1974 to replace gendered words with gender-neutral language. As Proposition 11 explains, "Instead of referring to the Governor as 'he,' the amendment repeats the word 'Governor.'"[34] Such measures can have broad impact. A 1986 Minnesota bill to make all statutes gender neutral by repeating job titles and other nouns promised to eliminate some 20,000 pronouns from the state's law books, though that probably increased printing costs, as nouns tend to be longer than pronouns.[35] And in 2003, Smith College revised its student constitution, to change generic *she* to *the student*.[36] When it comes to indefinites, however, repeating the subject only creates confusion, as example (6) shows.

One

Then there's gender-neutral *one*:

7. Everyone forgets *one's* passwords.
In 1770 Robert Baker, who thought that *she* derived from *he,* also ordained that the only acceptable gender-neutral pronoun was *one*.[37] But this option brought its own set of drawbacks. Grammarians had to keep reminding people who said *one . . . he* that the only pronoun that can follow *one* is *one*. Insisting on the *one . . . one* rule can lead to too many *ones,* as in this sentence: "One should do one's best when one is diagramming one's sentence." It's not surprising that, even in the eighteenth century, when grammarians sought to codify the language and formalize its style, the British felt that *one* could be too formal, and many Americans found it completely pretentious. As for "Everyone forgets one's passwords," one simply doesn't say this, even in England.

Coin a new pronoun—or find one elsewhere

The last option is to coin a new pronoun altogether. Some writers find that the best way to deal with the missing word is to make up a new word:

8. Everyone forgets *thons* passwords.

Thon is one such word, a gender-neutral pronoun coined in the nineteenth century to use for *he or she*, a man or a woman. Such gender-neutral words are also meant to refer to people generally, and to be used when reference to gender would be inappropriate, irrelevant, distracting, or unnecessarily revealing. *Thon* and any of the other coined pronouns can be generic, referring to an unnamed person. Or *thon* can be nonbinary, referring to a specific person, whether male, or female, or gender-nonconforming.

Typically, these additions to the pronoun paradigm are coined words like *ze, ip,* and *heer*. But what if you could find a pronoun already used by English speakers? In 1789, William Marshall labeled the gender-neutral pronoun *ou*, common in Gloucestershire dialect, an error.[38] But in 1792, James Anderson wondered whether Marshall's *ou* could be a useful replacement for *he, she,* or *it*. Anderson felt that the lack of a gender-neutral pronoun was a major defect in English. He rejected generic *he* to refer to "neutral" words like *friend, servant,* and *neighbor,* because "the effect is confined to the *male,* which ought equally to include the *female*." *Ou* might be the answer to the missing word.[39]

Others besides Anderson also looked to the shires to find a suitable pronoun. An English newspaper in 1863 suggested *er,* a gender-neutral pronoun used in rural districts in the west of England.[40] And in 1899, a writer identified as "Kokni" (Cockney, get it?) wanted to adopt *un,* a gender-neutral pronoun still in use in Dorset.[41]

The need to supply a new word was clear to occasional amateur writers as well as to those more professional or learned. A 1794 attack on singular *they* offers what may have been the first gender-neutral pronoun showdown, as a group of New Bedford women known as the Belle Assembly silenced a man calling himself Alonzo, who tried to shame them for using singular *they*. Here's the sentence that provoked Alonzo's wrath: "How ungenerous it is to pitch upon *some one* of our acquaintance, tell private stories of *them,* and then industri-ously report *them* to be the author!"[42]

But the women defended their mismatch of singular with plural by reminding Alonzo that English has no way to express—or in this case, to mask—gender identity: "With regard to our using the plural pronoun *them* in conjunction with the definitive pronoun *one* . . . we wished to conceal the gender." And they laid down a challenge: if Alonzo doesn't like singular *they,* he'll just have to "coin us a substitute."[43]

All talk and no action, Alonzo did not offer a new pronoun, and those English writers who wished to conceal the gender, or who simply found singular *they* natural, continued to rely on it, as they had done for centuries. But not everyone resorted to *they.* In 1909, the columnist Daphne wanted to hide the gender of the person she was writing about. Daphne complained, "I have been looking in my old school grammars to find a pronoun common to both genders. I can only see 'he, she, or it'. . . . There ought to be a sexless pronoun." Daphne wondered aloud about this lapse committed by "the men who made English": if "language was made to conceal our thoughts, then why did not the men who made English think of a word for my purpose? I must do the best I can and say 'he or she.' "[44]

Not long after James Anderson called for a pronoun of indefinite gender and the Belle Assembly sought a gender-masking one, the poet and critic Samuel Taylor Coleridge became the first literary celebrity to try to solve the missing word problem by extending the use of the pro-noun *it,* "in order to avoid particularising man or woman, or in order to express sex indifferently."[45] (See exactly what he said on the facing page.) It's fortunate that Coleridge's readers responded to this extension of *it* indifferently, but the semantic hole in the language remained unfilled.

It wasn't the only candidate for repackaging as a gender-neutral pronoun. In 1883 one writer, prompted by a call for a new pronoun in the *Atlantic* in 1878, suggested *whose* instead of singular *their* or the compound *his or her:*

It would not take us long to become accustomed to hear the minister say at the close of an appeal for a generous contribution: "I hope each member of the congregation will give liberally according to whose several ability."

That anonymous writer concluded with one of the few comments on pronouns that consider race as well as gender:

> In the eye of the law, of course, "his" and "their" include both sexes, irrespective of race, color, or previous condition, but in the colloquies of everyday life a new combination pronoun is required, and the sooner the philologists come to the rescue the better it will be for all concerned.[46]
>
> —"Something for Grammarians to Consider,"
> *The Republic* (1883)

ANIMA POETÆ

A NEUTRAL PRONOUN

QUÆRE—whether we may not, *nay* ought not, to use a neutral pronoun relative, or representative, to the word "Person," where it hath been used in the sense of *homo, mensch,* or noun of the common gender, in order to avoid particularising man or woman, or in order to express either sex indifferently? If this be incorrect in syntax, the whole use of the word Person is lost in a number of instances, or only retained by some stiff and strange position of words, as—"not letting the *person* be aware, *wherein offence has been given*"—instead of—"wherein he or she has offended." In my [judgment] both the specific intention and general *etymon* of "Person" in such sentences, fully authorise the use of *it* and *which* instead of, he, she, him, her, who, whom.

Samuel Taylor Coleridge entertained the idea of using *it* as the much needed gender-neutral pronoun. (University of Illinois Library, used by permission.)

An 1839 call for someone to fill in the blank with "a really personal pronoun in the third person singular, without gender" insisted that none of the current options, *he, she, it,* or *they,* can do the job:

> We say, "If any lady or gentleman shall buy this article _____ shall have it for five dollars." The blank may be filled with he, she, it, or they; or in any other manner; and yet the form of the expression will be too vulgar to be uttered.[47]
>
> —"New Words," *Mercury and Weekly Journal of Commerce* (1839)

Perhaps inadvertently, perhaps out of reluctance to use *they,* but surely with no sense of irony, the writer employed the generic *he,* one of the forms "too vulgar to be uttered," to address potential word coiners: "If anybody will get us well out of the difficulty . . . *he* will be entitled to the thanks of all persons who love to talk" (emphasis added).

And in 1851, the women's rights advocate John Stuart Mill complained that the lack of a gender-neutral pronoun forced him to use generic *he,* which was "more than a defect" in English because it presumed "one-half the human species" to represent the whole, while rendering the other half invisible:

> The pronoun *he* is the only one available to express all human beings; none having yet been invented to serve the purpose of designating them generally, without distinguishing them by a characteristic so little worthy of being made the main distinction as that of sex. This is more than a defect in language; tending greatly to prolong the almost universal habit, of thinking and speaking of one-half the human species as the whole.[48]
>
> —JOHN STUART MILL, *A System of Logic* (1851)

We'll see in the next chapter that, although Mill proposed a gender-neutral revision to the 1868 British voting law that would give women the right to vote, he did not attempt to find a replacement for generic *he*. But as Chapter 3 reveals, it wasn't long before word coiners began filling in the blank with their own inventions. I call these attempts to supply the missing word "the words that failed," because none of these many coinages—and as we find in the Chronology of Gender-Neutral and Nonbinary Pronouns, there were more than 200—got much recognition at all, let alone the thanks of all persons who love to talk.

The Politics of He

The exclusion of the sex from political life has hitherto been secured by the simple use of the masculine pronoun.

—*The Times* (1873)

Pronouns are political. In 1870, the suffragist MP Jacob Bright asked the British Parliament to revise the voting laws so that words referring to men also included women.[1] But an editorial in the *Times* objected that the pronoun *he* in the election law did important work by excluding women from the polls. For the staid London newspaper, the idea of women voting offended both nature and grammar:

> An old prejudice exists, embodied in Acts of Parliament and in the usages of grammar, that [men and women] should be considered as distinct, and that the grammatical idioms of gender correspond to real differences of nature. . . . The fact that the exclusion of the sex from political life has hitherto been secured by the simple use of the masculine pronoun, without any special legislation, illustrates how absolutely inconceivable and unnatural the idea of Women's Suffrage has hitherto seemed. If it were ever to be realized, we should have to revolutionize the commonest modes of thought and expression; to

guard our most familiar language, to watch our pronouns, and to check our most constant assumptions.[2]

—"Mr. Jacob Bright's Bill to Remove the Electoral
Disabilities of Women" (1873)

Perhaps you thought that *he* was generic. After all, language treatises from William Lily's *Short Introduction of Grammar* (1549) to the fourth edition of William Strunk and E. B. White's *Elements of Style* (1999) promoted the generic masculine as the approved way to watch our pronouns. The inclusive masculine has even been enshrined in British and American law. Both the UK Act of Interpretation (1850) and the US Dictionary Act (1871) declared that, in the law, words referring to men also include women. But as the *Times'* position shows, there's no getting around the fact that generic *he* is problematic: sometimes *he* includes both men and women, and sometimes, despite laws that specify that masculine words include women, *he* means "only men."

If you haven't seen generic *he* around much lately, that's because the feminist call in the 1970s for an end to sexist language led to a sharp decline in generic *man* and *he* in edited prose. Nevertheless, some language authorities tried to hold on to the generic masculine in the face of such opposition. In 1977, Vermont Royster, the former editor of the *Wall Street Journal,* lamented that "anyone in the writing business is in for trouble whenever the masculine pronoun 'he' is used in referring to a person of indefinite sex." But Royster was hopeful that women would relent when they "become secure enough . . . to lose their semantic sensitivity," and generic *he* would once again be standard.[3] Clinging more strongly to the dying *he,* the third edition of Strunk and White's popular *Elements of Style* (1979) warned against trying to replace generic *he* with the phrase *he or she,* which sounds "boring or silly," or worse yet, with generic *she:* "Try it and see what happens." *Elements of Style* even insisted, with no data to back up the claim, that generic *he* "has lost all suggestion of maleness. . . . It is never incorrect."[4] But the authors were wrong. *He* had never lost its maleness, and by 1999, although continuing to recommend the form, the *Elements of Style* conceded that "many writers find the use of the generic *he* or *his* . . . limiting or offensive."[5]

Votes for women

The *Times* was wrong to oppose votes for women, but it was right that pronouns in statutes designate who has access to political power and who is excluded from the democratic process. Grammarians have told us for centuries that *he* also means "she," but does generic *he* mean that women can vote? Nineteenth-century suffragists argued that it did. Or does *he* in the voting law mean voting is for men alone? Antisuffragists, like the writer in the *Times,* argued that, when it comes to votes for women, *he* excludes women from political life. The meaning of *he* was so contentious that both England and the United States had to pass specific and unambiguous laws to guarantee that women could vote.

The fight for universal suffrage was a long and difficult one, much of it involving direct action, violence, imprisonment, hunger strikes, and even death. In both England and the United States there was also a lot of talk about the language of the election laws, and a lot of that wrangling concerned the politics of the pronoun *he.*

Opponents of votes for women in England insisted that according to centuries-old common law, women had never voted. But that wasn't strictly true. The first statute to officially deny the vote to English women didn't date back to the Norman Conquest in 1066, it was the Reform Act of 1832, which specified that "every Male Person of full Age . . . shall be entitled to vote," provided they had enough money.[6] Then a voting bill called the Representation of the People

Act of 1867 substituted *man* for the earlier law's *male person:* "Every Man shall ... be entitled to be registered as a Voter."[7] And with that change, people wondered, does this bill give women the vote?

There was a legal reason as well as a grammatical one to think that *man* in the new voting law might actually be generic, referring to "a human being," not "a male person." In 1850, Parliament had passed the Act of Interpretation, which stated that "In all Acts ... Words importing the Masculine Gender shall be deemed and taken to include Females ... unless the contrary as to Gender ... is expressly provided."[8] According to law, *man* and *he* could include 'woman' and 'she.' But English antisuffragists maintained that, so far as the election laws were concerned, *man* and *male person* were synonymous, and so the change in wording changed nothing in the voting act.

John Stuart Mill, the philosopher and committed suffragist who had earlier called for a gender-neutral pronoun and had recently been elected to Parliament, introduced an amendment to remove any doubt from the new voting law by replacing *man* with *person,* a word that would assure women the vote because it clearly included

Interpretation of certain Words for future Acts.   IV. Be it enacted, That in all Acts to be hereafter made Words importing the Masculine Gender shall be deemed and taken to include Females, and the Singular to include the Plural, and the Plural the Singular, unless the contrary as to Gender or Number is expressly provided; 15

Detail from the 1850 Act of Interpretation, formally the bill called Act for Shortening Language used in Acts of Parliament. An attempt to repeal the act in 1851 on the grounds that it would permit women to vote failed when the Attorney General assured members of parliament that, despite the *he-means-she* clause, women were still ineligible to vote. (Image published by permission of ProQuest. Further reproduction is prohibited without permission. Image produced by ProQuest as part of the House of Commons Parliamentary Papers. www.proquest.com)

all human beings.[9] But Mill's amendment failed in a vote of 196 to 73, confirming that *man* was not generic after all. In a reform act that otherwise opened up access to the polls to males who couldn't vote before, *man* continued to mean "no women allowed."

Asking Parliament to change *man* to *person* was an admission that the generic masculine of the Interpretation Act had failed. During the debate on the voting law, another suffragist, the MP George Denman, asked Chancellor of the Exchequer Benjamin Disraeli whether the Reform Act "intended by the use of the word 'man' instead of the words 'male person' . . . to confer the suffrage on women." Disraeli replied that it did not. The Interpretation Act, Disraeli explained, contained an escape clause: masculine words were generic "unless the contrary as to gender is expressly provided," and Disraeli told the Commons that, when it came to votes for women, "the necessary provision" to exclude women had been made.[10]

Disraeli's definition of *man* as gender specific stated the government's position, but it remained unclear how courts might read the word. For one thing, despite the chancellor's assertion, the new voting law did not explicitly bar women from voting. That's why, soon after it went into effect, one barrister appointed to register voters ruled that *man* in the new law did in fact include women.[11]

But the courts read the law differently. Ruling in *Chorlton v. Lings,* a case involving Manchester women who wanted to vote, Chief Justice William Bovil, of the Court of Common Pleas, found that "man" in the 1868 voting law excluded women:

> There is no doubt that, in many statutes, "men" may be properly held to include women, whilst in others it would be ridiculous to suppose that the word was used in any other sense than as designating the male sex. . . . I do not collect from the language of this Act, that there was any intention to alter

the descriptions of the persons who were to vote ... and if
so important an alteration of the personal qualification was
intended to be made as to extend the franchise to women, who
did not then enjoy it, and were in fact excluded from it by the
terms of the former Act, I can hardly suppose that the legislature would have made it by using the term "man."[12]

—*Chorlton v. Lings* (1868)

Chorlton became the official reading of the voting law: regardless of
what the Interpretation Act says about gendered words, a suffrage bill
must specifically include women or they cannot vote. That prompted
Jacob Bright—supported by his sister and other Manchester suffragists denied the vote in *Chorlton*—to propose an amendment that
would add the words of the Interpretation Act directly to the voting law: "Wherever words occur which import the masculine gender
the same shall be held to include females." As we've seen, the *Times*
opposed Bright's bill when it came for a final vote in 1873, and it was
soundly rejected by the House of Commons.

That's not to say that the Interpretation Act had no impact at
all. British courts did sometimes find that *man* and *he* "included
females," but only when that didn't mean giving women rights that
the men of government didn't want them to have. British women
would continue to be equal to men when it came to paying taxes
or fines, but most would have to wait fifty more years for the right
to vote. Despite repeated introductions of specific women's suffrage bills, and reminders that the Act of Interpretation prescribed a
gender-neutral definition of *man* and *he,* English women who owned
property did not get the vote until 1918, and the rest got the vote ten
years after that.

Watching our pronouns

In its response to Jacob Bright's proposal, the *Times* warned that, if women ever vote, "we" had better watch "our" pronouns. That's not a generic *we*, it's the men-only *we* referring to the male readers of the *Times*. The United States was also busy watching its pronouns, trying to determine whether *he* in statutes also meant "she." The smart money had it that the American *he*, like its English counterpart, did not include the right to vote. But in the United States pronouns weren't just about voting. A New York State law banned imprisoned saloon keepers—referred to by the pronoun *he*—from continuing to operate their bars. In 1854, the state legislature debated an amendment to add *she* to a revision of the Liquor Code in order to prevent wives from operating the saloons when their husbands were in jail. Legislators decided that the amendment wasn't necessary because the code already stipulated that *he* means "she" and *she* means "he," and besides, women would soon be able to vote.[13]

That optimism was premature. American women wouldn't vote for another seventy years, but language specifying that "*he* also means 'she'" began to appear in other American statutes. As an 1868 federal law taxing alcohol and tobacco specified, "words of the masculine gender, as applied to persons, . . . mean and include the feminine gender," which is to say that women as well as men had to pay the "sin" tax for drinking and smoking.[14] And in 1871, the Dictionary Act declared that all masculines in US federal law included women, just as the British Act of Interpretation had done in 1850.

The relevant part of the Dictionary Act, like its British counterpart, included an escape clause: "Unless the context shows that such words were intended to be used in a more limited sense."[15] That "more limited sense"—where *man* meant "only males"—didn't stop American suffragists from invoking generic *he* in their quest for voting rights, though it did enable courts and legislatures to deny women equal treatment under the law.

There was always a good reason to deny women their rights— or so it seemed to those men doing the denying. In 1869, the *Chicago Tribune* observed that women could not vote in Illinois because the state constitution limited voting to "every white *male* citizen." According to the *Tribune,* modern women could do just about anything, they could even own their own property—so not letting them vote actually did them a favor: it excused them from paying a poll tax, which eligible voters had to pay to be allowed to vote.[16]

A similar paternalism played out in England. When the militant suffragist Emmeline Pankhurst's Women's Franchise League proposed a bill in 1889 to provide that masculine words included women in all acts involving the vote, a Yorkshire newspaper reasoned that it would be fine to let unmarried women vote if they owned property, but not married women, "for their interests are protected by their husbands."[17]

Is it a crime to vote?

Not surprisingly, suffragists in England and the United States didn't agree that being spared the vote either protected women or improved their lives. American women claimed both repeatedly and unsuccessfully that, by virtue of the Constitution, the Dictionary Act, and the grammarians, *he* in voting laws must include women. In 1871 the American suffragist J. F. Byrnes articulated what would become the legal and grammatical case for women to vote:

> ➤ The penal code refers to criminals as *he,* but the criminal laws punish women as well as men.

➤ The Fifth Amendment uses the pronoun *he* but protects women's right to remain silent as well as men's.

➤ The Thirteenth Amendment, which extends the vote to former slaves, refers to citizens as *he,* but *citizens* is a gender-neutral term including women as well as men.

Here's how Byrnes put it:

> In the language of this act, the masculine pronoun *he* is used with reference to the term *citizen,* whose right [to vote] it is intended to protect. If this fact be urged against women being included within the meaning of the act, the reply is, that the same term is used in almost every penal statute enacted in every State in the Union, and is taken for and accepted as a general term embracing every person liable to punishment for crimes committed. The term *he* is used in the Constitution of the United States in repeated instances. In article 5 of the amendments providing, "no person shall be held to answer for a capital or otherwise infamous crime," etc., the term occurs in this wise, "Nor shall *he* be compelled in any criminal court to be witness against *himself,*" etc. Here the term is used in connection with another masculine pronoun, *himself;* and yet it is a general term, and includes women, for they can no more be held to testify against themselves than men.[18]
>
> —J. F. BYRNES, "The Women of the United States: Their Political Rights under the Constitution and the Laws at Present in Force" (1871)

Susan B. Anthony echoed Byrnes when she addressed the pronoun issue in a number of speeches in the 1870s. Anthony, who famously asked if it was a crime for a citizen to vote, was arrested in 1872 and fined $100 (just under $2,100 in 2019) for "the alleged crime of having voted." As Anthony noted, the Fourteenth Amendment refers to *persons* and *citizens*, both gender-neutral terms:

> All persons born or naturalized in the United States and subject to the jurisdiction thereof, are citizens of the United States and of the state wherein they reside. No states shall make or enforce any law which shall abridge the privileges or immunities of citizens of the United States . . . ; nor shall any state deprive any person of life, liberty or property, without due process of law, nor deny to any person within its jurisdiction the equal protection of the laws.
> —The Fourteenth Amendment to the US Constitution (1868)

Anthony then argued that the Constitution makes women who meet these qualifications both persons and citizens, and as citizens, they cannot be denied the vote. As for pronouns, she says,

> It is urged, the use of the masculine pronouns he, his and him, in all the constitutions and laws, is proof that only men were meant to be included in their provisions. If you insist on this version of the letter of the law, we shall insist that you be consistent, and accept the other horn of the dilemma, which would compel you to exempt women from taxation for the support of the government, and from penalties for the violation of laws.[19]
> —SUSAN B. ANTHONY, "Is It a Crime for a Citizen of the United States to Vote?" (1873)

Anthony made this point more bluntly in a speech to Illinois suffragists. Keeping women from the polls is no act of gallantry, she maintained. But if men take on the burden of voting to spare women the rough campaigns, the raucous voting places, and the onerous act of casting a ballot, then to be consistent, men must also spare women the unpleasantness of taxes or the inconvenience of jail:

> If, for instance, in a penal law there are no feminine pronouns, women should be exempt from the penalties imposed. And if men are to represent woman in [voting], let them represent her in all. If a wife commits murder let the husband be hung for it.[20]
> —SUSAN B. ANTHONY, "Woman Suffrage" (1872)

Elizabeth Cady Stanton repeated this same reasoning in *The Woman's Bible* (1895) in her attempt to extend gender equality both to religion and to law. Stanton argued, in her commentary on Exodus, that in the absence of inclusive pronouns in both scripture and law, *he* must also mean *she,* and she asked, "If women can pay the penalties of their crimes as 'He,' why may they not enjoy the privileges of citizens as 'He'?"[21] The logic is both pointed and compelling. But the struggle for women's suffrage was far from over. In addition, there were frequent complaints of sacrilege lodged against Stanton's biblical commentary; and the complaints against the gender-neutral biblical translations from the 1970s to the present show that for many, the struggle for religious equality remains starkly unresolved.

In 1888, the Equal Rights Party took up Anthony's argument that *he* means "she" for voting. In a letter to John J. O'Brien, the chief of New York City's Election Bureau, party member Anna Johnson insisted that generic *he* in the state voting law gave women the vote:

> The English language is destitute of a singular personal pronoun, third person, of common gender; but usage sanctions

the employment of "he," "him" and "his" as of common gender. Therefore under "he" women can certainly register.[22]

—ANNA JOHNSON, "The Last Day of Registry,"
New York Tribune (1888)

We don't know whether O'Brien agreed with her argument, but it appears that Johnson may have voted in that election. In contrast, most women who tried the *he*-includes-*she* gambit were turned away from the polls. The refusal of American election authorities to honor the generic *he* prompted Elizur Wright, president of the National Liberal League, to call for a constitutional amendment to insert "*or she* after every *he*."[23] But Wright had no better luck changing people's minds in America than Jacob Bright had in England. Court after court found that women were citizens, to be sure, and as citizens they had an *obligation* to obey the law and pay the penalty when they broke the law. But beyond that, each legal *privilege*—practicing law, running a school district, and especially, voting—had to be granted by the legislature individually, separately, and specifically.

The battle for suffrage continued in England, too. In 1911, the House of Commons passed a bill that would extend voting rights to women who met minimum property requirements, but Prime Minister Herbert Asquith enraged suffragists when he abruptly substituted a different bill dropping the woman's vote altogether and instead extending the vote to all *male persons,* a throwback to the 1832 election law. Although Asquith's Manhood Suffrage Bill languished, women's suffrage had to wait until the passage of a new Representation of the People Act in 1918. That law ignored the Interpretation Act's stipulation that masculine words apply to women as well and continued to treat the sexes as separate and unequal. Its first three sections specified the voting requirements for *men,* who could vote at age twenty-one if they met certain residency requirements. Section 4 of the Reform Act gave voting rights to women over

House Joint Resolution 1, 1919, which would become the Nineteenth Amendment, contains no pronouns. (National Archives)

30, but only if they had enough money. Finally, in 1928, the United Kingdom's Equal Franchise Act dropped all property requirements and extended the vote to everyone twenty-one and over, regardless of sex.[24] It even incorporated language that John Stuart Mill and William Bright tried to enact sixty years earlier, referring to voters gender-neutrally as *persons*.

Similarly in the United States, women won the vote without any explicit legal concession that *he* includes *she*. In fact, the Nineteenth Amendment contains no pronouns at all: "The right of citizens of the United States to vote shall not be denied or abridged . . . on account of sex." Even so, legislatures continued to ignore the pronoun arguments of Byrnes, Anthony, Stanton, and the other suffragists, recognizing generic *he* only to suppress or penalize women, not to liberate them. Not surprisingly, only women's rights advocates seemed to think this was unfair.

Crime and pronouns

The suffragists were right: the men who made the laws may have wanted to keep women from voting, but they were happy enough to punish them using generic *he*. In 1848, a woman in England refused to obey a summons because the law authorizing the summons used the masculine pronoun. Although courts dismissed such readings as attempts to evade responsibility, an 1887 legal treatise reflected the assumption that the recipient of a summons was a man: "A summons for the attendance of a witness is served personally, or, if that cannot be effected, by being left with . . . his wife or servant."[25] And in 1867, the same year that Parliament declared women ineligible to vote because *he* means "he," a court in Portsmouth, England, decided that *he* means "she" in the case of a woman tavern owner being prosecuted for harboring an "unfortunate . . . infected with a contagious disease" (that is, a prostitute). The publican maintained that the statute didn't cover her because it used the masculine pronoun. But the magistrate rejected that defense because "the masculine gender would include the feminine."[26]

The generic pronoun applied to fictional criminals as well. In Agatha Christie's *A.B.C. Murders*, the detective Hercule Poirot, always precise in his diction, describes the murderer with generic *he:*

> That he is a madman in an advanced state of mania goes without saying. That his appearance and behavior give no suggestion of such a fact is equally certain. This person—and though I say he, remember it may be a man or woman—has all the devilish cunning of insanity.[27]
>
> —AGATHA CHRISTIE, *The A.B.C. Murders* (1936)

When it came to punishment, American courts interpreted generic *he* like their British counterparts. In 1896, for example, the Massachusetts Supreme Court denied a petition by a woman who had challenged her arrest because "the citation issued . . . against her was not grammatical, as it used the masculine gender instead of the feminine gender pronoun."[28]

If *he* was ambiguous in a statute, *she* was not. It was simply assumed that laws using the feminine pronoun never referred to men. For example, in 1909 Wisconsin considered a bill providing a fine of up to $500 (just under $14,000 today) and six months in jail for any stenographer who "reveals confidential information regarding her employer." A Kansas newspaper, calling attention to that pronoun, observed, "There are male stenographers too but they are not covered by the bill." The paper's editor, presumably male, smugly suggested that the purpose of the law was to protect the (male) employer from a charge of harassment "when he buys bon bons, and cut posies, and otherwise spends his money . . . for the typewriter girl."[29]

In rare instances, Parliament took care when drafting legislation to ensure that women were specifically included in a bill's pronouns. Though the government insisted that *man* in the 1868 voting law excluded women, British lawmakers explained that the use of *his or her* to refer to jurors in the Criminal Act passed the year before was no mistake, that it had been chosen deliberately to provide for a "jury of matrons" if need be.[30] But when California passed a constitutional amendment in 1911 giving women the vote, opinion was divided on whether the newly enfranchised women could serve on juries chosen from lists of registered voters. California statutes still called jury members *men* and referred to them as *he,* but since the state's Code of Civil Procedure contained a *he*-means-*she* clause, some judges began putting women into jury pools. However, at least one magistrate said "no" to women jurors because, as he put it so bluntly,

> A he is a he and not a she. If the code were meant to include women as possible jurors it would not say he but would say "he or she." Man is a man. Man is not a woman. Therefore, until the Legislature meets and changes the code in accordance with this view, women cannot sit on juries in my court.[31]
> —"Justice Frederickson: Can't Sit in My Court,"
> *Los Angeles Times* (1911)

In another instance a woman in Oak Park, Illinois, complained when her name was stricken from the jury pool because she was a woman. This time a judge found that, because of the state's *he*-means-*she* law, the extension of suffrage to women automatically made them eligible to serve on juries. But this was no radical departure from previous interpretations of generic *he,* since jury service was an obligation, not a perk.[32]

Even men sought to benefit from "*he* means 'she.'" After the Nineteenth Amendment was ratified, a murderer in New Jersey unsuccessfully appealed his conviction because there had been no women on the jury at his trial. The New Jersey Supreme Court rejected that appeal because, even though women could vote, since state law referred to jurors as *he*, without specific legislation they could not serve on juries.[33] Texas took an even stronger position on the all-male jury. In 1921, the Texas Supreme Court threw out six convictions made by juries with women on them, including one conviction for murder, because the state constitution provided, "Grand and petit juries in the District Courts shall be composed of twelve *men*."[34] The court refused to apply the Texas *he*-means-*she* law to the constitution, and it refused to interpret *men* in the constitution as generic. Opponents of women on juries routinely argued that women must be protected from hearing about the sordid crimes frequently discussed in open court, and that mixing the sexes in a jury room was "inconvenient," meaning that men had to watch their language.[35] Texas did not formally permit women in the jury pool until 1954. The positive impact of that change was felt immediately, and it had nothing to do with fairness or judgment by one's peers. As one male juror commented, with a woman on the jury, "we couldn't do any cussing."[36]

Some defendants in capital cases even argued that the masculine pronoun protected them from execution. In 1925, the lawyer for Sabelle Nitti, a Chicago woman sentenced to hang for murdering her husband, sought her release on the grounds that the Illinois capital punishment statute read, "he (the defendant) shall be sentenced to death if found guilty."[37] Nitti, an Italian immigrant later memorialized among the women who kill their husbands in the musical *Chicago*, was sentenced to hang on Columbus Day, an irony that was not lost on the press covering the story. In the end, the Illinois Supreme Court vacated Nitti's conviction, not because of pronouns or a reluctance to execute an Italian American on a day celebrating

Italian Americans, but for lack of evidence. The prosecution did not retry the case.

Sometimes, of course, law enforcement read the criminal code literally as "*he* means 'he.'" In 1934, the police chief in Indianapolis declined to stop "the Rabelaisian revelry of semi-nude woman dancers" because the relevant disturbing-the-peace statute used the masculine pronoun, rendering it, in his view, "inapplicable to women." But one local resident wryly observed that any eighth grader would know that the voyeuristic chief was wrong, because "custom justifies the pronoun for both genders."[38] And in 1975, an Episcopal court rejected the argument of the activist Rev. L. Peter Beebe, an Oberlin priest who favored ordaining women, that the use of masculine pronouns in the canons was generic and "not a demarcation of sex."[39] The church court found that *he* means "he" in scripture, but Beebe's generic interpretation of *he* ultimately prevailed when the Episcopal Church accepted women into its priesthood.

A suitable job for a woman

He clearly included *she* in the criminal code, but did the masculine pronoun include women when it came to jobs? That depended on the job. A woman could be a teacher or a secretary or a factory worker, even if *he* in regulations included women, but could a *she* be president? Even before the Seneca Falls Convention of 1848, two leading American abolitionists—both male—disagreed about whether *he* in the Constitution barred women from the presidency.

Article II of the US Constitution, specifying the president's qualifications and duties, uses the masculine pronoun four times. According to Lysander Spooner, that meant that male slaves could technically become president if they met the constitutional age and citizenship requirements, but a woman could not:

> The constitution, whenever it uses the pronoun, in speaking of the president, uniformly uses the masculine gender—from which it may be inferred that male persons only were intended to be made eligible to the office.
>
> —LYSANDER SPOONER,
> *The Unconstitutionality of Slavery* (1845)[40]

But Wendell Phillips objected that elsewhere, the Constitution uses the masculine pronoun to refer to women as well as men, and so calling the president *he* in Article II must also be generic:

> In grammars, as well as law, the rule used to be, that the masculine pronoun and the word "man" included the race.... The Constitution itself, in the 5th Amendment, has, "no person shall be compelled to be witness against HIMSELF ... " But, alas! according to Mr. Spooner, none of these shields cover the defenceless heads of the women![41]
>
> —WENDELL PHILLIPS,
> "The Constitution and Slavery," *The Liberator* (1845)

Spooner admitted that the Fifth Amendment's *himself* is generic. It applies to everyone, not just to men. But he insisted that when the pronoun refers to a specific person, as it does in Article II, that individual is always male.[42] Although Spooner's reasoning is not reflected in the grammar books of his day, his is the mantra advanced repeatedly in nineteenth-century America to deny women access to jobs in government and the professions: of course *he* may be generic, but not in this particular case.

In England, the 1870 Elementary Education Act, sponsored by the Liberal MP William Edward Forster, established universal schooling and provided for elected local Education Councils, whose members were referred to with the pronouns *he* and *his*. During one parliamentary debate on the bill, Forster explained that he used male pronouns, not to exclude women from school boards, but "because the use of those words was the best way to include them." When this paradoxical reasoning was greeted with laughter, Forster invoked the Act of Interpretation.[43]

Men in power accepted the generic masculine only when it didn't require them to give up too much. Women on school boards were one thing, but in a few cases in the United States, women as state school superintendents were seen to be taking "*he* means 'she'" much too far. In 1888, Kansas attorney general S. B. Bradford argued that, since the Kansas constitution used *his* to refer to all state officials, Agnes J. Carruthers could not run for state superintendent of public instruction, even though she was already the school superintendent of Saline county. Salina attorney T. F. Garver strongly objected that, since the Kansas law uses *he* to guarantee rights to women as well as men, neither pronouns nor biology should disqualify a woman from office.[44] Despite this support, Carruthers never did become the state's school chief.

Convinced that Americans were long past such folly or ignorance, in 1897 the *Idaho Statesman* reassured women that it was unnecessary to add *she* to every statute that contained a *he*: "No one need fear that the use of the pronoun 'he' and its variations will shut out any person to whom it is not personally applicable."[45] Yet as we've seen, women continued to be shut out because men read *he* to mean "men only."

But can women be lawyers?

In 1888, the Stenographers Association apologized for having to call women stenographers *he*:

> It is the misfortune of the English language that it has no pronoun capable of expressing in the singular number a substantive of either the masculine or feminine gender. . . . Let it not be supposed, however, that we are unmindful of the very large element of women in the shorthand profession.[46]
>
> —"Women Stenographers,"
> *New York Evening World* (1888)

And in 1909, a journalist blamed grammar for making him use *he* to refer to workers in paper box factories when most of them were women: "This use of the masculine pronoun . . . is forced merely through the English lack of the neuter gender."[47] *He* might mean "she" when it came to low-paid jobs for office and factory workers, but for lawyers, who required a license, court approval, and admission to the bar, generic *he* was problematic. Many people (men, to be sure) argued that *he* in references to lawyers meant only "he."

The policy on women lawyers varied from state to state, and even county to county. Lavinia Goodell was admitted to the Wisconsin bar in 1874, but citing the pronoun *he* in the law covering attorney qualifications, the Wisconsin Supreme Court denied her admission to the State Supreme Court bar. Chief Justice Edward G. Ryan refused to apply Wisconsin's *he*-means-*she* law in Goodell's case "in view of the uniform exclusion of females from the bar by common law." Declaring that women were destined to bear children and maintain homes, Ryan insisted they were not cut out for "forensic strife." His comments were so outrageous that in 1877 the state legislature passed a law specifically authorizing women to practice before the Supreme Court, and Goodell was finally allowed to practice before the Wisconsin high court bar.[48]

But practicing law in the highest courts didn't always mean that women could work in lower ones. In 1879, Belva Lockwood became the first woman admitted to the US Supreme Court bar, and she was the first woman to argue a case before that court. Under the slogan "I cannot vote, but I can be voted for," Lockwood ran for president in 1884 on the ticket of the National Equal Rights party, appearing on the ballot in nine states. But although she was admitted to the Frederick County bar in Maryland, she was denied admission to the bar in Carroll County on the grounds that Maryland law referred to lawyers as *he*. Pressing her case, Lockwood argued that state law stipulated that "the masculine includes all genders, except where such construction would be absurd and unreasonable." But Circuit Judge William N. Hayden denied Lockwood's petition on the very grounds "that it would be 'absurd and unreasonable,' in the exact words of the code, to apply the pronouns 'he' and 'him' to a woman."[49]

In 1885 the Oregon Supreme Court denied Mary A. Leonard admission to the Oregon bar, even though she was already a practicing lawyer in the Washington Territory, because Oregon's statutes referred to lawyers exclusively as *he*.[50] Leonard took her case to the US District Court, which did approve her application, and she became the first woman admitted to the Oregon bar.

But in Maryland, despite women's persistence, *he* continued to mean "he." In 1901, James McSherry, Chief Judge of Maryland's Court of Appeals, denied the bar application of Etta H. Maddox, the first woman to graduate from the Baltimore Law School, because

> the Act of 1898 regulating admission to the bar ... uses the masculine pronoun or adjective throughout in referring to the applicants. Unless this can be interpreted to include the femi-

nine gender, then the court can find no legislation upon which to base a right to admit the present applicant. By common law no woman could take part in any public affairs. It is clear that the act mentioned did not intend to enlarge the class allowed to practice law.[51]

— "Barred from the Bar: Women Cannot Practice Law in Maryland," *Frederick News* (1901)

Maddox, a founder of the Maryland Suffrage Association, then petitioned the state legislature, which to its credit passed a law in 1902 that specifically granted women the right to practice law in the state. However, changing the language of the law didn't necessarily change attitudes: yes, women could finally practice law in Maryland, but the state's male lawyers did not admit women to the Maryland Bar *Association* until the 1950s. In any case, Maddox, finally a lawyer, drafted Maryland's first women's suffrage bill. It did not pass. In fact, Maryland did not ratify the Nineteenth Amendment until 1941.

One year after Maddox was denied entry to the bar, and then admitted, the city of Baltimore appointed eight women as truant officers after the city solicitor cited the same *he*-means-*she* statute that had failed Maddox: "In all legislation a masculine term was held to include the feminine except where it would be absurd or unreasonable."[52] Apparently it was reasonable for women to chase after delinquent children but not to prosecute or defend them in court.

Shakespeare's Portia practiced law in Venice, but that was in another country, and on stage, not in a real courtroom. Portia notwithstanding, women lawyers in England had their own legal difficulties. Lucy Frances Nettlefold scored firsts in her Cambridge law exams but was barred by the Law Society—the group charged with certifying solicitors—from becoming an attorney. Nettlefold appealed on the grounds that the Solicitors Act of 1843 required admission of any qualified "person," a neutral word that did not exclude women. Although her attorneys included Lord Robert Cecil, a former prime minister and future winner of the Nobel Peace Prize, the courts turned down Nettlefold's suit because, despite the Interpretation Act, women had never before served as solicitors.[53]

Nettlefold—who had been forced to sue under her husband's name, Bebb—continued to support women's rights, and in 1919 she argued that a proposed Bill for the Regulation of Aerial Navigation must include women under such terms as *pilot, navigator, officer, mechanic,* and *person,* and that the pronoun *he* refers to them as well. Nettlefold cited the Interpretation Act's *he*-means-*she* provision and dismissed the excuse that had thwarted her own legal career:

> The objection raised . . . that women never had acted as solicitors . . . would not be applicable here . . . because flying is too recent to admit of a disqualification based on ancient custom, but still more because there have been successful women aviators, both here [in England] and in France and in the United States.[54]

> —L. F. NETTLEFOLD, "Women and Aviation" (1919)

The Aerial Navigation Act passed in 1920, but British women had already been flying planes for a decade—one had even founded England's first flying school. The *OED* cites the word *aviatrice,* "a woman pilot," as early as 1910—so, pronoun or no pronoun, British women flew if they wanted to.

Pushing back against generic *she*

Pronoun discrimination cut two ways, at least according to men who felt slighted by the occasional generic *she*. For example, an 1873 newspaper article on the "Science of Teaching" explains that teachers are referred to with feminine pronouns because teaching is women's work. In the (presumably male) writer's view, men teach only to replace those women who lack endurance or commitment.[55] A few years later we find a male teacher complaining that generic *she* turns men in the profession into "an accident." For him, the blatant sexism of generic *she* "violates the well-known principle in English grammar that the masculine, being the stronger, etc., may be used when reference is made to one of a class including both males and females." In an age of "woman's rights, woman suffrages, etc.," wounded male pride prompted the writer to urge men to "assert our rights while yet there is hope."[56]

As in teaching, so in music: an 1897 article in the *Springfield Sunday Republican* complained that " 'he' is our common gender pronoun in other connections, but not in music," where women make up the majority of the students, discouraging men from entering the field.[57] But as Belva Lockwood, Etta Maddox, Lucy Nettlefold, and countless others would attest, generic *he* hardly solves the problem of inclusiveness. Even after women secured employment rights, resistance to a truly gender-neutral interpretation of generic masculines continues. Flash forward to 2017: Jodie Whittaker would be the first woman to play the Doctor in the British science fiction television show *Doctor Who*, prompting a backlash from some of the more easily bruised male egos, who insisted that this was not a suitable job for a woman. As one of the milder tweets put it, "Um, the Doctor is a time LORD. Not a time LADY."

Her place is in the House, and in the Senate

The early women's rights movement focused on *votes* for women, but it also encouraged people to vote *for* women, fielding women candidates for elected and appointed office. Despite the proliferation of *he*-means-*she* laws, the masculine pronoun often barred the way. For example, a Texas statute specified that "the masculine gender shall include the feminine and neuter."[58] This prompted one man to object that Texas had abolished both grammar and gender, that the statute that required "sawing off the tips of the horns of vicious bulls might apply as well to female and neuter bulls." But the big issue for him was that "suffrage becomes promiscuous in Texas, and all the avenues of political preferment are open to all the sexes, masculine, feminine, and neuter." In other words, Texas women would be able to vote, and, perhaps worse still in the writer's opinion, to govern.[59]

As women continued to seek elected office, their opponents continued to use the issue of pronoun gender to keep them out. When Anna J. Baxter was elected county clerk of Jasper County, Missouri, in 1890, the first woman elected to public office in that state, her rival challenged her eligibility on the grounds that the law describing the qualifications for the office used the masculine pronoun. But an editorial in the *St. Louis Post-Dispatch* supported Baxter, who as deputy clerk was already doing the job in question. The paper also warned that, since the education law also referred to teachers with the masculine pronoun, refusing to interpret *he* as generic would produce an immediate teacher shortage, and it concluded that women shouldn't be punished just because English was missing a word:

> The want of a personal pronoun of the common gender in our language leads, as is well known, to the frequent use of the masculine pronoun alone, instead of the dual "he or she" and "his or her" in laws applying to either sex, and to give it an exclusive signification for the purpose of preventing the people from electing women to office, would be without any warrant in reason or public policy.[60]
>
> —"Mrs. Baxter's Eligibility,"
> *St. Louis Post-Dispatch* (1890)

Missouri attorney general John Wood agreed that the statutory *he* was generic and did not prevent Baxter from serving as county clerk.

Some states and territories allowed women to vote long before the Nineteenth Amendment. When the US Senate debated the admission of Wyoming as the forty-fourth state in 1890, Alabama senator John Tyler Morgan warned that, since the territory of Wyoming allowed women to vote, a new state of Wyoming could elect a woman to Congress. But Ohio senator Henry B. Payne countered that he hoped Wyoming would send two women senators to Washington. Even though the Constitution uses the pronoun *he* for members of Congress, Payne was certain the Senate would declare "that 'he' was a pronoun of the 'common gender.'"[61] Wyoming was duly admitted to the Union, and so far, all its senators have been men. Wyoming has elected three women to the US House of Representatives, though it did take the state more than a century to elect the first one.

As more women sought elected office, more people wondered if women could be barred by a pronoun. When the suffragist Mary E. Lease considered running for the US Senate in Kansas in 1892, a critic insisted that she could not serve because "the Constitution says 'He.'" Although Lease did not run, the *New Orleans Picayune* suggested that the question of whether *he* may include *she* would be a matter for the courts, adding that if the Supreme Court decided that the constitutional "'He' might embrace the gentler sex, Mrs. Lease would be delighted."[62] But Senator George Vest, of neighboring Missouri, was not delighted by Lease's candidacy, complaining, "the Constitution is against it." Reporting on this story, the *Pittsburgh Dispatch* supported her right to run, and to its credit, the paper disputed any restrictive interpretation of *he*:

> It is, of course, not worth while to dispute that the language was employed with the presumption on the part of the Constitution-makers that the Senators would be of the male

sex. But the pronoun does not make a constitutional enact-
ment to that effect.... Her constitutional rights and those of
Kansas, if she should be selected by that State, are not to be
swept away by imaginary constitutional restrictions that are
wholly the creation of prejudice.[63]

    —"No Such Restrictions," *Pittsburgh Dispatch* (1892)

In 1891, Nebraska voters had the opportunity to elect Prohibition
Party candidate Ada M. Bittenbender to the US Senate. Although
Bittenbender, the first woman to be admitted to the Nebraska bar,
lost by a wide margin, she then stood as a candidate for judge of the
Nebraska Supreme Court. Answering objections that she would
be ineligible to serve if elected, Bittenbender argued that the Fourteenth Amendment guaranteed her right to run for the office, and
that the state constitution referred to judges as *he* and *his* "simply
because the English language has no third person singular pronoun
for the common gender." An editorial in the *Nebraska State Journal*
advised voters that grammar was not a problem, and that the best
way to test a woman's suitability for office was simply to elect her.[64]

In contrast, in 1906, Ohio attorney general Wade H. Ellis took a
narrow view of statutory masculines, declaring that "In the law the
pronouns 'he' and 'his' are ... the sole indications that the Legislature intended the appointment to be conferred upon male persons."
Ellis explained that only in the absence of such intent can the masculine include the feminine.[65] Such contorted logic suggests that
despite the *he*-means-*she* laws, there is no such thing as generic *he*,
since any masculine noun or pronoun not accompanied by its feminine counterpart signaled the legislature's intent to exclude women.

With women increasingly successful in state and local elections—
often, but not always, in positions like education—there was increasing talk of women running for the US House of Representatives.
Sarah Platt Decker, a prominent Denver resident, considered such

a run in 1909, prompting concern that the constitutional *he* would prevent her, or any other woman, from serving if elected. Out-of-state newspapers frequently weighed in when women ran for office. The *Davenport Daily Times,* an Iowa paper, could not resist invoking a sexist stereotype: "It is quite possible that some woman candidate may be found willing to confess to being 25 years of age, but how she would manage to avoid collision with that word 'he' in the constitution has not yet been suggested." Even so, the paper conceded that it would be up to Congress to determine whether or not to seat an elected representative.[66]

The *Des Moines Daily Tribune* took a stronger but equally anti-feminist stand against women in Congress, arguing that "congressman admits of but one interpretation" and reminding readers that no official communication ever used the word *congresswoman.* Furthermore, the Constitution refers to representatives as "he," and " 'he' refers to a man, nothing more nor less." In the *Tribune's* view, if a woman were elected to Congress from Colorado, she would be disqualified "by an accident in our language which provided three sets of pronouns as arbitrary symbols of the three genders." The paper held out one faint hope in the form of an equal pronoun rights amendment: "Perhaps in time the women can get the constitution amended to read 'he or she,' or, possibly, 'she' exclusively."[67]

But not in Maryland. There the Board of Election Supervisors would not let Ada Smith Lang run for the Maryland House of Delegates in 1909 because no language in the state constitution explicitly gave women the right to hold office. An editorial in the *Baltimore Sun* supported the decision to keep women off the ballot:

> It would seem to be absurd... to elect a person to the Legislature who does not possess the right to vote, and it can be safely assumed that the question of the eligibility of females

for office did not once present itself to the minds of the members of the convention of 1867.[68]

—"Against Mrs. Lang," *Baltimore Sun* (1909)

Even Mrs. J. Williams Funck, the head of Maryland's Woman's State Suffrage Association, agreed that a woman should not serve in the legislature if she can't vote, though Funck was optimistic that when women did get the vote, they would have plenty of women candidates to choose from.[69] Lang, who vowed to sue, later ran unsuccessfully for the US House in 1920 and for the Senate in 1934.

Can she be he?

Generic *he* resurfaced as an election issue in 1916, when five women ran for Congress, and Jeanette Rankin, of Montana, became the first woman elected to the House of Representatives. Days after Rankin's victory, the *Minneapolis Star Tribune* asked, in this front-page headline, "Can 'She' Be 'He', a Congressman, and Be Woman?" That led to further questions: "As a matter of grammar, SHE cannot be HE. But as a matter of law? And politics?"[70]

As we've seen, the Constitution uses masculine pronouns to describe the qualifications for office. And so a strict constructionist from Philadelphia complained that Montana's voters could not "amend the masculine pronoun from the federal Constitution."[71] But the *Washington Post* consulted Barton Payne, a prominent Chicago judge who would later become Secretary of the Interior, who dismissed the fear—or the hope—that the masculine pronoun barred the way for Rankin.[72]

Even so, John P. Irish, a leading California Democrat and vocal opponent of votes for women, invoked the same constitutional grammar to register his objection to Rankin:

> Can 'She' Be 'He',
> a Congressman,
> and Be Woman?
> ───
> Students of Law Worry Over
> Status of Feminine Repre-
> sentative-Elect.

Headline in the *Minneapolis Star Tribune* after Rankin's House victory.

The use of the pronoun "He" in the constitutional qualifications of a member of that House is by plain intention of the
constitutional convention a permanent limitation of membership to men.... "He" is held to include both genders only in
penal statutes and in the revenue laws.... "He" is not a bisexual pronoun ... and members [of the House] who vote that it
is will be guilty of perjury, for they will not have upheld the
constitution.

—"The Woman Congressman,"
Oakland Tribune (1916)

Irish feared that manners would trump law, that a misplaced sense of
gallantry would cause Congress to violate the Constitution "because
there is a lady concerned."[73] And Oakland writer J. W. Dutton cited
Noah Webster's dictionary to disqualify Rankin because *he* means
"the man or male person named before."[74] But the editors of the
Woodland Daily Democrat argued that, regardless of the pronoun,
Rankin was eligible because the noun *representative* "is no more masculine than feminine."[75]

Opposing such views, another writer was sure that Rankin's election would prove once and for all that *he* is a gender-neutral pronoun,
a concept enshrined in grammar books as well as law, but not in

actual usage. Besides, a woman in the House could actually improve, not just the government, but also the English language:

> The use of 'he' as a common pronoun referring to 'person' is well established in law and good usage. But it has not become idiomatic. The tendency in conversation is to use the anomalous 'they' despite its plural form, merely because it is of common gender. Perhaps the controversy over Miss Rankin's eligibility, which is altogether likely to be settled in her favor, will help to popularize the usage of 'he' as a common gender pronoun.[76]
>
> —"A Common Gender,"
> *Marshalltown Evening Times-Republican* (1916)

To complete this debate over the scope of constitutional *he,* the *Nebraska State Journal* proclaimed that Rankin's election underscored the inadequacy of the English pronoun system. The paper looked to women lawmakers to fix the problem not by backing generic *he,* but by legislating a new pronoun:

> The need of a common gender pronoun is now official. Some technicality burdened brain has discovered that Miss Rankin of Montana may be ineligible for a seat in congress because at one place the constitution refers to a congressman as 'he.' Now as a matter of fact few days pass in any life without the use of the masculine pronoun to include both men and women.... There is a longstanding demand for a pronoun equivalent to 'he or she' and 'him or her' but the desired word has not appeared.... When the congresswomen get the balance of power in congress they will doubtless fill by law the gap in the language which causes all this trouble.[77]
>
> —*Nebraska State Journal* (1916)

The *Morning Oregonian* did find one terminological hurdle facing Rankin: what to call her? Although most commentators fretted over the difficulties Rankin would face navigating the sweary, smoke-filled caucus rooms of the Capitol, the *Oregonian* wondered whether Rankin would be "the lady from Montana," "the person from Montana," or "the member from Montana"—which the paper characterized as "non-committal, polite and sufficiently elegant"—or would she simply be "Representative Rankin"?[78] In 1895, Colorado had faced the same problem, with three women serving in the state's General Assembly. One writer moaned about legislative debates and speechifying where "every sentence abounds with 'he or she,' 'his or her,' 'him or her,' until the ears and brains of the Representatives are weary."[79] The writer offered no solution for Colorado's pronoun problem. In the end, these women simply carried out their legislative functions, and both the language and the political system survived.

Then there was Maryland's pronoun problem. The Maryland legislature had not ratified the Nineteenth Amendment, and in 1921 the state was still trying to bar women from public office because of statutory *he*. The League of Women Voters had to sue the state after Attorney General Alexander Armstrong ruled that "the use of the masculine pronoun in connection with an office barred a woman as incumbent." But other Maryland politicians were finally ready to move on. Philip B. Perlman, Maryland's secretary of state, argued that pronouns do not bar a woman from serving in public office. Perlman's view prevailed, and in November, Mary E. W. Risteau became the first woman elected to the Maryland House of Delegates.[80] Yet even after women were admitted to the legislature, not through pronoun interpretation but because the House of Delegates was empowered to determine its own membership, the pronoun *he* was used from time to time to bar some women from *appointed* offices in the state. The state's pronoun problem was not settled until 1937, when Maryland attorney general Herbert O'Conor declared that the pronouns *he* and *his* were used in statutes "for ease of expression rather than . . . to prohibit the appointment of women," finally ensuring women's eligibility for all Maryland state positions.[81]

The long decline of generic *he*

Besides generating debates over the scope of *he* for voting and for holding office, nineteenth-century feminism prompted a general male backlash, some of it involving pronoun gender. Critics of women's rights chastised the movement for making men "watch their pronouns." They defended their precious generic *he*. They dared suffragists to invent a new pronoun. They even blamed these new women for singular *they*, though that usage arose centuries before women's suffrage—it even predates the right of men to vote. But the nineteenth-century woman's movement did impact language, and the increased presence of women in public life contributed to the gradual decline of generic *he*, a usage that finally collapsed in the late twentieth century.

This sarcastic description in 1864 of Elizabeth Cady Stanton's political activity, titled "The Pronouns Mixed," alternates gender references in order to mock suffragists, but it was motivated by a sense that the generic masculine was under attack:

> We admire Mrs. Stanton's spunk—she is a gentleman of genius; she is a gentleman of parts; she has honorably achieved wide influence among the gentler sex of both genders. It is highly proper that she should not only sign a Presidential call, but go into the Convention as a delegate, take others of her female brethren with him. Perhaps we are getting the pronouns a little mixed; what we mean to say is that this is a free country, and is going to be freer, and that every man or

woman of either sex has a perfect right to speak her mind and follow the lead of his own progressive ideas, and we hope she will do it.[82]

— "The Pronouns Mixed," *Jeffersonian Democrat* (1864)

Other writers simply assumed that, if generic *he* was in fact objectionable, then it was the job of the feminists—one wag at *Appletons'* called them "the women's rights women"—to come up with an alternative, and the *Somerset Herald* wrote, "We think the next Woman's Rights convention would and should object to [generic *he*]," creating a new pronoun instead.[83]

Similarly, a writer aptly calling himself "Fogy" apologizes for using the generic *he,* attributing the construction to "the dark age, when woman was considered inferior to man." But, he goes on,

in these days of "woman's rights," [generic he] is inappropriate; the same rule that confers upon our mothers and sisters . . . the privilege of working out poll-taxes on the road and standing up in rail and street cars, doubtless makes it necessary to use nouns and pronouns of both genders in all sentences in which reference is had to the entire human race.

—FOGY, "Hotch-Potch," *Freemont Weekly Journal* (1871)

By trivializing women as fighting for the "right" to stand on the streetcar or to work on a road crew in lieu of paying tax, Fogy dismissed the rights that women's activists sought, the vote and access to professional and economic power, so his support of gender-neutral language seems at best insincere.[84]

In contrast, in 1895 the social radical and eugenicist Moses Harman assailed the discriminatory force of generic *he,* to which "women writers, teachers, lecturers acquiesce," and which makes women "a lower class." Declaring that "They have rights who dare to take them," Harman warned women that the defects of vocabulary are "the causes that enslave themselves and their sisters." As a remedy, Harman considered replacing generic *man* with generic *woman,* though he settled on the Latin *homo* instead, and he called for the adoption of *en* as a gender-neutral pronoun.[85] In 1902, the activist Bertha Moore reprised Harman's theme, recommending singular *they* because generic *he* is "prejudicial, detrimental and unjust."[86]

Similarly, in 1913 William T. Miller, a Boston schoolteacher, argued that generic *he* was no longer appropriate in an age of women's rights. He called for a new pronoun to use when a teacher scolds, "Not a pupil should leave his seat!":

> Surely, in these Suffragette days, a girl pupil should not be advised to stay in "his seat." . . . We very evidently could utilize a new word which shall be more consistent than this makeshift rule. Many suggestions have been made to cover this need, but no word has as yet been adopted into common use.[87]
>
> —WILLIAM T. MILLER, "Some Words Our Language Needs," *Boston Globe* (1913)

In 1914, a British suffrage journal joined the pronoun fight, encouraging women to take the lead replacing generic *he*: "It would seem to be the duty of good Suffragists to evolve a singular pronoun of the third person and of common gender. They would be blessed of many extempore speakers." In the absence of a new pronoun, though, the writer relied on generic *he,* explaining in a note that "for this article the masculine imports also the feminine."[88]

American women were finally voting in 1921, but the *Gulfport Herald* lamented one consequence of the Nineteenth Amendment:

Some women ... are insisting that the grammatical or historically approved use of man, he, his or him to refer to both man
and woman, be subjected to the amendment—and this they
consider fundamental, constitutional and foundational. ...
The modern woman feels that man is "putting something
over" by use of the words he, him, his, although they are of
common gender when used with reference to a class and used
as a collective noun.[89]

—"A Common Pronoun," *Gulfport Daily Herald* (1921)

In 1922, the *Arizona Republic* suggested that feminism would
prove to be the death of generic *he:* "We do not think the feminists
will always stand for the discrimination involved in 'his' when referring at the same time to both males and females."[90]

And in 1934, the educator Philip Ballard disparaged the type of
grammarian "who would remould the language by artificial means,"
which, in Ballard's example, meant an invented gender-neutral pronoun. He recounted, having forgotten the details of time and place,
a feminist attempt to redress the grammatical "tyranny of man,"
who has three personal pronouns, by adding *shim* to the woman's
paradigm:

At a women's conference some years ago a member got up and
pointed out that the tyranny of man appeared no less in the
laws of grammar than in the laws of the land. While the masculine personal pronoun had three distinct forms, he, his, and
him, for the separate cases of the singular, the feminine pronoun had only two, she and her. She suggested as a remedy for
this gross piece of injustice that the feminine pronoun should
be declined she, shis, and shim.[91]

—PHILIP B. BALLARD, *Thought and Language* (1934)

The attitude that new pronouns are women's work, or women's fault, continues to the present. Almost 100 years after the Seneca Falls Convention focused attention on women's rights, the bruised male ego, unable to roll back women's suffrage and the increased presence of women in realms formerly the preserve of men, was still clinging to generic *he,* a sure sign that the pronoun was in trouble. The Canadian humorist Stephen Leacock, a social conservative who opposed the woman's vote, blamed women for voting out generic *he:*

> Another of my antipathies among the pronouns is the perpetual extension of the use of *"his or her"* where we used merely to use *his* when I was young. In those rude days women didn't count for so much as now, except as angels, heroines and guiding stars, all dollar-a-year jobs. But the women's vote has set up a sort of timid deference that is always afraid of omitting or insulting them.... This *his or her* stuff gets particularly troublesome after such words as *anybody, everybody, somebody* and *nobody etc.* It tangles us in such forms as:—
>
> Everybody nowadays has to have his or her ration card and if anybody lends his or her ration card to somebody then he or she must be careful to return it to him or her or else the inspector will make trouble for her or him.[92]
>
> —STEPHEN LEACOCK, "My Particular Aversions" (1944)

This nostalgia for the good old days, when men were gallantly nongeneric and women knew their place, did nothing to reverse social progress, and in the end they failed to prop up a dying generic *he.* As Leacock's words suggest, even before the feminism of the 1960s and '70s, support for generic *he* was on the wane. As far back as 1941, W. Worthington Wells wrote in his syndicated column on language, "The use of 'he' in addressing a mixed group is not considered the best construction."[93]

What added to this realization that generic *he* was on the way out was the growing realization that legislating the meaning of pronouns through broad measures like the 1850 Act of Interpretation in Britain or the 1871 Dictionary Act in the United States, which are still in force today, had failed to make the masculine pronoun generic in the law. The decades-long debate over the right of women to vote, hold office, and enter certain professions, showed that generic *he* was not generic after all, except when it came to requiring women to pay their tax bill or putting them on death row. Women won the right to vote through legislation addressing that issue, and in some states they were allowed to hold office, or become lawyers, not through new readings of existing law, but only after legislation was passed expressly opening up those opportunities to women.

Even as recently as 2016, at least one scholar proposed rewriting the American Constitution to clarify the legal meaning of *he*. When Hillary Clinton ran as the first woman candidate for president from a major political party, Richard Albert, a professor of constitutional law at Boston College, suggested that it was time to replace the outmoded references to the president and other elected official as *he*, not through the difficult task of amending the Constitution, but by rewriting the founding document from beginning to end to bring it up to date.[94] Creating a new Constitution would be harder than amending the existing document, and there's no guarantee that a constitutional convention would produce a gender-neutral document. But in the absence of such revision, Albert was confident that calling the president *he* posed no legal impediment to a woman: if a woman takes the oath of office, "no one will sue the chief justice for violating the Constitution. If [Clinton] wins, there will be no problem with her becoming the country's 45th president—no matter what the Constitution says."

Clinton did not win, so that hypothesis remains to be tested. But Albert's confidence that constitutional reference to "the president . . . *he*" will pose no problem may be premature. For one thing, the rabid birther challenges to Barack Obama's presidency suggest that political enemies will throw whatever they can at an officeholder they oppose. But more to the point, the long history documented here of challenges to generic *he* in American and British statutes, together with failure of *he*-means-*she* laws to clarify legislative intent, suggests that the constitutional meaning of *he* remains far less certain than it should be. That is why a number of states have rewritten their constitutions using gender-neutral language, some adopting *he or she,* and others avoiding pronouns whenever possible.[95] It's clear that the only surefire way to avoid a problem with statutory gender reference is to make constitutions and laws unambiguously gender-blind.

As for generic *he,* the years have not treated it kindly. The feminism of the 1970s pushed hard against sexist language. The most visible results of this are the spread of the honorific *Ms.,* a marriage-neutral title coined as early as 1901; an increase in gender-neutral job titles like *letter carrier, flight attendant,* and *firefighter;* a decline in the use of gender-neutral *man;* and the death of generic *he.*

He didn't vanish overnight. But during the 1970s, a distaste for gratuitous gender reference in formal writing quickly showed up in textbooks. By 1980, the popular college textbook *Writing with a Purpose* was explaining, "Many people now urge that the linguistic discrimination implied in this traditional use [of generic *he*] should be avoided whenever possible." Instead of *he,* the text advised students to use the compound *he or she* or to recast their sentence to avoid the gender issue altogether.[96] In the next chapter we'll look at the pronouns that were created to replace generic *he.* None were recommended by the style guides or the grammar books, and none achieved widespread use. But they're not dead yet: a few have persisted. I call them the words that failed—that's the title of the next chapter—because most of the invented pronouns crashed and burned. But there's renewed interest in them today, with lots of discussion and a small but not insignificant number of users. Although as we'll see in Chapter 5, it's singular *they* that has now become an approved alternative, and for many it is now the pronoun of choice.

The Words That Failed

> Surely great big men who can invent such fine
> words as "radioactinium" and "spectroheliograph"
> should be able to devise a little useful pronoun.
>
> —*Daily Gazette* (1920)

John Stuart Mill sought grammatical equality for women
and Samuel Taylor Coleridge wanted a pronoun that would not specify gender. These goals, separately and together, spurred nineteenth-
century word coiners in their quest for the missing word. In 1852
an anonymous writer complained that generic *he* refers only to men;
coordinate *he or she* is "inelegant and bungling"; and singular *they*
violates grammatical rules. To remedy this, the writer called on "one
of our grammar makers" to craft a new pronoun.[1]

Some of these "grammar makers" were only too willing to comply. Sometimes they created a pronoun that would secure gender
fairness and inclusivity, or at least what counted as fairness and
inclusivity at the time. Other times, their goal was just good grammar. And occasionally, these two goals converged. Some of the
word coiners were women. Most were men. Some may not have felt
that binary pronouns fit them, but if so, they didn't mention it. A
few of the coiners were crackpots, others serious reformers. And in

at least two cases, they were legislators. What they had in common was that their words were bound to fail.

Legislating pronouns

When three women were elected to the Colorado legislature in 1894, the *Rocky Mountain News* asked state lawmakers to coin a gender-neutral pronoun:

> The legislature will have an opportunity to cover itself with glory by inventing a new pronoun, which will stand for both sexes, for use in the election law. Since the ladies are entitled to equal recognition with the men they are distinctly below their rights so long as the pronoun "he" is required to do duty for both sexes. There has been a demand for a bi-personal pronoun and with legislative sanction it would soon pass into general acceptance.[2]
> —"Coin a Word," *Rocky Mountain News* (1894)

The *Denver Evening Post* agreed, though the paper was skeptical about lawmakers' linguistic ability, noting that "average legislatures have heretofore been more noted for violations of grammar than practice or knowledge of it." The *Chicago Tribune* added its two cents in the interests of getting rid of verbosity in the Colorado General Assembly, where "everything must be he or she will do so and so and the repetition becomes monotonous."[3] Colorado's legislature did not enact a pronoun law. But two correspondents wrote to the *News* to suggest that the lawmakers adopt *shee,* or the paradigm *hesher, hiser,* and *himer.*[4]

Then, in 1922, two states formally entertained the idea of legislating pronouns. Mississippi state senator W. A. Ellis, who also advanced a bill giving women in the state the same right to vote as men, tried but failed to establish *hesh, hiser,* and *himer* as Mississippi's official gender-neutral pronouns. Ellis explained that his proposed bill grew "out of the exigencies of the times on account of woman's new political freedom."[5] The measure would "legalize" and "make valid" *hesh, hiser,* and *himer* not just in the law, but wherever English was used in Mississippi, and it would save the state "many bottles of ink and many pages of paper."[6] The *Okolona Messenger* added its support: "Since woman's sphere is so widened that she takes part in matters which were then considered wholly within the province of the sterner sex, such a word is needed and should come into use to lessen the burden on the language."[7] Initially approved by a Senate Committee of the Whole, Ellis's pronoun bill, proposed in a year when the Mississippi legislature considered both women's suffrage and an anti-lynching law, ultimately failed—by only one vote.

This seemed destined to become the year of failed pronoun legislation, as the state of Missouri also considered legalizing yet another gender-neutral pronoun, *idn,* in 1922. Judge A. N. Gossett, a delegate to the Missouri Constitutional Convention that year, proposed an amendment to recognize *idn,* a gender-neutral pronoun to be used in the state's laws instead of *he, she, it,* and even *they.*[8] Gossett assured the convention that he was not offering his pronoun "to arouse risibility," and assured delegates that Latin, Greek, French, and German already had gender-neutral pronouns.

Risibility was aroused, however, when a delegate asked for the French or German equivalents of *idn,* and Gossett had to admit that he did not actually speak either language. And more risibility followed in the press, as the *Nebraska State Journal* insisted that *idn* stands for "I don't know."[9] Gossett defended *idn* in the *Christian Science Monitor.* Though an "ugly duckling," *idn* would avoid the clumsy or ungrammatical alternatives of *he or she* and singular *they.* The *Monitor* agreed that "there would be some satisfaction from getting rid of the 'his or her or their' necessary for safety in legal documents and for accuracy oftentimes in conversation and ordinary writing."[10]

As it turned out, the convention presented Missouri voters not with a promised new constitution, but with a set of constitutional amendments that did not contain an *idn* clause. In the end, the state's voters rejected all of the proposed amendments including those specifying that Missouri's elected officials be *male persons,* so even if Gossett's gender-neutral pronoun had made it out of committee, *idn* would have failed to become the law of the state.

But there's still a missing word . . .

Legislating gender-neutral pronouns didn't work in Missouri or Mississippi, partly because no one took the proposals seriously, but more important, because laws mandating pronouns don't work: people use the pronouns they like, not the ones they're told to use. That didn't stop the word coiners, who felt that the need for a new word would eventually weaken the public's resistance to language change.

The earliest coined gender pronouns that I have found so far for English are *E, es,* and *em.* In 1841, Francis Brewster took time from his medical practice to write a grammar in which he labeled his new pronouns "masculor feminine." *Masculofemina* is Latin for "man-woman, or hermaphrodite," and Brewster's use of this unusual term is the first hint at nonbinary gender in a grammar book.[11] *E* was reinvented several times, but Brewster's contribution was universally ignored. In 1878, an anonymous coiner explained that if *I* can be the pronoun for the first person, then *E* can be the pronoun for the third.[12] That prompted Brewster to remind the public that he had coined *E* forty years earlier, but the public

MASCULOR FEMININE.

	Sing.	Plur.
Nom.	E.	They.
Poss.	Es.	Their.
Obj.	Em.	Them.

F. A. Brewster, *English Grammar.* (Courtesy of the Yale University Library.)

remained unimpressed.[13] *E* was proposed again in 1912,[14] and again in the mid-1970s.[15] In 1978, the Broward County School Board, in Florida, adopted *e* and *ir*—comprising elements from both the masculine and feminine pronouns—in order to comply with federal regulations that required gender-neutral language. The board offered teachers and administrators this dialogue about a student who missed the bus to show the new words in action:

QUESTION: Why did e miss ir bus?
ANSWER: E was afraid to go home.
QUESTION: Who was e with?
ANSWER: E was by ir self.

One of the six women on the seven-person school board disapproved: "I think the English language is in danger. I'd prefer they didn't make up words."[16] Apparently the Broward schools did not use *e* for long.

In another little-noticed round of early pronoun creation, *ne, nis, nim,* and *hiser* were all coined around 1850. *Ne* combines *n* with the endings of the masculine pronoun, while *hiser* is a blend of *his* and *her.* We know nothing about who coined these words, or why, and the evidence for dating these pronouns remains indirect: an unsigned 1884 comment in the *New York Commercial Advertiser* by a writer who disapproved of *thon,* an even newer gender-neutral pronoun that was receiving lots of attention. *Thon,* a blend of *that* and *one,* had just been announced with great fanfare by the composer Charles Crozat Converse. But the *Advertiser* didn't think *thon* had much chance of success, declaring that all such coinages were bound to fail "because the supposed need is not strongly felt" and it's hard to get people to adopt new words "unless they spring up naturally and, as it were, spontaneously."[17] According to the *Advertiser,* most English speakers opted for *one,* or they followed the worthiness doctrine, "the sound rule of rhetoric which recognizes the masculine pronoun as dominant." The writer even preferred singular *they*, used freely by such giants of English prose as Joseph Addison and Richard Steele of *The Spectator*, who did not have to suffer under teachers described by the writer as "the grammar mongers who bestride education in our day."

In fact, the grammar mongers bestriding education were faithful to their eighteenth-century predecessors, who demanded that everyone from schoolchildren to professional writers stick with generic *he*. The grammarians took pride in rooting out the errors of famous authors like Addison and Steele, not to mention Shakespeare and Milton, when these literary giants strayed from the rules. Yet the fact that English had no effective pronoun to refer to the author of this 1884 pronoun critique suggests that *he or she*, *they*, *ne*, and *thon* weren't the answer, and there is indeed a missing word.

If there was a serious effort to introduce *ne*, *nis*, and *nim*, as the *Advertiser* suggested, it didn't leave a paper trail. As for *hiser*, that coinage popped up first in 1879, and other pronouns besides Brewster's *E* appeared before Converse announced his new word in 1884, so before we get to *thon*, let's look at the other early coinages.

In 1864, a writer identified as Philologus offered *ve*, *vim*, *vir*:

> To secure precision without violating a plain rule in grammar or employing a tedious circumlocution, we need an additional word in our language—a personal pronoun of the third person, singular number, and common gender.... Might we not, in this age of improvement, by some means supply this much-needed word? How would the following answer? Nom. *ve*, poss. *vis*, obj. *vim*.... A little practice would make the use of the word facile, and thus precision, perspicuity, and brevity would be secured.[18]
>
> —PHILOLOGUS, "An Epicene Personal Pronoun Needed," *The Ladies' Repository* (1864)

But *vir* is not really gender neutral. Philologus is certainly a man (*-us* in Latin is a masculine suffix) and he gets *vir* from the Latin word for *man,* the same word that gives us English *virile.* Another writer offered *ze,* a pronoun that doesn't carry any gender baggage, suggesting that Noah Webster endorse the coinage. But Webster was already dead, and dictionary endorsements don't really get anyone to use new pronouns.[19] *Thon* and *heer* appeared in several major dictionaries, but these seals of approval failed to give them any traction.

Failure didn't stop the word coiners. Soon after *ze* was proposed, two readers wrote to the popular language columnist Richard Grant White, suggesting *en,* from French (not the gender-neutral pronoun *on,* as one might expect, but the preposition *en*), giving this example: "If a person wishes to sleep, *en* mustn't eat cheese for supper."[20] White rejected these imports, or any other innovation, insisting that if English needed a new pronoun, it would have found one long ago.

Like most men, White saw nothing wrong with either generic *he* or generic *man.* But *man,* like *he,* proved far from inclusive. The Seneca Falls Convention of 1848 had seen the official launch of the American women's movement, a call for women's rights that eventually led to the passage of the Nineteenth Amendment in 1919. One of the reasons it took seventy years for women to get the vote was the attitude of antifeminists like White, who used his readers' call for a gender-neutral pronoun to sneer at the feminists of his day: "Any objection to this use of *man,* and of [generic *he*], is for the consideration of the next Women's Rights Convention." If they want "to free the language of the oppression of the sex," all they need to say is, "If one wishes to sleep, one mustn't eat cheese for supper." If only rooting out oppression were this easy.

White was a nineteenth-century language guru, the equivalent of Henry Fowler or William Safire in the twentieth century, and even though his comments were negative, they sparked a discussion about the need for a new pronoun. The *Boston Recorder* lamented the lack of a gender-neutral pronoun in English that would help writers avoid the error of singular *they* and the "not quite accurate" generic *he*. The *Recorder* asked, "Cannot some of the philologists or grammarians, at a single bold dash, move an amendment in this matter, which shall be carried by acclamation?"[21]

But it turns out that most philologists and grammarians don't relish the business of coining new words, leaving the field open for amateurs. One amateur identified as "L" wrote to the *Recorder* suggesting *han, hans,* and *hanself,* words han described as odd and uncouth, but which han had been using "sportively among my friends."[22] Even though L proclaimed hanself no expert, han pointed out that the pronoun system is slow to change, noting that it is easier to incorporate "a hundred new nouns and adjectives, and fifty new verbs," than one new pronoun. Needless to say, *han* proved to be a dud.

The prospects for change were dim, but the search for the missing word continued. In 1869, the influential *Appletons' Journal* put out a call for a new gender-neutral pronoun, and like White, the *Appletons'* editor suggested that feminists—*Appletons'* called them "the women's rights women"—should be the ones to coin the needed word:

> As the laws of the grammars stand, the use of "he," when "she" may be meant, is an outrage upon the dignity and an encroachment upon the rights of women. It is quite as important that they should stand equal with men in the grammars as before the law—so we hand this duty of amending the language over to Mrs. Stanton and Miss Anthony.[23]
>
> —"Table Talk," *Appletons' Journal* (1869)

Men seemed eager to blame women for the pronoun problem. If finding a new pronoun was the *job* of the women's movement, then singular *they* was the *fault* of the women's movement. As *Appletons'* put it just five years later, "The instincts of justice are stronger than those of grammar, and hence the average man would rather commit a solecism than ungallantly squelch the woman in his jaunty fashion."[24]

Perhaps in response to *Appletons'*, the pronoun *um* was coined in 1869.[25] *Um* was rediscovered as a shortened form of *them* in 1878[26] and again in 1879[27] and 1884.[28] And it appeared yet again in 1910, when Walter Scott Priest, a well-known Wichita pastor, used *um* to refer to a donor to the church fund who did not want um's gender revealed. The congregation laughed when the pronoun accompanied the gift's announcement, but Priest persisted, offering plural *ums,* and the possessives *um's* and *ums'*.[29]

Not every new pronoun was greeted with laughter. In 1877, the editors of the *Cincinnati Enquirer* replied to a reader's suggestion of gender-neutral *ita* with this stinging rejection: "Very few persons have thoughts too tremendous to express in the English language. Such as have are at liberty to invent a language of their own—or make signs."[30] In another attack on new pronouns in 1884, a blatantly antifeminist screed in the *Atlanta Constitution* called the recent inventions of *hiser, hisen, thon,* and *lin* "barbarous" because women don't merit their own pronoun: "If, as General Butler once decided, a woman is not a person, the masculine gender will be sufficient to embrace her, when either man or woman has to be included."[31] Benjamin Butler, a Union army general who served as a military governor of New Orleans, had issued the notorious "Woman Order," which declared that women who insulted or abused Union soldiers were not to be considered women, whose legal status was protected, but prostitutes, who could be treated with violence and contempt. That analogy would be fresh in the minds of Atlanta readers, whose sense of chivalry combined with their disdain for Yankee pronouns would not permit any meddling with the worthiness doctrine.

At about the same time, another Georgian, Captain John Dozier, the head of the West Georgia Agricultural and Mechanical College in Hamilton, went public with his own pronouns, *se, sis,* and *sim,* which he had coined in 1874 "for the good of the country."[32] Dozier, perhaps trying to heal the rift between North and South, took *se* from the Latin "himself, herself, itself," as in the phrase *per se.* But C. M. Arnold independently took credit for *se, sis, sin,* predicting that these pronouns would succeed because of "the prevalence of the Latin language among the educated class."[33] *Se* appeared again in 1948 (with *sim*);[34] in 1973;[35] and in 1975.[36] *Se, sim,* and *sis* were coined yet again in 1982 by the MIT physicist Kenneth McFarlane, who offered two additional pronoun sets: *sey, sem, seir, semself,* and *ti, tis, tisself.* A bemused reporter who didn't believe that any of these inventions were likely to succeed said that the professor really needed "a long vacation."[37]

Meanwhile, the nineteenth-century push to find the missing word continued unabated. An 1878 article in the *Atlantic Monthly* labeled the need to fill in the blank "desperate, urgent, imperative." Its writer called on "the eminent linguists" to coin a pronoun, adding, "I do not believe there is a writer in the country that is not hampered every time he—no, she—There! I've run against the old snag."[38]

Alice L. Heath, who called herself "a progressive teacher," responded in 1879 by combining the masculine and feminine pronouns to create *hesh, hiser,* and *himer,* though she hedged her bets with the alternative pronouns *e, es,* and *em* (Heath was apparently unaware of Brewster's earlier attempt to introduce these pronouns).[39] Heath understood that English changes from the bottom up, as speakers discard words they no longer need and adopt others in order to say what needs to be said. But she disliked slang, a bottom-up source of many new expressions, and she found a place for a mandated, top-down pronoun change: "Our language is our servant and if it can be improved without crime, why not improve it?" Heath acknowledged that *hesh* had drawbacks: she disliked its harsh initial sound—as in *Heath*—but she was committed to finding a suitable replacement so *he* could no longer mean both exclusive *he*, "only men," and generic *he*, "men or women." With no apparent awareness of the irony, Heath resorted to a generic masculine in her call for a neutral pronoun:

> It becomes us to put aside our fastidiousness, our instinctive dislike to a new word, and welcome the time when an intelligent *man* with something valuable to say will not have to halt in the middle of a sentence feeling *himself* stranded, go back and begin again or else flounder ungrammatically through to the bitter end; and all because our language is deficient in that one direction. It will be small consolation at such a time to be told of the beauty and sacredness of our mother tongue.[40]
>
> —ALICE M. HEATH, "The New Pronoun,"
> *Holt County Sentinel* (1879)

Other wordsmiths forged blends out of *he* and *she*. In 1890, the *Irish Times* recommended *hi, hes,* and *hem* for their brevity, their resemblance to *he* and *she*, and their "conformity to the existing endings." The paper did admit that, as with any new word, "the eye and ear experience a shock at first."[41] But although other blends of *he* and *she* would continue to crop up for decades, in the years immediately following 1884 the gender-neutral pronoun to beat was *thon*.

The year of *thon*

1884 was a golden year for gender-neutral pronouns. In the spring, William D. Armes, an instructor at the University of California at

Berkeley, issued a call for a new pronoun that would "express personality without denoting gender" while avoiding singular *they*
and the wordy *he or she*.[42] It was not long after that when Charles
Crozat Converse, who was a lawyer as well as a well-known hymn
writer, announced in the popular literary magazine *The Critic* that
he had coined *thon* to fill the pronoun gap in English. Converse
didn't root his coinage in either feminism or grammatical correctness. He argued instead that it would improve the efficiency of communication. Converse reported that he had thought up *thon* some
years earlier—perhaps as early as 1858—after many failed attempts
involving borrowings and other coinages. He didn't specify these
failed pronouns, but he did say that *thon* blended *that* and *one,* and
he instructed readers to pronounce the initial *th* as in *that,* not *thing*.
Converse saw *thon* filling three important requirements for any new
word: communicating our thoughts, doing so accurately, and doing
so "with despatch." Plus, *thon* fit the modern aerodynamic spirit:
"The philological atmosphere is full of winged words, the aim, in
the making of them, is a minimum of word-body with a maximum
of flying power."[43] His comment on the word-body/flying-power
ratio shows that Converse was familiar with the research of late
nineteenth-century engineers on wing shape, airflow, and lift, work
that eventually led to the development, not of a successful pronoun
in 1884, but of the airplane in 1903.

Converse's pronoun sparked a national conversation. The pros
and cons of *thon* were discussed in highbrow journals and in daily
newspapers. The *Boston Globe* conceded that Converse's pronoun
had "more common sense than is usual with such inventions,"
but believed that people would still resort to *they*.[44] Some writers actually adopted *thon*—not in large numbers, to be sure, but
enough to keep the word in circulation. *Thon* was even picked up
by three dictionaries, and four decades after Converse announced
his coinage, the pronoun earned a mention in the second edition

of journalist H. L. Mencken's monumental study, *The American Language*.[45]

The *Critic* logged some of the first responses to *thon* in its next few issues. Two correspondents worried that *thon* was too easily confused with *thou*. This may seem a stretch, since *thou* was hardly common by 1884, but it did appear in place of *thon* several times in otherwise carefully edited publications. For example, the *Winfield Courier* reported in 1885, "'Thou,' the proposed new pronoun (impersonal, singular number) is being taught by some of the teachers in the public schools in Lewistown, Missouri."[46] And years later, in 1927, a reader asked the *Nebraska State Journal*, had the pronoun *thou* "been added to the language?"[47] Presumably *thou* was even rarer in 1927 than it was in the 1880s, but even so, it was clearly more common than *thon*.

Some readers preferred *one* to *thon*,[48] others the blends *hi, hes, hem*—though the *Critic* warned that these were too similar to *he, his*, and *him*.[49] And one writer defended singular *they*, on the analogy of singular *you*.[50] But a number of language experts did praise *thon*.[51] The prominent philologist Francis A. March said, "It seems to me a

> **ANSWERS TO QUESTIONS.**
>
> Questions, return postage included, should be addressed to Frederic J. Haskin, director, Nebraska State Journal Information bureau, Washington, D. C.
>
> Q. Has the pronoun thou been added to the English language?
> B. D. W.
>
> A. While it appears in some dictionaries, this pronoun suggested in 1858 can not be said to be incorporated into the English language. It is a contraction of that one, and is meant to be used as the third person singular, common gender.

Either the author of this query or the typesetter at the newspaper wrote *thou* for *thon*, an error missed by the editor and the proofreader. In any case, the editor responds that the word has failed. (© 1927 *Lincoln Journal Star*, used by permission.)

very happy suggestion. I hope that it may be received favorably and in due time adopted." And Harvard's Charles Eliot Norton, a distinguished authority on American letters, wrote to Converse:

> Such a pronoun would undoubtedly be a convenience, did it exist. The difficulty lies in its being yours. All forms of speech have grown, and I do not recall an instance of the use by a civilized race of any word, not a noun or a verb, deliberately invented by a philologer, however ingenious.
> —CHARLES ELIOT NORTON, "Thon," *The Critic* (1884)

Merrill Edward Gates, the president of Rutgers and a friend of Converse, felt that *thon* would not only provide fodder for small talk, but might also prove a boon to the language:

> We have amused and interested ourselves by often using it in the family, in conversation. Beyond controversy, it is a great convenience.... If thon is at once received, Mr. Converse will occupy the distinguished and almost unique position of the living father of a new Saxon word for our Anglo-Saxon-English-sentence-building tongue. I wish thon success.
> —MERRILL EDWARD GATES, "Thon," *The Critic* (1884)

But not everyone agreed. A reader identified as "Peck's Sun" dismissed Converse as a "grammatical crank," objected that *thon* was unnecessary, and warned that the new pronoun would drastically increase the cost of already overpriced schoolbooks. Sun warned that adopting *thon* would lead to the reintroduction of *thee, thou,* and *thine:* "America would become a nation of Quakers as to speech, without their many virtues." Peck's Sun saw but one solution: "Shoot the thon!"[52]

Not everyone opposed *thon*, but some praise for the new pronoun seemed faint at best. In 1900, under the headline "New Pronoun for the New Woman," the *Des Moines Register* took a tone of paternalistic amusement as it connected "uppish" feminists with an inclusive pronoun:

> Exactness in language has long demanded it, but especially since the forward movement of women. Time was when it did not grate on feminine sensibilities to use the masculine gender, as in the sentence, "Each student will prepare his thesis," but now the sex is more uppish.... Young women see no reason why they should be indefinitely included under the masculine pronoun, and threaten, in case a professor says "each student will prepare his thesis," not to understand that they are included, and to present no theses.[53]
>
> —"New Pronoun for the New Woman,"
> *Des Moines Register* (1900)

Similarly, in 1910, the *Baltimore Sun* endorsed *thon,* if it was indeed an endorsement, by blaming women's rights advocates for reconfiguring traditional gender roles:

> Not so many years ago the need for the new pronoun was not pressing. ... The word 'American,' for example, then meant a male citizen only. An American woman was called an American woman. There were then no female wrestlers or male milliners. But today the old barriers of sex grow shadowy and faint. Women are taking the citadel of the decadent sterner sex by storm. Already the female barber, baseball player, anarchist, theologian and horse trainer are commonplace. And men grow feminine as the dear girls grow masculine. The Chicago women's clubs demand that all schoolboys be taught plain sewing and home cooking. Men eat chocolates, patron-

ize manicures, go to matinees. Thus 'thon' seems to meet a growing want.... Perhaps it might be well, while the subject is under discussion, to attempt the creation of an entirely new gender, for the purpose of facilitating reference to the growing caste of manly women and womanly men.[54]

—"Proposing a New Gender," *Baltimore Sun* (1900)

On a more positive note, in 1884, the *Times-Picayune* paraphrased a comment in the *Chicago Rambler* that the Woman's Rights Association should invent a singular pronoun for either gender, "as it is chiefly owing to the great part women are taking in the works of the day that the need for such a word has arisen."[55] And that same year, Converse's suggestion of *thon* prompted a reader from Taunton, Massachusetts, identified only as "Z," to ask *The Critic* to find another badly needed word, a title by which a man may address a "lady whom he knows only by reputation"—that is to say, a marriage-neutral alternative to *Miss* and *Mrs.*[56] That call would ultimately be answered by *Ms.,* which appeared not long after, in 1901.[57]

There were other *thon* alternatives. The writer Edgar Alfred Stevens agreed with Converse that English needed a gender-neutral pronoun, but thought that *thon* had "little grammatical merit" because its etymology was obscure and it had no inflections (that's not quite right: Converse did offer the possessive *thons*). Stevens wrongly believed that the pronoun *it* was initially meant to refer both to men and women. After considering and rejecting Latin *unus,* "the one," and *talus,* "such a one," he suggested French *le,* rounding out the set with *lis* and *lim,* to parallel *he, his, him.* Like the proposers of *vir* and *un,* Stevens seemed curiously untroubled by the fact that *le* derives from a French masculine and is hardly gender neutral. Faced with so many options, he proposed a pronoun showdown: "Let each individual who has a word to suggest make it known, and then let our writers adopt and use the best one."[58]

Emma Carleton, who regretted that until now "no man [has] risen to supply the missing word," offered her own invention, *ip*, which she pointed out "has a short, sharp, distinctive sound which will prevent it from being confounded with any other word now in the language"—no confusion with *thou* or *he*. Plus *ip* was both strange and familiar: it smacked of Latin, without actually being Latin, and it was "a word unlike any pronoun now in use, yet with a family likeness to the impersonal pronoun 'it,' and susceptible of being declined similarly."[59] A few years later a pronoun coiner came up with *id*, which also smacks of Latin,[60] while another observer, who clearly missed Converse's derivation of *thon* from the two native English words *that* and *one*, praised *thon* for its Greek roots.[61]

In the years that followed, *thon* remained new and strange, though occasionally there was a writer who chose to deploy it in the spirit of reform. For example, in 1895 Henry Williams introduced *thon* in a revised edition of his widely used college textbook, *Outlines of Psychology*, giving the example, "Every student should acquaint thonself with some method by which thon can positively correlate the facts of thons knowledge." Williams explained this in a note to readers:

> As the English language lacks a pronoun for the third person, singular number, common gender, the author hopes he will be pardoned for using the above new word. He also hopes the word will soon become euphonious to many a student in English.[62]
>
> —HENRY WILLIAMS, *Outlines of Psychology* (1895)

It's not clear who would like the sound of *thonself*, but in a response to the announcement of Williams's new book, Eugene Lewis objected that *thon*, "so warmly welcomed by the professors," had not succeeded: in the decade between the introduction of the new pronoun by Converse and the publication of Williams's text-book, Lewis had "neither heard nor seen it used."[63]

Despite objections that no one was using *thon*, the word was included in Funk & Wagnalls's brand-new *A Standard Dictionary of the English Language* in 1897. The dictionary clearly positioned *thon* as a proposal rather than a word in common use. Here is the entry, in full:

> **thon** [THON's, *poss.*; THON, *obj.*] That one; he, she, or it; a pronoun of the 3d person, common gender, a contracted and solidified form of *that one,* proposed in 1858 by Charles Crozat Converse, of Erie, Pennsylvania, as a substitute in cases where the use of a restrictive pronoun involves either inaccuracy or obscurity, or its non-employment necessitates awkward repetition. The following examples, first as ordinarily written and afterward with the substitution of the genderless pronoun, illustrate the grammatical deficiencies of the English language in this particular and the proposed method of removal: "If Harry or his wife comes, I will be on hand to meet *him or her* (or whichever appears)." "Each pupil must learn *his or her* own lesson." With the substitution of *thon:* "If Harry or his wife comes, I will be on hand to meet *thon (i.e., that one* who comes)." "Each pupil must learn *thon's* lesson (*i.e., his or her* own)."[64]
>
> —*A Standard Dictionary of the English Language,* vol. 2,
> Funk & Wagnalls Company (1897)

The supplement to the *Standard Dictionary* offered *thon* as a solution to the error of singular *they*:

> A pronoun must agree in number with its antecedent. An indefinite antecedent is often mistaken for a plural, as in the sentence "If any one has been overlooked *they* may raise *their*

hand." This error arises from the lack in our language of a singular pronoun of common gender. No one but a lawyer would care to say "If any one has been overlooked, *he or she* may raise *his or her* hand." The common solutions are: (1) to alter the construction, using the definite article where it is necessary instead of the pronoun; as, "Anyone who has been overlooked may raise *the* hand," or, "If any of you have been overlooked you may raise your hand." (2) To use *he* in its general sense as representing both masculine and feminine. . . . To meet this deficiency of the language, *thon* has been suggested.

> —*Supplement to A Standard Dictionary of the English Language,* Funk & Wagnalls Company (1903)

(The *Standard* omitted the fact that Converse was himself a lawyer as well as a composer.)

Thon also appeared in the *Century Dictionary,* though it was relegated to the dictionary's supplement with a note that the word was little used. As if to demonstrate its rarity, the *Century* provided a citation from W. J. McGee, the Director of Ethnology at the Smithsonian Institution, who used *thon* only once in an essay otherwise replete with generic *he* and even an occasional *he or she.*[65]

Thon was picked up in Merriam-Webster's *Second New International Dictionary* (1934) as well, though it did not appear in the (first) *New International Dictionary* in 1909, and by *Webster's Third* (1961) it had disappeared, presumably from lack of use. The *Second* identifies *thon* as a contraction of *that one* and defines it not as a current word, but "a proposed genderless pronoun of the third person."

Though most fans of the word tried *thon* and then abandoned it, a few diehards held on to *thon* well into the twentieth century. From the 1950s to the 1970s, the organist, music critic, and social activist Caldwell Titcomb campaigned to spread the pronoun. Titcomb

> Brit. physicist.] See ATOMIC THEORY.
> **thon** (thŏn), *pron. sing. & pl.; nom.* THON; *poss.* THON'S
> (thŏnz); *obj.* THON. [Contr. of *that one.*] A proposed
> genderless pronoun of the third person.
> **thon** (thŏn), *pron. & adj.* That yonder. *Scot., N. of Eng.,*
> & *Ir.*
> **thon** (thŏn). Var. of THEN. *Obs. exc. Dial.*
> **thon'der** (thŏn'dĕr), *adv. & adj.* Yonder. *Chiefly Scot.*
> & *N. of Eng.*

The definition of *thon* in *Webster's Second*, 1934. (By permission. From Merriam-Webster.com ©2019 by Merriam-Webster, Inc. https://www .merriam-webster.com/dictionary/thon)

may have sounded *thon*'s last hurrah in 1978, when he reminded the *New York Times* columnist Tom Wicker that *thon* was still a desirable option more than a century after it was coined.[66] After that, *thon* pretty much went dark, overshadowed by other nonbinary pronouns like *xe* and *hir,* and the inexorable forward march of singular *they.*

Thon would have been an easy choice for Word of the Year in 1884, had we been picking words of the year back then. But it was never the *only* choice. Amid the flurry of comments on common-gender pronouns at the time, a correspondent identified only as "M. S. R." of Pawtucket, Rhode Island, wrote to *The Current* to ask, tentatively,

> Has anyone proposed the contractions *his'er* and *him'er* (*his or her* and *him or her*)? How would that do? It sounds almost familiar already. Let every person decide in *his'er* own mind what is right, and then let *him'er* abide the issue.[67]
>
> —M.S.R., *The Current* (1884)

The *Current's* editor missed the chance to inform M. S. R. that yes, we'd seen *hiser* before—perhaps as early as 1850, certainly as recently as two months past—and the editor lacked the foresight to predict that *hiser* would come into its own, though only briefly, in 1912.

The age of *hiser*

If 1884 was the year of *thon,* it was also the year that reintroduced *hiser* to America's literary community. One Charles P. Sherman, of Philadelphia, independently offered his own recipe for blending *his* and *her* to get *hiser* in reply to Wolstan Dixey's support of gender-neutral *one.*[68] Sherman thought Dixey's example—"Every man or woman is the architect of one's own fortune"—just didn't sound right, though Sherman's version—"Every man or woman is the architect of hiser's own fortune"—doesn't seem much better. Sherman rounded out *hiser* with *himer,* though he indicated that he would also accept the alternative spellings *hyser* and *hymer.*[69]

It was clear that Dixey's *one* had no future as a gender-neutral pronoun. The same was true for the various invented pronouns, including *thon* and *hiser.* But new pronouns kept appearing. Charles Dietz offered *twen* in 1884, along with *twens* and *twem,* or *twon,* a blend of *two* and *one.*[70] And another writer unhappy with *thon* created a blend with the feminine first: *hersh* and *herm.*[71]

Things didn't end with *hiser* and *hersh,* as word coiners came up with multiple ways to fuse the genders. "Suggester" offered *hae, haes* (or *hais*), *hain.*[72] George Washington Eveleth, who styled himself a friend of Edgar Allen Poe (Poe never reciprocated), offered *zyhe, zyhe's, zyhem,* combining "Anglo-Saxon *he*" with "Danish *zy,* 'she' "[73] (*zy* isn't Danish; Eveleth got that wrong). *Hom* was proposed by a Prof. Davis (along with *ho, hus,* and *hum,* a serious proposal capable of yielding the comic sequence *ho, hum*),[74] and the compounds *his-her, him-her,* a "hermaphroditic pronoun to represent both sexes," was coined by "a Maryland lady sojourning in New Haven."[75] Its inventor claimed that *his-her* "has the advantage of being free from fantastic form or unfamiliar sound." That seems odd given the example provided: "Neither he nor she gave *his-her* address," which sounds both fantastic and unfamiliar.

1890 brought *hi, hes, hem,* touted as short and familiar,[76] and *zie,* an option that continues to pop up today. Then came *hor, hors,* and *horself,* which "would be convenient for the writers of popular novels" (the reason was not stated, though gender-neutral pronouns would appear in later twentieth-century science fiction).[77] And in 1900 the *Louisville Courier Journal* reminded readers that *heesh, hizzer,* and *himmer* had failed years ago, and any new pronouns would suffer the same fate.[78] The *St. Paul Globe* joked in 1903 that *hesh, hish, hush, hoosh* would lead to *hash,* a blend of a different kind.[79] And in 1910, E. P. Jots, of New Decatur, Alabama, wrote seriously to the *Baltimore Sun* to suggest that *hier* was better than *thon.* Jots got *hier* by blending *hi(s)* with *(h)er,* but hier was also willing to recast the pronoun as *heir,* which could generate even more confusion.[80]

Like Jots, many coiners underscored the tentativeness of their proposals by offering multiple suggestions, a further sign that no consensus pronoun would emerge from the hundreds of pronouns being coined. Even so, in 1912 the national spotlight fell on a single set of blends, *he'er, his'er,* and *him'er,* "duo-personal" pronouns introduced by the prominent Chicago School Superintendent Ella Flagg Young, at a meeting of the city's school principals.

Young told the *Chicago Tribune* that she invented the words "in an instant" on her way to that meeting.[81] But despite the *Tribune's* breathless headline, "Mrs. Young Invents Pronoun . . . Makes Principals Gasp," Young did not actually coin *he'er.* That honor goes to another Chicagoan, Fred S. Pond, an insurance broker who had proposed *he-er, his-er,* and *him-er* some months earlier, along with the possessive *hisers* and the reflexive *himerself.*[82] Pond, who later told Young about his creation, argued that the standard options were inadequate: *he or she* was awkward, and the generic *he* could be embarrassing when it included women in contexts that were clearly masculine. Pond illustrated how to use the inclusive *heer* for a mix of gender-stereotyped activities: "Speaking of your friend from the

country, does heer enjoy wrestling, racing, football, sculling, prize
fights, dancing, opera and the theater?"—a catch-all example even if
it's not the sort of sentence anyone might actually say. Pond rejected
singular *they* as substituting one error for another, and he acknowledged that the coinages "sound strange and perchance ludicrous."
But Pond hoped that people would get used to his pronouns, as they
had gotten used to other strange, new words like *xiphioid, xystus,*
and *zinziberaceous*—though it doesn't seem likely that anyone, anywhere, got very comfortable with those obscure technical terms for
swordfish, portico, and "something resembling ginger."

A month after she claimed *heer, hiser,* and *himer* as her creations,
Ella Flagg Young decided to share authorship of these words with
Fred Pond. Although Pond coined the pronouns on his own, in a
half-hearted apology Young insisted that "language belongs to all,"
and she revised her story about the pronouns suddenly popping into
her head on the way to a meeting. Instead, they came out of an earlier
collaboration:

> Mr. Fred S. Pond of Chicago and myself had talked over the
> duo pronoun before I ever mentioned it. Mr. Pond and myself
> agreed there was need for a terse form of mentioning the third
> person without identifying that person by gender.... We
> developed the words.[83]
>
> —ELLA FLAGG YOUNG, "Wanted: A Duo-Personal
> Pronoun," *New York Sun* (1912)

Young never explained why she changed the backstory of *heer,* or why
she claimed the coinage as a joint effort and not Pond's alone, but her
revisionism raises the possibility that Chicago's superintendent of
schools, a suffragist and well-known progressive educator, the first
woman to head a big-city school system and to serve as president of
the National Education Association, had plagiarized a pronoun.

Young insisted that she did not want to use her position as school superintendent to impose new words. In fact, she didn't use them much herself. In the *New York Sun* interview where Young finally shared credit for *heer* with Pond, she avoided her new pronoun while reeling off *his or her,* a generic *himself,* and the hyperformal *one,* all in quick succession—every pronoun option except *heer* and singular *they:*

> No person, no matter how exalted *his or her* station may be, is qualified to make a part of the language without the aid of others.... Since none of us is custom or law unto *himself,* what right has *one* to foist upon us some word? *One* can merely suggest.
>
> —ELLA FLAGG YOUNG, "Wanted: A Duo-Personal Pronoun," *New York Sun* (1912)

Young maintained that the success of *he'er, him'er* and *his'er* would hinge on approval both by experts and by users of the language. It took little prompting for experts and amateurs alike to weigh in. The lexicographer Isaac K. Funk wrote to the *New York Times* that he preferred *thon,* citing its definition in his *Standard Dictionary.* But Funk was willing to give *heer* a chance. He grudgingly admitted that Young's pronouns, "like Wagner's music, are better than they sound," then added this warning: "New words as a rule are very grudgingly admitted to good society."[84] Even so, Funk waited less than a year to admit *heer, hiser,* and *himer* into his *Funk & Wagnalls,* where the words are documented both by a letter to the dictionary from Fred Pond and by a citation from Ella Flagg Young:

> **heer** He or she a suggested personal pronoun, third person, singular number, indicating a common gender. Compare HIMER, THON

There has ever seemed to exist a general surprise among all English-speaking peoples that their language contains no form of the personal pronoun in the third person singular expressive of the common gender.

As illustrative of the elimination of our present awkwardness and often incorrect use of the English language, I give you the following: "Nearly, if not every writer, whoever *heer* may be, has a style of diction peculiarly *hiser* own (or *hisern*) which distinguishes *himer* from all others."

FRED S. POND, in *Letter to Standard Dict.* Feb. 8, '12

himer Him or her a suggested objective case of *he* or *she,* indicating a common gender. Compare HISER and THON.
hiser His or her a suggested possessive case of he or she indicating a common gender. Compare HIMER and THON.

A principal should so conduct *his'er* school that all pupils are engaged in something that is profitable to *him'er.*

E. F. YOUNG, in *The Chicago Tribune,* Jan. 7, '12, p. 7, col 6
—*Funk & Wagnalls New Standard Dictionary of the English Language,* Funk & Wagnalls Company (1913)

Even though few people adopted *heer, himer,* and *hiser,* the pronouns stayed in *Funk & Wagnalls* until the dictionary ceased publication in the 1940s. But the critics didn't hold back. Young's counterpart in the Milwaukee schools immediately attacked the new pronouns, though instead of focusing on the issues of grammar and equity that they address, Superintendent Carrol G. Pearse, who followed Young as president of the National Education Association, rejected *he'er, his'er,* and *him'er* as newfangled "reform spelling."[85] More to the point, St. Louis Schools Superintendent Ben Blewett announced his preference for generic *he,* insisting that "pronouns are generic, not genderic," and that "generically we are all men," at least, in Blewett's view, until the feminist revolution takes hold:

In fact when women achieve their ambition to enter all the walks of life in competition with men the feminine form of pronoun may come into general use.... Miss Young is represented as suggesting "he'er." Why not: "She'er" and why not "her'er" instead of "him'er"?[86]

—BEN BLEWETT, "Blewett Not in Favor of He'er, His'er or Him'er," *St. Louis Post-Dispatch* (1912)

Picking up on *she'er*, an editorial in the *St. Louis Globe-Democrat* expressed no surprise that the *she*-first "cogendrous pronouns" in Blewett's mocking comments are not as pleasing to the ears.[87] The *New York Tribune* joined the antifeminist crusade with the opposite take on what's pleasing to the ear: "In this age of feminism, if we must have such a word wouldn't it be better to change the order and make it 'heris' [her-his] and 'herim' [her-him]? Besides, it would be more euphonious."[88] And the *Topeka State Journal* insisted that Young's pronouns were unnecessary, since "the women are rapidly acquiring control of everything, and plain old fashioned 'hers' can be used in nearly every instance."[89]

Students weighed in as well. Instead of asking "What's your pronoun?" an editorial in Indiana University's *Daily Student* blamed feminists for everyone's pronoun problems, going back all the way to Eve:

In former years, since Eden was depopulated, it has been the custom to generalize in the pronoun, using the masculine form whenever possible. That was in the days when a woman made no pretensions toward equality with man. The suffragette movement has had disastrous results. Now we cannot generalize into Him or He or His. If Ella Flagg Young has her way, we'll be saying Him'er, His'er, and He'er, divid-

ing up our old-time supremacy with the feminine gender. As
a step toward recognition of the woman in other things, we
denounce this new pronoun, and call on all male philologists
to stomp it out.[90]

—*Daily Student*, Indiana University (1912)

The *Daily Student* did not explain how a man stomping out a pronoun
would aid the "recognition of women in other things." As we'll see in
the next chapter, today the same sort of rhetoric is aimed at nonbinary pronouns, often attacked as political correctness run amok.

More tempered was the response to gender-neutral pronouns at
the University of Missouri. Unhappy with either the male-first *heer*
or the faux-feminist *she-er*, the *University Missourian* acknowledged
that the drive for gender equity had rendered the generic *he* problematic: "The enlarged part that woman now plays in affairs has
increased the repugnance to its use."[91]

He'er and other gender-neutral pronouns continued to be associated more with feminism than with grammar reform. Writing after
American women got the vote, and apparently unaware of the animated pronoun debate, Thomas W. Gilmer rejected the generic masculine: "In view of the nineteenth amendment . . . she is more likely
to include him." Gilmer then offered his own gender-balancing paradigm of *hesh, shis,* and *shim,* assuring readers that these innovations
"would sound natural after a little usage."[92] But Gilmer's pronouns
did not sound natural, and they got so little usage there was never a
chance that they would sound natural.

Although many people felt that the expanded role of women in
positions of influence was long overdue, the first wave of feminism
did not sit well with George Harvey, the influential editor of *Harper's
Weekly,* who offered the bleakest view of *he'er, his'er,* and *him'er,* warning that any attack on generic *he* signaled the end times for language:
"When 'man' ceases to include women we shall cease to need a language, and won't care any more about pronouns."[93]

Though *heer* was in their dictionary, even *Funk & Wagnalls*'s own staff couldn't resist attacking the word. In 1915, Frank H. Vizetelly, lexicographer and usage expert at the dictionary and a nationally recognized language pundit called "Dr. Viz" by his fans, labeled *heer, himer,* and *hiser* "uncouth," adding that "to the modern cultivated eye they seem repulsive; their appearance seems to do violence to the genius of the language."[94]

And that same year, James C. Fernald, another *Funk & Wagnalls* lexicographer, dismissed *thon* and *heer* as life preservers for sentence emergencies that are always "impossible to inflate.... and [are] now shelved among the curiosities of the dictionary." Clinging desperately to his shipwreck metaphor, Fernald advised writers to navigate around sentences that would produce awkward gender references, just like a "steersman" guiding a ship around an iceberg. Since the *Titanic* had gone down six years earlier, Fernald's images of malfunctioning life preservers and steering out of the way of icebergs hardly seem apt.[95]

With *thon* and the trio of *heer, hiser,* and *himer* shelved among the curiosities of the dictionary, the hunt for the missing word went on, led by word coiners who were either unaware of earlier suggestions, or thought they could do better. In the spring of 1912, an Illinois business executive offered *heor, hisor, himor,* which seem remarkably similar to a number of recent coinages.[96] And in 1920, the *Sacramento Bee* coined a new pronoun and proclaimed that " 'Hir' Will Be the Bee's Word for 'He or She.' "[97] This prompted the *Oakland Tribune* to use the *Bee*'s new pronoun in a sentence: "[Hir] looks as if the one using it doesn't know how to spell."[98] That must have stung, for despite its optimistic headline, the *Bee*'s reporters used *hir* only sporadically in their stories, though they did so into the 1940s. *Hir* was reinvented and ignored again and again in the years to come. And as we'll see in the next chapter, *hir* is enjoying a revival as a nonbinary pronoun today.

Then came *hizzer,* offered by the *Asbury Park Press* because "the women vote now." Pointing to Calvin Coolidge's preelection mes-

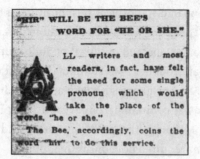

"HIR" WILL BE THE BEE'S
WORD FOR "HE OR SHE."

LL writers and most
readers, in fact, have felt
the need for some single
pronoun which would
take the place of the
words, "he or she."

The Bee, accordingly, coins the
word "hir" to do this service.

Despite its promise, the *Sacramento Bee* used *hir* only sporadically for the next twenty years to replace he or she.

sage, "Let no voter abdicate their sovereign right of self-government at the election on Tuesday by failing to vote," the *Journal* called the use of singular *they* a "technically lawless act. . . . But it was only such lawlessness as one commits who violates a stop signal in order to escape a collision." The paper went on to quip that presidents "like to obey the laws they are sworn to enforce" but that they "should be relieved from a choice between lawlessness and foolishness."[99]

And the blends kept on coming, with the next decades producing *hesh, shis, shim;*[100] *he-she, his-her, him-her;*[101] *hos;*[102] *hesh, hizzer, him-mer;*[103] *heesh;*[104] *hes* or *shes, shim;*[105] *che, chis, chim;*[106] *himorher; hes, hir, hem; his'n, her'n;*[107] *hesh, himer, hiser, hermself;*[108] and, in a Chinese cookbook of all places, *hse.*[109]

A letter to the *Times*

England got into the pronoun game as well. A year after all British women got the vote in 1928, the prominent suffragist Lady Annette E. Matthews wrote a letter to the *Times* to argue that Prime Minister Stanley Baldwin's use of generic *he* in a radio address demonstrated the need for a "bi-sex" pronoun, "which would remove from the newly enfranchised woman elector the absurd position of being left to the imagination, or appearing as an afterthought in parenthesis."[110]

Matthews's letter sparked a flurry of follow-up letters to the *Times*—almost all from men—recommending gender-neutral coinages like *vey, su,* and *tu,* along with *hesh* and *hier,* singular *they,* and even the generic *her* common in one local dialect. But mostly they cautioned that, although the political system had now changed, English pronouns required no feminist meddling.

Then, in 1930, A. A. Milne, who published his first *Winnie the Pooh* book in 1926, addressed the pronoun issue in his introduction to *The Christopher Robin Birthday Book.* Milne explained that he used *he or she,* and sometimes generic *he,* but in a perfect world, everyone would say *heesh:*

> You notice that I say 'he or she'. If the English Language had been properly organized by a Business Man or Member of Parliament, instead of living from hand to mouth on almost anybody who happened to be about with a pencil, then there would be a word which meant both 'he' and 'she', and I could write, 'If John or Mary comes, heesh will want to play tennis', which would save a lot of trouble. Also I could have made a much better thing of this Birthday Book. As it is, most of the quotations refer definitely to one sex, and more often to 'he' than to 'she'. But you must not let this worry you. If Aunt Emily's birthday is on July 2nd— well no, let us hope it isn't; but if it were on April 2nd—no, that's wrong. Well, what I mean is that the motto for May 11th, '*He*'ll know what to do', can be read, if necessary, as '*She*'ll know what to do', and so on and so forth, and vice versa and otherwise. I hope that's clear.[111]
>
> —A. A. MILNE, *The Christopher Robin Birthday Book* (1930)

The *Birthday Book* gives a quote or motto from one of Milne's books for each day of the year. The motto for July 2 is "He just happened to hiccup while signing his name" (*Now We Are Six*), and Milne seems to suggest that *he* can't mean 'she' because women like the imaginary Aunt Emily don't hiccup in public. But the motto for May 11, where *he* includes either sex without seeming rude, reads simply, "*He*'ll know what to do" (*The House at Pooh Corner*).

Milne was no social radical, at least so far as hiccups and grammar were concerned. Many discussions of gender-neutral and nonbinary pronouns today offer a truncated version of the Milne quote. But what people miss is the fact that Milne starts off with *he or she*, shrugs that off in favor of *heesh*, and then goes on to explain why generic *he* is just fine. Despite what Milne said, neither the business types nor the MPs of the day—Milne assumed they would always be men—were naturally predisposed to favor gender-neutral language. Nor were they any good at designing language, which belongs, not to experts, but, as Milne ruefully suggests, to anyone with a pencil or a voice. What Milne is acknowledging is that no one really takes the advice of a pronoun coiner, and anyway, he insists, *he* can be read as *she*, not always, to be sure, but certainly on May 11th and at other appropriate times of the year as well. I hope that's clear.

Still, the need for what Lady Matthews called "a bi-sex pronoun" encouraged the word coiners to persist. In 1932, Arthur L. Dakyns, of Manchester, took second prize of one guinea in a *Manchester Guardian* Saturday Competition for his list of ten most-needed words, which included another blend of *he* and *she*, the "indefinite gender" pronouns *ha, ham,* and *shas.* Another contestant, not named, offered *tra, trem, tres,* words which did not win anything.[112]

It may seem counterintuitive, but some word coiners formed their gender-neutral pronouns, not from blends, but entirely from the masculine. Back in the USA, that's how a man named Lincoln King derived his "bisexual pronouns" *ha, hez,* and *hem.*[113] A few years later, the spelling reformer Mont Follick came up with *hie, hiez, hie.*[114] And in the 1970s, a more recent period of pronoun coinage sparked by the second wave of feminism that began in the 1960s, Donald Darnell, a professor of communications at the University of Colorado, Boulder, used the forms *ho, hom, hos, homself,* based not on *he* but on the Latin *homo,* "person," as in *homo sapiens,* though many readers would simply think the words come from *he.*[115]

The 1970s drive to eliminate sexist language saw more blended pronouns that put women first: *she, heris, herim* (1970), *shis, shim, shims, shimself* (1972), *she, herm* (1976), *sheme, shis, shem* (1977), *hir, hires, hirem, hirself* (1979), and *shey, shem, sheir* (1982).[116] But not all feminists chose this option. Writing in the preview issue of *Ms. Magazine* in 1971, Casey Miller and Kate Swift argued that "the problem of the generic personal pronoun is a problem of the status of women," and they offered *tey, ter,* and *tem* as their candidates for the missing word. Miller and Swift repeated the complaint that *he or she* is awkward, and they disapproved of singular *they* as ungrammatical—not surprising, since both Miller and Swift were professional editors. But they were eager to rid English of its sexism, and they were not averse to coining new words, though they complained that previous coinages lacked "the transparently logical relationship to existing pronouns that is necessary if a new word is to gain wide acceptance." *Tey, ter,* and *tem* were intended to echo *they, their,* and *them,* providing the best way to "kick the habit" of generic *he* without making a plural pronoun singular. Miller and Swift's coinage was widely noted, and it remains in circulation, but it has never been widely adopted.[117]

There have been other gender-neutral pronouns—many of them offered with little comment or fanfare, or any awareness of earlier discussions of the missing word. For example, in 1971 Don Rickter, of Arlington, Massachusetts, coined *xe* as a "unisex" pronoun to be used for God to avoid "a patriarchal hierarchy."[118] Although his proposal appeared in a national Unitarian journal, nothing came of it. Other suggestions have included *thir* (ca. 1930), *se, sim, sis* (1938), *che, chis, chim* (1959), *kin* (1969), *co* (1970), *ta, tamen* (1971), *ze, zim, zees, zeeself* (1972), *per* (1972), *na, nan, naself* (1973), *se, ser, sim* (1973), *ne, nis, ner* (1974), *j/e, m/a, m/e, m/es, m/oi; jee, jeue* (1975), *ve, vis, vim* (1975), *ey, eir, em; uh* (1975), *po, xe, jhe* (ca. 1977), *E, E's, Em; hei, heis em, ems* (1977), *ae, e, ir þe (the), im, ir(s)* (1978), *et, ets, etself* (1979), *hann* (1984), *a, un, a's, gee, hem, hes, che, chim, chis, chimself* (1985), *han, hans; ala, alum, alis* (1989), *de/deis; den/din* (1991), *mef, ws, wself* (1992), *ree, hurm* (2002), *het, hes, hem* (2003), *hu* (2006), and *yo* (2007). As we will see in the Chronology of Gender-Neutral and Nonbinary Pronouns, there are more than 250, and more are surely on the way.

Critics of word coinage typically argue that in order to succeed, words must arise naturally and spread across a speech community. But for a word to arise naturally, first someone has to create it, and other people have to find it useful enough to repeat it. It's true that most purpose-made words achieve only limited popularity or fail outright. But as words like *google* and *xerox* show, some recently invented words may thrive as well.

These coined, gender-neutral pronouns failed because not enough people adopted them. Some of these pronouns never reached a wide audience. Others looked too strange on the page, sounded too foreign to the ear, or proved too difficult to decode or pronounce. *Thon* and *heer* are notable for getting into dictionaries, though that did not help them succeed. *Hir,* enjoying some resurgence as a nonbinary pronoun, is now in the *Oxford English Dictionary,* and *ze* has been approved for international use as a high-value two-letter word by the Collins *Scrabble Dictionary,* though as the book goes to press it is still waiting for approval by the Merriam-Webster *Official Scrabble Players Dictionary,* which governs US competition. As we'll see in the next chapter, a few of the coined pronouns, notably *co, ze, xe, ter, hir,* and *jhe,* are visible enough that they frequently appear among the answers to the increasingly common question, "What's your pronoun?" But even these words haven't spread beyond their still small circle of users.

And yet, despite the repeated failure of invented pronouns over the past two centuries, word coiners keep cranking them out, and small groups of English speakers do adopt them. Gender-neutral pronouns have been popular in science fiction. For example, Ursula K. Le Guin revised her novel *The Left Hand of Darkness* (1969), changing her original generic *he* to generic *she,* and finally to the gender-neutral coinages *e, es,* and *en.* And Marge Piercy used *per, pers* in *Woman on the Edge of Time* (1976). These two pronoun paradigms are discussed and actively used by participants in trans- and nonbinary-gender chat sites, and among some college students, particularly in the United States and the United Kingdom, though they have not spread to the general population of English speakers and writers. Yet the fact that gender-neutral and nonbinary pronouns are invented over and over again, often by people completely unaware of previous attempts to find the missing word, suggests that speakers of English do feel that a word is missing from the set of personal pronouns.

There appears to be no time from the late eighteenth century to the present when someone wasn't wondering about "the missing word" or creating a pronoun to "fill in the blank." In 1942, for example, the *Atlanta Constitution* columnist Dudley Glass, apparently unaware of previous efforts, wrote that someday, "when I revise the grammar and the dictionary I shall . . . substitute a pronoun of neuter gender, standing for either 'he' or 'she.' It is a reflection on British-American inventive powers that no such pronoun exists."[119]

Of course you don't have to use gender-neutral pronouns to be aware of them. The answers to 13, 18, and 40 across in this 1930

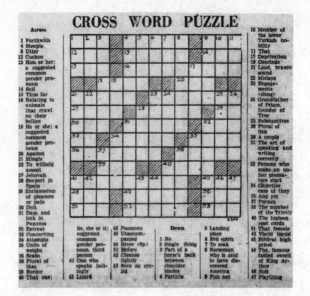

Gender-neutral pronouns frequently appeared in crosswords. This 1930 puzzle has three of them. (*Brooklyn Daily Eagle*, used by permission.)

crossword from the *Brooklyn Daily Eagle* show that, even though few English speakers actually used them, solvers were expected to be familiar enough with *himer, hesh,* and *thon* to complete the puzzle.[120]

Until the 1970s, most people were content with the existing options, generic *he* and singular *they*. But as we saw in the previous chapter, generic *he* has always been problematic. At best it was ambiguous—it might include women, or it might not. At worst, it was not generic at all, but a grammatical ploy to deny women the vote and keep them out of the boys' clubs of government and the professions. As for singular *they*, we'll see in Chapter 5 that it's finally getting the recognition it deserves as the oldest and most viable of all the third-person singular gender-neutral, nonbinary, and inclusive pronouns.

| ## *Queering the Pronoun*

"You don't have a pronoun yet for me."

—RIKI ANNE WILCHINS, *Read My Lips* (1993)

"In these new genders, exist new pronouns."

—TAYLOR MAC, *Hir* (2014)

To "queer" something is to view it in a new light, particularly one that upsets traditional categories of gender and sexuality, a sense of the verb that arose in the 1990s.[*] The latest development in language and gender is queering the pronoun. So far we've seen many wordsmiths inventing pronouns to neutralize gender and thereby include both men and women. But what happens to pro-

---

[*] This new sense of the verb *queer* appears in Merriam-Webster's online dictionary. The earliest citation for this sense in the *Oxford English Dictionary* is from 1993. The *OED* adds this definition: "To make (more) relevant, accessible, or susceptible to audiences or perspectives representing diverse sexual and gender identities." As I noted in the introduction, the terminology of sex and gender is currently in flux and is sometimes the subject of controversy. In 2014, for example, Facebook let users designate their gender from a drop-down menu that offered *male, female,* and fifty-six additional options. In this chapter, I will try to use sex and gender terms neutrally and consistently, though some of the sources that I cite use *sex* and *gender* interchangeably and a few may take a more biased or confrontational approach.

nouns when gender isn't binary, or when there's a mismatch between the sex someone's assigned at birth and who they really are? Here's one answer: in her 1993 memoir, Riki Anne Wilchins writes that her trans friend Holly politely advised strangers who were struggling to use the correct gender terminology, "Don't give it a second thought. You don't have a pronoun yet for me."[1]

But as we've seen, there were pronoun options available for Holly, even if Holly was unaware of them. Two of these pronouns were front and center in Taylor Mac's 2014 play *Hir*. In the play's first act, Paige, mother of trans teenager Max, formerly Maxine, explains Max's pronouns:

> In these new genders, exist new pronouns. Max is no longer a she or a he. So you call Max "ze" instead of the pronouns "he" or "she" and you must use the pronoun "hir" [*pronounced "here"*], H. I. R., in place of the pronouns "her" or "him." Max gets very upset if you refer to hir as a she, he, her, or him. Ze wants you to refer to hir as a hir or ze. Ze also gets upset when you emphasize the "ze" as if commenting on the pronoun when speaking to hir. For example, if you were to say, "What is ZE doing today?" ze will not like that. Ze, understandably, is not to be treated as a sideshow oddity. Ze wants you to say "ze" or "hir" as if this had been part of your regular speaking vocabulary your entire life. Any breach in decorum will cause hir to write in hir blog about how awful hir troglodyte fascist heteronormative mother is. It's fantastic.[2]
>
> —TAYLOR MAC, *Hir* (2014)

Although this scene is played partly for laughs, in more and more contexts new pronouns for the new genders are serious and they need no long explanation. That's why I overheard a volunteer at the Urbana Farmer's Market simply say, "My pronoun is *they*," while chatting with a customer about the heirloom tomatoes. There was no comment, no explanation. None was needed. In fact there are so many pronouns for gender-nonconforming persons that Taylor Mac announces on the web, both playfully and seriously, "Taylor Mac . . . uses 'judy' . . . not as a name but as a gender pronoun." But judy is also aware that new pronouns need some explanation, which is why Paige says what she does, and why Mac inserts a stage direction telling the actor how to pronounce *hir*.[3]

Pronouns were political during the fight for suffrage, and they remain political today, though the focus of the debate has expanded from women's rights to encompass the rights of LGBTQ persons, particularly those who identify as trans, nonbinary, or gender-nonconforming, including their right to designate a pronoun.

The earlier waves of "missing word" commentaries were sparked by debates over grammatical correctness, the problems faced by writers, and the issues raised by feminists. The gender-neutral pronouns that came out of these debates are inclusive representations of men and women, to be used when gender is unknown, irrelevant, or distracting, or when speakers or writers think it important to conceal the gender of a specific person. Today's question "What's your pronoun?" signals that *gender-neutral* pronouns are now doubling as *nonbinary* ones, pronouns that identify specific, known persons. This can be confusing, since a word like *hir* can be both a gender-neutral pronoun and a nonbinary one.

To repeat, nonbinary pronouns—the "gender pronouns" as many are now calling them—refer to specific, named people. Taylor Mac's pronoun is *judy*. Max's pronouns are *ze* and *hir*. Going beyond the conventional categories of male and female, these pronouns expand the ways that people are able to indicate their gender identity to encompass anyone who is trans or nonbinary, as well as those who choose an altogether different term to characterize their gender, like gender-nonconforming, genderqueer, Two-Spirit (a term used only by Native Americans), or genderfluid, among others. Such terminological variation spills over into grammatical discussions, where some prefer the term *neopronoun* for new pronouns. Or, as the question "What's your pronoun?" suggests, people can just call them pronouns.

Nonbinary pronouns look the same as gender-neutral ones, but they're used differently. We typically associate gender-neutral pronouns with indefinites like *everybody, someone, the student, the lawyer, the president, the person*—words that are inclusive, or that have become gender-inclusive over the course of time, as in these examples:

➤ Everyone forgets *their* passwords.

➤ Let no voter abdicate *their* sovereign right of self-government at the election on Tuesday by failing to vote. [Calvin Coolidge, 1926]

➤ The writer should respect *their* subject's pronoun.

➤ The person, whoever it was, had come in so suddenly and with so little noise, that Mr. Pickwick had had no time to call out, or oppose *their* entrance. [Charles Dickens, *The Pickwick Papers*, 1837]

➤ The author wanted us to run the piece anonymously, but first we needed to know that *they* were who *they* said *they* were. [Michael Grynbaum, *New York Times*, 2018]

Here's an example of nonbinary *they:*

➤ Alex likes mustard and ketchup on *their* burger, but no way do *they* like onions.

Like singular *they*, neopronouns can be either gender-neutral or nonbinary:

➢ If a person wishes to sleep, *en* mustn't eat cheese for supper. [Richard Grant White, 1868]

➢ The author wanted us to run the piece anonymously, but first we needed to know that *zie* were who *zie* said *zie* were.

➢ Alex likes mustard and ketchup on *hir* burger, but no way does *E* like onions.

It may seem like a modern concept, but awareness of gender nonconformity goes back centuries, and with it has come the issue of what pronoun to use. The lexicographer Kory Stamper cites seventeenth-century medical texts deploying singular *they*, or even *it*, to refer to hermaphrodites, people displaying both male and female sex characteristics.[4] And in 1792, as if anticipating today's interest in the nonbinary, the Scottish philosopher James Anderson argued that to better reflect the sexual diversity he found in the world around him, English grammar would be better off with thirteen grammatical genders instead of two or three. Among the categories that Anderson created: a separate gender to refer to castrated animals; another for men and castrated men; yet another for "females and castrata"; another for males and inanimates; and just to be fair, another for females and inanimates. He also found it inconvenient that the feminine *her* had to do double duty as both object and possessive, while the masculine used the distinct forms *him* and *his*. Finally, Anderson's dream of a revised pronoun system would have not just one, but two indefinite plurals to take the place of *they*.[5] Anderson was a thinker, not a doer. Confining most of his writing to economics and philosophy, he didn't actually coin any new pronouns to go with his new gender categories. Fortunately for us, his recommendations for thirteen third-person plural pronouns, far too complicated for any grammar, were largely ignored.

1st, To denote male animals alone, which might constitute the - - -	Gender, Masculine.
2d, Female animals alone, - - -	Feminine.
3d. Inanimate objects alone, - - -	Neuter.
4th, Animate objects which either expreſs general claſes, or a whole genus, or where it is not neceſſary to specify sex at all,	Indefinite.
5th, Animals known to be castrated, and meant to be distinguiſhed as such,	Imperfect, or Soprano.
6th, Males and females, known to be such, though not meant to be separated,	Matrimonial.
7th, Males only, part perfect, and part castrated, known and meant to be distinguiſhed, but not separated,	Masculine Imperfect.
8th, Females and castrata, - - -	Fem:imperfect.
9th, Males, females, and castrata, - -	Mixt imperfect.
10th, Males and inanimates conjoined, -	Masc. mixt.
11th, Females and inanimates conjoined,	Fem. mixt.
12th, Males, females, and inanimates conjoined,	United.
13th, Males, females, or inanimates, either separated or conjoined, where no distinction of gender was meant to be adverted to in any way. This is precisely the power of our present pronoun they.	Universally indefinite.

A chart of thirteen English genders proposed by James Anderson in 1792. (University of Illinois Library, used by permission.)

What's different about pronoun discussions today is that more and more people are taking the gender debate away from the medics and grammarians and making it their own.

According to the *OED*, the word *transsexual* appeared in English early in the twentieth century with the meaning "applicable to or suitable for members of both sexes," but starting in the 1950s it was used to refer to persons whose gender identity does not match the sex they were assigned at birth, although today it's much more common to use the words *transgendered* (now disfavored) and *transgender*, which appeared in this sense in the 1970s. As Ruth Tam has shown, discussions of appropriate pronoun use among trans persons have become increasingly prominent since the 1990s,[6] to the point where, in the past five years or so, they have come up in lawsuits as well as government regulations, school policies, and in the administrative rules that guide private businesses and organizations. And as we saw when the

University of Tennessee tentatively broached the subject of pronoun inclusivity in 2015 and was loudly and abruptly slammed by the state legislature, they have also become the stuff of partisan politics.

Looking at the politics of generic *he*, we saw that pronouns are little words with a big impact, standing as they often do between people and their rights. But pronoun power extends ever further. In hir 1993 novel *Stone Butch Blues*, the late trans activist Leslie Feinberg stressed that using the right pronoun is not just a matter of being polite to genderqueer persons, or guaranteeing them equal opportunity—it can also be a matter of their survival. In a restaurant scene in the novel, the character Jess tells a friend, "You can call me whatever you want, just try to remember the right pronoun in a public place. It could get real ugly."[7] Similarly, in a 1994 memoir about her own trans experiences, Kate Bornstein described the psychological damage triggered when a friend who had not seen her since her transition used the pronoun *he* for her by accident: "Attached to that simple pronoun was the word *failure*, quickly followed by the word *freak*."[8] Yet in 1993, after more than 200 years of missing-word proposals, Riki Anne Wilchins, writing of her experience as trans in the mid-'90s, reminded readers that the missing pronoun was still missing: "There were no anti-trans discrimination laws, and no public discussions about transphobic violence, gender-neutral bathrooms or pronouns, or other issues faced by gender variant people."[9] There were indeed both binary and nonbinary pronouns available for trans persons in the 1990s, yet as Wilchins's friend Holly put it so starkly, the sense persisted that "you don't have a pronoun yet for me."

Today, Holly might be able to find a suitable pronoun in just a few clicks. A web search as this book goes to press suggests that currently the most popular nonbinary pronouns are *they, xe, zie, e, ey, per,* and *ve*. But it's also clear that many trans persons use a binary pronoun, the *he* or *she* that reflects their identity. And some prefer no pronoun at all.

An early case of "What's your pronoun?"

The gender-nonconforming evangelist Jemima Wilkinson may have been the first American to sidestep the conventional he-she binary. Although Wilkinson likely stopped short of saying, "My pronouns are *he, him, his,*" Wilkinson showed a marked preference for the masculine, the "worthiest" gender.

Here's what happened. In the fall of 1776, Jemima Wilkinson, until then an ordinary eighteen-year-old Quaker woman, fell ill with a mysterious fever, recovered, and claimed to have died and been reborn as the ungendered embodiment of the divine spirit sent back to earth to preach. Rejecting the conventional gender binary, Wilkinson took a new name, the Public Universal Friend, switched to a combination of traditionally male and female attire, and founded a sect called the Universal Friends. Wilkinson further challenged traditional gender roles by encouraging the women in the sect to own property and serve as heads of households.

The record is muddy on Wilkinson's pronoun choice, and followers, critics, and neutral observers referred to her both as the Friend and as Jemima Wilkinson. One account insists that followers always spoke of Wilkinson in the third person as *the Friend,* never using any pronoun.[10] Another story reports that some of the Friends, though not all of them, "call[ed] her *him*" as a sign of respect.[11] And Wilkinson's many critics, who considered the Friend a fraud, routinely used *she* and *her,* perhaps using the "less-worthy" feminine pronoun to scorn this false prophet.[12]

What we do know is that the Friend, who had a clear preference for blending men's and women's dress, was a gender pioneer who assumed an identity that presented both as a combination of masculine and feminine and also as nonsexual, a radical self-presentation that might be labeled trans or genderqueer today. But we are concerned with pronouns rather than the complex biology and psychol-

Unfinished portrait of Jemima Wilkinson by John Mathies, 1816. It's not clear what the pronouns of this early American gender-nonconforming evangelist actually were. (Yates County History Center, used by permission.)

ogy of gender, and it's fair to say that we have no real idea of what Wilkinson's pronoun might have been, or whether the Friend ever considered the pronoun question seriously.

"I'm Orlando. My pronouns are *he, they,* and *she.*"

Virginia Woolf was another gender pioneer, but unlike Wilkinson, who wrote very little and so remains a mystery, we know Woolf from her well-regarded writing as well as from accounts by her contemporaries. Woolf's *Orlando,* hailed as the first trans novel, was published in 1928, the year that English women finally achieved full suffrage. In a pivotal scene, the thirty-year-old Orlando, born during the reign of Queen Elizabeth I, falls into a deep sleep as a man and wakes up, a week later, as a woman. Unfazed by this sudden and unexplained sex change, Orlando then proceeds to live as a woman for the next several centuries. In a brief, four-sentence passage shortly after Orlando wakes up, Woolf tracks Orlando's gender transition by rapidly shifting her protagonist's pronouns from *he* to *their* to *she:*

> Orlando remained precisely as he had been. The change of sex, though it altered their future, did nothing whatever to alter their identity. Their faces remained, as their portraits prove, practically the same. His memory—but in future we must, for convention's sake, say "her" for "his", and "she" for "he."[13]
>
> —VIRGINIA WOOLF,
> *Orlando: A Biography* (1928)

The pronoun *they,* coming between *he* and *she,* fuses Orlando's before-and-after genders at the moment of transition, but it tells us too that Orlando's gender has now become ambiguous, and decidedly nonconforming.

Manuscript evidence further illuminates Woolf's thinking about her character's gender. Woolf typically destroyed the early drafts of her work, but she sent the handwritten manuscript of *Orlando,* with all her interlinear corrections, to be bound in fine leather and presented to Vita Sackville-West, the model for Orlando, with whom Woolf had a long affair and to whom she dedicated the book. This manuscript reveals that Woolf initially considered using *his or her,* or possibly *his/her,* in the passage that describes Orlando's awakening: "The sound of trumpets died away, & Orlando stood for a moment in all {his her} beauty, stark naked. Then he/she dressed himself."[14] The printed version leaves out this confusion of pronouns: "The sound of the trumpets died away and Orlando stood stark naked."

It is evident from the manuscript that Woolf tentatively considered changing Orlando's name along with Orlando's pronoun:

```
The sound of trumpets died away, & Orlando stood for a moment
        ⌠his⌡
in all ⌡her⌠ beauty, [?] stark naked.   Then he/she dressed himself;
```

Transcription of the manuscript version of *Orlando* showing Woolf's initial treatment and her revision of the pronouns during Orlando's transition from male to female. The final printed version of the passage, which drops the pronouns, shows that Woolf continued to revise her work while preparing it for the press. (Stuart N. Clarke, used by permission.)

> We shall in the future allude to him as her; ~~& alter the masculine o at the end of his name to the feminine a.~~ . . . But while we make these superficial changes, we must beg the reader to remember that Orlando the man & Orlanda the woman were one & the same person . . . and that the change of sex did nothing to alter her / their identity.
>
> —VIRGINIA WOOLF, *Orlando* manuscript (1928)

Orlando remained Orlando in the printed novel, and regardless of the pronoun, which Woolf insisted was merely "conventional," what the novelist stresses is that the male and female Orlando are "one and the same person." Woolf inserted *their* interlinearly in the manuscript, and settled on *their* for the printed version: "The change of sex, though it altered their future, did nothing whatever to alter their identity."

Orlando's sex change, which occurs during the character's unexplained transformative sleep, sounds like a secular version of what supposedly happened to Jemima Wilkinson, who fell asleep a woman and awoke as the non-gendered Universal Friend. In any case, with Orlando's transition complete, the narrative switches to *she*, perhaps because Woolf felt there was no other suitable pronoun available. Woolf uses other gender-ambiguous language from time to time to refer to Orlando who, like Woolf and her friends, behaves in decidedly gender-bending ways, but Orlando moves through the rest of the novel with the pronouns *she* and *her*. As someone enmeshed in the British literary scene, Woolf may have been aware of the gender-neutral pronoun discussions of the day, but this brief passage at the moment of Orlando's transition is the only one in the novel where the author steps out of the frame to discuss what she labels ironically "such odious subjects" as sex and sexuality, and to point to pronouns as gender markers.

The politics of nonbinary pronouns

Woolf tells us in the transition passage from *Orlando* that identity is deep, but pronouns are simply convenient tools for writers. Orlando's exploits in the novel highlight gender dynamics, but except for the one scene we've just looked at, *he, she,* and *they* perform their conventional functions. Even so, Woolf's use of pronouns to register Orlando's transition have a subtext that evokes the politically charged pronouns of Susan B. Anthony and other suffragists, of politicians like John Stuart Mill and Jacob Bright, of lawyers like Belva Lockwood and Lucy Frances Nettlefold, and of the preservers of the patriarchy like Richard Grant White and other men worried that they would have to watch their pronouns. And pronouns were political as well for many of Woolf's contemporaries, who took the time to propose or oppose new pronouns for the new woman.

As we see from a number of more recent examples of trans pronoun preference, pronouns have once again become more than just conventions. In 1952, Christine Jorgensen became an American celebrity after front-page reports of her hormone replacement therapy and gender surgery in Denmark. Jorgensen, a World War II army veteran, left the United States in 1951 as *he* and returned a year later as *she*.[15] More recent still, both Caitlyn Jenner and Chelsea Manning announced that they would use *she* after publicly coming out as trans women. And at least three successful trans candidates in recent elections—Christine Hallquist, who won the 2018 Democratic gubernatorial nomination in Vermont; Danica Roem, elected to the state legislature in Virginia; and Andrea Jenkins, who was elected to the Minneapolis City Council in 2017 and became the first African American openly trans woman to be elected to public office in the United States—are referred to in the media as *she*. And there's Chloe Bressack, the trans teacher from Florida whom we met in Chapter 1, whose pronoun is *they*.

There are some indications that *they*, already the most common gender-neutral pronoun, is now the nonbinary pronoun of choice. A 2017 nonbinary/genderqueer survey of pronoun use reported that 80% of the 9,932 respondents chose *they*, up slightly from previous years. Respondents, English speakers worldwide who were asked to self-identify as trans, genderqueer, or nonbinary before participating, were given a list of pronouns and asked to choose one or more. Most picked a single option; another large group chose two or three. The second most popular option was the traditional binary *she* and *he*, selected by 57%, with 29% picking *she* and 28% picking *he*; another 13.6% chose to alternate *he* and *she*. The next group, 10.7%, repeated their name instead of using any pronoun. Of the coined pronouns, *xe* was an option for 8.2%, and *zie* for 6.1%. Other coined words polled much lower. The survey also permitted write-ins, and respondents added 295 "other" pronouns, including *thon*, which got one solitary vote, evidence, if any is needed, that *thon*'s not dead yet.[16]

It's not clear how accurately these reported preferences reflect actual usage. What people indicate in response to a survey may differ significantly from what they say or write in less self-conscious situations. Plus, people may use more than one pronoun. As *Sacramento Bee* columnist Erika Smith put it, "I talked to my friend . . . who prefers 'they,' but usually goes by 'she' in professional settings [because] 'it's easier and people just don't get it.'"[17] But the survey does confirm a general sense that singular *they* and the traditional binaries *he* and *she* tend to be a lot more popular than the neopronouns among trans and nonbinary persons.

On the other hand, when it comes to discussions of "What's your pronoun?" the coined words capture much of the interest, both online and off, and every website that offers advice about pronoun choice—many of these are affiliated with universities—proposes some version of *xe, zie, per,* and *E,* along with *they, she,* and *he.* Some discussions also refer to the "Spivak" pronouns, a set that includes *e, ey, em, eir,* or variants of these, all of which were created earlier but were promoted as gender-neutral alternatives by the mathematician Michael Spivak in the 1980s and thereafter on LambdaMoo and other online discussion groups. Although Spivak pronouns routinely pop up in discussions, they have never achieved widespread use outside their early online niche.

Online dating sites now offer gender and pronoun options as well: Tinder subscribers may pick from thirty-seven gender choices, and OkCupid lets users choose one of three pronouns, *he, she,* or *they,* or they can enter their own.[18]

In 2018 OkCupid announced that it was "the first and only leading dating app to create a dedicated space on profiles for LGBTQ daters to share their pronouns." Users may choose one of three "conventional" pronouns or enter their own. (Match.com, used by permission.)

And Starfriends, an inclusive dating site created by the partner of the person who conducted the nonbinary/genderqueer survey, allows new users to designate a pronoun from the list generated by the site's previous users or to enter a pronoun not already on that list.[19]

Trans pronouns and the law

Pronoun preference varies among trans persons, so it's not surprising to find pronoun variation in laws dealing with broader issues of sex and gender as well. For example, in 2004 the United Kingdom passed the Gender Recognition Act, which outlines the steps a person must take in order to have their gender change recognized for new birth certificates, passports, and other official documents, and also for claiming gender-based government benefits. The act recognizes two genders, male and female, and assumes a transition from one to the other, with the "acquired" gender controlling in terms of how benefits will be assigned. Its explanatory notes refer to individuals prior to a change by the pronoun of their birth gender. After a change, the instructions vary.

When the act was passed, women could retire earlier than men. For a female-to-male transition, the accompanying explanation of how to claim retirement benefits shifts midstream from *woman* to *person*, and the pronoun *she* becomes *they*. But the instructions that accompany the law use masculine pronouns both before and after a male-to-female transition, and when speaking of general entitlements, the act's instructions refer to all trans persons with the dual *he or she* and *his or her*.

Pension ages for men and women will equalize after 2020, and their retirement age will increase from 65 to 68 in the coming years. That means the instructions for persons changing gender will have to be revised, and that revision may be accompanied by pronoun changes as well. At the same time, the Gender Recognition Act itself is up for revision, and as part of that revision, a member of the House of Lords asked the government to "adopt the use of 'they' as the singular pronoun in all future legislation in preference to gendered pronouns."[20]

American Social Security benefits are gender-independent, and gender-change instructions either avoid pronouns or use *he or she*.[21] The US State Department permits gender change for passports. Trans persons must file a new passport application and provide what the government considers to be appropriate medical documentation. Instructions for the DS-11, the general passport application form, use the dual *he or she*.[22] These federal forms avoid singular *they*, though *they* has the advantage of being both familiar and more inclusive. The lexicographer Steve Kleinedler warns that *he or she* erases nonbinary identities, and he encourages anyone responsible for preparing such official documents to use singular *they* instead.[23] Eventually singular *they* may find acceptance in official government documents in Britain or the United States, but it's not clear when that might happen.

For the most part in the United States, gender-contingent rights, including the right to use a gender-specific bathroom or to designate a pronoun, are handled at the state and local level, with some jurisdictions restricting gender-identity rights and others protecting lesbian, gay, trans, and gender-nonconforming persons from discrimination in employment, housing, and general public accommodation. When pronoun complaints reach US courts, they form part of a broader claim of gender or sexual-orientation discrimination, and they are typically treated on a case-by-case basis. For example, in 2014, Valeria Jones, who identified as neither female nor male and opted for a gender-neutral pronoun but did not specify which one, sued their employer, a Portland, Oregon, catering service, because other employees insisted on referring to Jones as *she*. Jones's complaint charged that coworkers repeatedly made "specific references to plaintiff as 'miss' or 'little lady' [and used] pronouns [that] seemed uncalled for even if the pronoun usage was difficult to change." Although Jones alleged that the gender harassment forced them to quit work, the court dismissed the suit as having no legal merit.[24]

In contrast, the Equal Employment Opportunity Commission (EEOC) has supported the rights of trans employees. In a 2013 case involving a Postal Service worker, the EEOC ordered that "supervisors and coworkers should use the name and gender pronoun that corresponds to the gender with which the employee identifies, both in employee records and in communications with and about the employee."[25] The EEOC reaffirmed this position in a 2015 case involving a trans woman who was a civilian employee of the US Army. The commission found that the employee's supervisor and colleagues routinely treated her as a man, forbidding her from using the women's restroom, calling her "sir," and using male pronouns, all of which created a hostile work environment. In a consent decree, the Army agreed to conduct sensitivity training and to ensure the use of appropriate language, including pronouns, to reflect the employee's gender identity.[26] Although EEOC precedents have some legal force, it's not clear that the commission would continue such policies under a more conservative administration.

Cases dealing with gender-identity discrimination against prisoners also touch on pronoun issues, though the courts tend to view language rights as unimportant unless they are accompanied by charges of physical abuse. In 2008, a trans prisoner whose pronoun was *she* sued Oregon authorities in federal court, charging that, in the words of the court, "prison officials refuse[d] to refer to him [*sic*] with female pronouns and titles." Although the plaintiff, Anny May Stevens, had legally changed her name and gender, the court found that prison officials had no obligation "to refer to Stevens using female pronouns." Indeed, the court itself referred to Stevens with "male pronouns in order to conform to, and not create confusion with, the documents in the record." Preferring a sticks-and-stones interpretation of the law, the court concluded that "verbal harassment alone does not violate the Eighth Amendment," the constitutional protection against cruel and unusual punishment.[27]

But words can be harmful, and an earlier case involving both verbal and physical abuse saw a different outcome. In *Giraldo v. California Department of Corrections* (2007), a trans woman prisoner charged that she had been sexually assaulted and horrifically abused by male cellmates in Folsom State Prison. Prison officials asked the court to refer to Giraldo using masculine pronouns so that the jury would not think a woman was being kept in a men's prison.[28] The trial judge rejected that request, and an appeals court eventually found that the state had a special obligation to protect its prisoners from foreseeable harm by taking gender identity into account, a ruling that emphasized physical safety but that could also include honoring an inmate's chosen pronoun, particularly as the use of appropriate pronouns has a positive impact on mental health, and the use of inappropriate pronouns can form part of a general pattern of harassment and abuse.

In a 2015 case in Georgia involving both verbal and physical abuse, Ashley Diamond, a trans woman sent back to prison for violating her probation, charged that authorities disregarded her safety by housing her with violent offenders in a maximum-security men's state prison. Diamond, represented by the Southern Poverty Law Center, petitioned for the right to wear women's clothes and undergo hormone therapy, to be moved to a less dangerous facility, to be protected from sexual assault, and, in terms of language, to be addressed using gender-appropriate pronouns. The US Department of Justice had previously determined that standards of care "for inmates with gender dysphoria" include "outwardly conforming one's gender expression and role to match one's internal sense of gender identity, *including through pronoun usage,* grooming, and dress," along with hormone therapy and sex reassignment surgery, as determined to be appropriate on a case-by-case basis by qualified healthcare providers.[29] The case, which was profiled in the *New York Times,* chronicled how prison authorities placed inmates like Diamond in situations where they were likely to be assaulted, denied them appropriate medical and psychological care, and, as we see in this courtroom exchange between the defense counsel and a deputy warden, even used pronouns to punish trans inmates:

> "It is a male facility, sir, and he is, indeed for what I have been told from my experience, it is a male offender," testified Janet Brewton, a deputy warden, who added that she had been responsible for overseeing transgender women inmates since 1996.
>
> "So for 20 years, you've been referring to transgender inmates with the male pronoun because you view the facility as a male facility?" Ms. Diamond's lawyer, David Dinielli, asked.
>
> "That is correct, sir," the deputy warden said.[30]
> —DEBORAH SONTAG, "Judge Denies Transgender Inmate's Request for Transfer," *New York Times* (2015)

In settling the case, Georgia agreed to provide hormone therapy for trans prisoners. But perhaps to avoid having to deal with Diamond further, the state then released her from confinement months before she was eligible for parole.

A higher profile case, though it did not charge physical violence, led to another pronoun protection order. In 2013, Pfc. Chelsea Manning was court-martialed and convicted under the Espionage Act for giving confidential government documents to WikiLeaks, which subsequently made them public. Manning, who had legally changed her name to Chelsea, then sought to begin her transition from male to female. She petitioned the court to be referred to under her new legal name, Chelsea Manning, rather than her previous "dead name," and to be referred to with the gender-appropriate pronouns *she* and *her*. Although the Army opposed Manning's request, the appeals court ordered that "reference to appellant in all future formal papers filed before this court and all future orders and decisions issued by this court shall either be neutral, e.g., Private First Class Manning or appellant, or employ a feminine pronoun."[31] The Army eventually agreed to begin Manning's hormone therapy and to consider gender surgery for her, but that decision became moot when, in 2017, President Obama commuted Manning's sentence and she was released from custody.

Intentionally using the wrong pronoun may constitute hate speech, but in the United States, hate speech is protected by the First Amendment unless it is clearly threatening. That position was affirmed most recently in *Matal v. Tam* (2017), a case in which the US Supreme Court ruled that the government could not prohibit a racially disparaging trademark. In that decision, Justice Samuel Alito quoted a 1929 dissent by Justice Oliver Wendell Holmes, Jr.: "Speech that demeans on the basis of race, ethnicity, gender, religion, age, disability, or any other similar ground is hateful; but the proudest boast of our free speech jurisprudence is that we protect the freedom to express 'the thought that we hate.'"[32]

In contrast, both Canada and the United Kingdom criminalize hate speech—and that may include intentionally using the wrong pronoun. For example, the British Columbia Human Rights Tribunal ruled in 2019 that William Whatcott, who described himself as a Christian activist, had violated the Human Rights Code by publishing discriminating statements against Morgane Oger, a transgender woman running as a candidate in an election for the provincial legislative assembly. The flyers that Whatcott distributed locally and posted online refused to recognize Oger's gender and referred to her using masculine pronouns. Whatcott insisted that his words were protected under Canada's free-speech guaranties, and that denying these protections would expose him to "the possible lifetime deprivation of his liberty to evangelize, to manifest his religion in the public square, and to use the pronouns he chooses." He further told the tribunal, "Please be advised . . . I will not use the fake pronouns you describe[,] 'she' or 'her.'" Rejecting this argument, the court found that Whatcott's words were not protected speech, and it ordered him to cease his disparaging behavior and to pay both court costs and punitive damages to Oger.[33]

In the United Kingdom, using the wrong pronoun, while not illegal by itself, can result in a harassment warning. Although both the Antiharassment Act of 1997 and the Equality Act of 2010 prohibit discrimination against anyone on the basis of gender or gender reassignment, these laws do not specifically state that using the wrong pronoun or otherwise misgendering someone—intentionally classifying them as the wrong gender in order to harass them—constitutes harassment. Nonetheless, in 2018 the Home Office launched an antiharassment campaign warning, "If you target anyone with verbal, online or physical abuse because of their religion, disability, sexual orientation, transgender identity or race—you may be committing a hate crime." Print and television ads ran this message under the campaign slogan, "It's not just offensive. It's an offence."[34] An op-ed essay in the *Telegraph* complains that in 2016, "British police detained and questioned 3,300 people for using inappropriate language on social media."[35] Like the Antiharassment and Equality Acts, the 2003 Communications Act does not specifically address misgendering, but Section 127, which uses the generic masculine pronoun, could be interpreted to criminalize incorrect pronoun usage. It labels a person guilty of an offense "if he . . . sends by means of a public electronic communications network, a message or other matter that is grossly offensive . . . or that he knows to be false."

These laws are silent on the question of intent, but it's not likely that anyone would be convicted of accidental pronoun misuse. So far there don't seem to have been any convictions for misgendering. Even so, UK free speech advocates have expressed concern that the increasing intervention of police in social media disputes concerning the use of incorrect pronouns—some of them involving journalists or other high-profile figures—could chill online speech.

Schools even more than prisons routinely find themselves dealing with gender-recognition issues, and some schools have established policies that include support for students' right to their own pronouns. In 2016, a joint policy by the US Department of Justice and the Department of Education under President Obama ordered schools to acknowledge students' gender identity. The policy emphasized that students be allowed to use the restroom appropriate to their gender identity and required that in all school records and comments with and about students, "school staff and contractors will use pronouns and names consistent with a transgender student's gender identity."[36] A year later, the new Trump administration's Departments of Justice and of Education abruptly withdrew those gender protections.[37]

Even in the absence of ongoing federal support for gender-inclusive policies, some school districts have set their own accommodations for transgender students, and many of these include a section on pronouns. For example, in 2016 the Chicago Public Schools (CPS) adopted new guidelines to support transgender and gender-nonconforming students. These included a provision for a "Preferred Gender Pronoun," or PGP, defined as "the pronoun or set of pronouns that an individual would like others to use when talking to or referring to that individual. Common examples in the CPS policy include 'they,' 'their,' 'ze,' 'he' and 'she.'"[38] (Although CPS is not alone in using the term, calling pronouns "preferred" suggests that gender is an option, not an essence, and there's a growing movement to drop *preferred*.) As we saw in Chapter 1, Florida's Leon County also had a pronoun-sensitive policy for students, though it did not protect the Tallahassee schoolteacher Chloe Bressack when Bressack chose *they* as their pronoun and *Mx.* as their honorific.

Various gay-straight alliances—groups supporting gay, transgender, and nonbinary students in school—also recommend pronoun options, though many also caution that some students may not want to announce their gender identity. Here's a representative pronoun chart from GSAFE (formerly known as the Gay-Straight Alliance for Safe Schools):

A (Short) List of Pronouns

The list of pronouns being used in the English language is ever growing, so below we have included a short list of some of the ones we know. This is not meant to be an exhaustive list, and we plan to keep it updated as much as we can. If you know of a set of pronouns that should be on this list, let us know!

Subject Pronoun	Object Pronoun	Possessive Pronouns	Reflexive Pronoun
___ *is an activist.*	*I am proud of* ___ .	*That is* ___ *book.* *That book is* ___ .	*That person likes* ___ .
she	her	her/hers	herself
he	him	his	himself
ze*	hir	hir/hirs	hirself
ze*	zir	zir/zirs	zirself
e or ey	em	eir/eirs	eirself or emself

*Additional alternate spellings for "ze" are "zie," "sie," "xie," and "xe."

(cont.)

Subject Pronoun	Object Pronoun	Possessive Pronouns	Reflexive Pronoun
___ is an activist.	I am proud of ___.	That is ___ book. That book is ___.	That person likes ___.
per	per	per/pers	perself
hu	hum	hus/hus	humself
they**	them	their/theirs	themselves
vey	vem	veir/veirs	veirself
fae	faer	faer/faers	faerself

**More and more people are using "they," "them," and "their(s)" as singular, gender-neutral pronouns, even though those are often considered plural pronouns. When using "they" as a singular gender-neutral pronoun, you would still conjugate the associated verbs as you would for the plural version. So you would say "they are an activist" or "they like to go shopping," not "they is an activist" or "they likes to go shopping."

—"Pronouns Are Important," GSAFE

Another group, Trans Student Educational Resources (TSER), takes a more radical position, rejecting the idea of pronoun preference altogether and declaring that all pronouns are gender neutral. For TSER, using the correct pronoun is not a choice, it's a requirement:

There are no "male/female" or "man/woman" pronouns. All pronouns can be used for any gender and are gender neutral. We also do not use "preferred pronouns" due to people generally not having a pronoun "preference" but simply having "pronouns." Using "preferred" can accidentally insinuate that using the correct pronouns for someone is optional.[39]

—Trans Student Educational Resources

TSER's pronoun chart offers these options: *she, he,* singular *they,* and either *ze/hir/hirs/hirself,* or *ze/zir/zirs/zirself.* Acknowledging that other choices exist, TSER recommends, "Always ask someone for their pronouns." Even the term *gender-neutral* proves problematic. One "Pronoun Dos and Don'ts" posted in the lobby of an Urbana community theater in connection with a performance of Taylor Mac's *Hir* counsels, "Don't refer to pronouns such as 'they/them/their' or 'zie/hir/hir' as 'gender-neutral pronouns.' While some trans people identify as gender-neutral, many see themselves as gendered, but as gender-nonconforming. Better language is 'non-binary pronouns.'"[40]

Given both the growing sensitivity to pronoun choice, and the variable usage of both traditional gendered pronouns and nonbinary options, variation that shows no sign of ending any time soon, the consensus on the many sites that provide advice on gender issues in general and pronouns in particular is to ask for a person's pronoun and to try to use it. Such advice frequently counsels patience, since conventional pronoun use is hard to change, and people of good will may sometimes slip and use an inappropriate word. And, of course,

1	2	3	4	5
(f)ae	(f)aer	(f)aer	(f)aers	(f)aerself
e/ey	em	eir	eirs	eirself
he	him	his	his	himself
per	per	pers	pers	perself
she	her	her	hers	herself
they	them	their	theirs	themself
ve	ver	vis	vis	verself
xe	xem	xyr	xyrs	xemself
ze/zie	hir	hir	hirs	hirself

The pronoun options card developed by the University of Wisconsin–Milwaukee LGBT Resource Center in 2011, updated in 2016, has been widely reproduced and distributed across the United States. The first line represents two alternative paradigms, *fae, faer, faers* and *ae, aer, aers.* (©2011, 2016 U-W Milwaukee LGBT Resource Center, used by permission.)

since not everyone may be ready or willing to declare their gender identity, it's also important to remember that "What's your pronoun?" is a question that not everyone wants to answer.

Pushing back against pronoun choice

The Trump administration's rollback of protections for transgender students is part of a larger retreat on gender and minority rights. We have seen how the pushback against the first and second waves of feminism, and against women's suffrage and women's rights in general, spilled over into attacks on the linguistic reforms associated with these movements. The demand that generic *he* be truly generic was countered by antisuffragists who insisted that *he* was generic when it needed to be, and besides, it was the only correct grammatical form. And yet, despite such regressive attitudes, universal suffrage prevailed. Generic *he* declined as well, a decline hastened in part by the demand that *he* be replaced with an unambiguously neutral pronoun and the push for gender-neutral terminology promoted by the feminism of the 1960s and 1970s. But although that second-wave feminism saw renewed interest in coined pronouns, along with growing acceptance of singular *they*, it was not until the current focus on nonbinary language that words like *zie* and *xe* reentered the public debate. In turn, that renewed interest is generating some opposition from social and political conservatives.

● ● ●

In Ontario, misgendering a person may violate the law, and an Ontario Human Rights Commission brochure warns that in employment, housing, or education, using the wrong pronoun may constitute harassment. However, the commission does not go so far as to recognize an individual's right "to insist on any one gender-neutral pronoun in particular."[41]

Ontario's law made headlines in 2016 when the conservative University of Toronto psychologist Jordan Peterson announced on his widely viewed YouTube channel that he would not use gender-neutral pronouns. University administrators urged Peterson to comply with the law, but Peterson doubled down by rejecting the right of the government, or of a private citizen, to compel him to use *ze* and *hir* against his will. That in turn sparked a debate between conservatives and progressives that has gone well beyond pronouns, and consequently well beyond the scope of this chapter. However, it is a sign of the power of language to express identity that a part of speech—a pronoun—has managed to reignite the culture wars to the point where, once again, grammar is front-page news.

Like earlier objections to the linguistic aspects of women's rights, American opponents of nonbinary pronouns claim that their position has nothing to do with discrimination. Instead, they say, it's purely rational and objective, a simple matter of grammar and biology. They even claim that forcing someone to use a pronoun against their will constitutes compelled politically correct speech in violation of the free-speech protections of Canadian law and the US Constitution.

Many argue as well that their position reflects both scientific and religious beliefs that there are only two genders, or two sexes (the terms are used interchangeably in these debates). Or, if neither science nor religion is your cup of tea, they fall back on the grammatical gender binary. Two genders/sexes in the Garden of Eden. Two genders/sexes formed by X and Y chromosomes. Two grammatical genders in the English pronoun system, masculine *he* and feminine *she* (the third English grammatical gender, the neuter, represented by the pronoun *it*, tends to be omitted from these debates, as is the fact that other languages recognize more or fewer than two grammatical genders, including some that have no grammatical gender at all). As any "defender of good grammar" knows, there's no such thing as singular *they*, since a plural pronoun can never double as a singular. You could remind them that *you* was originally plural, but ideologues tend not to pay attention to linguistic facts.

In 2018, the conservative columnist Abigail Shrier argued that laws requiring deference to the pronoun choice of students, patients, or employees violate constitutional religious protections.[42] For Shrier, if you hold fast to the belief "that sex is both biological and binary," then the government requiring you to use singular *they* or *zie* constitutes a kind of "forced conversion." Covering both the religious and secular objections, she claimed, like Peterson, that state-mandated pronouns also violate legal protections against compelled speech.

In the United States, the broad protection against forcing someone to speak was articulated in *West Virginia v. Barnette* (1943), where the US Supreme Court found that students may not be made to salute the flag in violation of their religious belief.[43] The Court concluded, "If there is any fixed star in our constitutional constellation, it is that no official, high or petty, can prescribe what shall be orthodox in politics, religion or other matters of opinion or force citizens to confess by word or act their faith therein." Shrier extends that reasoning to argue that no one may be forced to violate their belief—whether religious or grammatical—that pronouns must agree with their antecedents in number, and that "forced reference to someone else as 'ze,' 'sie,' 'hir,' 'co,' 'ev,' 'xe,' 'thon' or 'they'" is unconstitutional. Safe to say that's a leap of reasoning that neither the *Barnette* court nor the framers of the Constitution would have imagined possible.

And yet a recent dissent in a major antidiscrimination case reflects this growing insistence among conservatives and libertarians that the First Amendment protections of speech and religion should invalidate those antidiscrimination laws that seek to regulate language in the workplace and the classroom. In 2020, the US Supreme Court ruled that "an employer who fires an individual merely for being gay or transgender violates Title VII" (*Bostock v. Clayton County, Georgia,* US Supreme Court, No. 17-1618, 2018; Title VII of the 1964 Civil Rights Act prohibits discrimination in employment, including discrimination "based on race, color, religion, sex, or national origin"). In his dissent in that case, in a section ominously headed "Freedom of speech," Justice Samuel Alito warns that the decision in *Bostock* "may even affect the way employers address their employees and the way teachers and school officials address students." And he adds, "After today's decision, plaintiffs may claim that the failure to use their preferred pronoun violates one of the federal laws prohibiting sex discrimination." Alito refers specifically to antidiscrimination regulations both in New York City and at some universities that require the use of gender pronouns, not just the traditional binaries *he* and *she,* but also singular *they* or a coined pronoun such as *ze* or *hir,* implying that such regulations violate the First Amendment protection against compelled speech.

Alito's comment raises the question of whether a First Amendment defense—"You can't make me say your pronouns!"—could neutralize an antidiscrimination regulation designed, not to silence or compel speech, but to protect the speech of those minority workers and students whose voices may otherwise be silenced by what the framers viewed as the tyranny of the majority.

The so-called scientific argument used to prop up binary pronouns is flawed: biologists now understand that sex is expressed through the complex interaction of multiple genes, not a simple pairing of X and Y chromosomes, and psychology has reinforced the understanding that gender identity and biological sex do not always align the way that the English pronoun system expects them to.[44]

The constitutional argument is flawed as well. Although it's true that the First Amendment prohibits the government from restraining or compelling most speech, there's no constitutional protection for obscene speech, threats, or incitement to violence. And *Barnette* notwithstanding, the Constitution does compel some speech, including the presidential oath of office, the Miranda warning, certain loyalty oaths, and the Surgeon General's warning on tobacco products.

Given that constitutional backdrop, antidiscrimination legislation covers language in public contexts, not in private social interactions, and it only targets language that reveals a clear intent to harass or discriminate. Those regulations that do address pronoun choice are designed to protect individuals from a hostile environment at school, at work, in prison, in interactions with health care professionals, and in shops, restaurants, hotels, and other places doing business with the public. These regulations—like those requiring bakeries to sell their wares to all customers, not just those who meet a religious litmus test[45]—do not target personal interaction outside such environments, and their aim is to protect vulnerable minorities whose speech rights have been historically fragile. In addition, given the clear preference for the conventional pronouns *he, she,* and singular *they* by everyone, no matter what their religion, sex, gender identity, or, as we'll see in the next chapter, their grammatical convictions, it is frankly bizarre for anyone to frame new pronouns as orthodox, and the defenders of the older *he* and *she* as an oppressed minority.

As it turns out, rants against politically correct pronouns aren't really necessary, since most top-down directives about which words to privilege and which to avoid don't change language use. Mandating respect for pronoun choice in a prison or a classroom or an office won't catapult *xie* into the *Associated Press Style Book* or resurrect *thon* from out-of-print dictionaries. The defenders of traditional pronouns have nothing to fear from legal or institutional directives about language. And they have nothing to gain by clinging to the pronoun recommendations of Strunk and White. That's because language changes when enough people use a word of their own accord, not because of science, religion, a rule book, a YouTube video, an op-ed, or a dissent in a Supreme Court antidiscrimination case. Parents, teachers, employers, and usage critics all readily acknowledge that they feel obliged to make the same corrections over and over because, when it comes to telling people what to say or write, nobody is really listening to them.

In Taylor Mac's *Hir*, Pearl advises, "Ze wants you to say 'ze' or 'hir' as if this had been part of your regular speaking vocabulary your entire life." The key words are "as if": the pronoun *hir* has a following offstage as well as on, and it may eventually become part of the "regular speaking vocabulary" of English, but it still has a long way to go. Similarly, Shrier argues, "Individuals need not be religious to believe that one person can never be a 'they.'" That's very true, and yet belief and practice don't always align. Singular *they* has survived centuries of condemnation by grammarians and usage critics, and it persists today despite the widespread belief that it is grammatically incorrect.

More to the point, directives about pronouns don't aim to silence speech. Instead, their goal is to validate the words of those whose voices have been consistently silenced. Official support for nonbinary pronouns reinforces the need to maintain respectful, neutral interactions on the job, in the classroom, in the marketplace, and in other public situations where regulation is traditionally seen as appropriate—no different from rules against the use of racial, ethnic, or religious slurs, swearing, or harassment in such situations. Using such words in the workplace may not be illegal and it is not unconstitutional, but it may be in poor taste and it can still get you fired.

Pronouns are good business

Private enterprises are often quicker than governments to recognize that sensitivity to gender issues may be good for business. In the 1950s, for example, the American business community began discussing the need for a marriage-neutral title like *Ms.*, though that term, coined as early as 1901, did not achieve widespread use until it got the backing of feminists in the 1970s. Today the nonbinary title *Mx.*, pronounced "mix," which appeared as early as 1977, is starting to spread as well, particularly in the United Kingdom. *Mx* as a gender-neutral or nonbinary title is being recognized by an increasing number of UK institutions, from the government's National Health Service and its Revenue and Customs division, to major banks like the Royal Bank of Scotland and NatWest, to prestigious universities like Oxford and Cambridge. *Mx.* is less common in the United States, though both the *New York Times* and the *Wall Street Journal* permit the ungendered honorific in reference to people who have indicated their preference for it, and it is the title chosen by Chloe Bressack, whose pronoun is *they*. Recently United Airlines added *Mx.* to its drop-down menu of booking options.[46] It has also been recognized by dictionaries, not because these reference books have a social agenda, but because people are using the term. The *Merriam-Webster Unabridged* has an entry for *Mx.*, as does the *Oxford English Dictionary*, the latter noting that "*Mx* was originally offered as an alternative to *Mr, Mrs, Miss*, and *Ms*, as a means to avoid having to specify a person's gender, but has frequently been adopted as a title by those who prefer not to identify themselves as male or female."

Abigail Shrier argues that "gender activists" are trying to steal words like *he* and *she* from conservatives who see them as essential to their way of life. That claim is both inflammatory and inaccurate, given that trans persons are a minority, estimated to be about 0.6%

of the US population, or about 1.4 million people,[47] and contrary to what conservatives might believe, significant numbers of the trans population use *he* or *she* as their pronouns. Shrier further suggests that singular *they* represents some kind of grammatical aberration that conservatives and others have a legal right to resist. Such resistance may be constitutionally protected, but it is also futile. As we will see in the next chapter, singular *they* has been in common, frequent, and thoroughly grammatical use in English speech and writing since the 1300s. It has survived unscathed by the nineteenth- and twentieth-century attacks on its grammaticality and has become the pronoun of choice to replace the no longer popular and rarely generic, generic *he*. Singular *they* is a word that comes close to being one-size-fits-all, used by supporters of gender equity and nonbinary rights as well as those who oppose such rights. It's used as well by people who theoretically oppose singular *they* on grammatical grounds—or even constitutional ones—but who use it when they're not paying attention, just because singular *they* has been good, idiomatic English for seven hundred years.

The Missing Word Is They

The word they is being used as a pronoun of the common gender every day by millions of persons who are not particular about their language, and every other day by several thousands who are particular.

—FRED NEWTON SCOTT (1885)

It turns out that the missing word isn't missing after all. It's singular *they,* and it's been filling in the blank in sentences like "Everyone forgets their passwords" for centuries. Well-educated English speakers and writers routinely use singular *they,* and today's language authorities find it not just acceptable, but sometimes even mandatory.

The *Oxford English Dictionary* traces singular *they* back to 1375, in the medieval romance *William and the Werewolf.* Except for the old-style language of the poem, the usage is not all that different from how we might use singular *they* to refer to an unnamed person today. Here's the Middle English:

Hastely hiȝed *eche wiȝt* . . . til þei neyȝþed so neiȝh . . . þere william & his worþi lef were liand i-fere.

In Modern English:

> *Each man* hurried . . . till *they* drew near . . . where William
> and his darling were lying together.

And just to confirm that singular *they* wasn't rare back then, the *OED* gives a second example from the same period, from *Three Kings of Cologne,* ca. 1400 (emphasis added):

> *Noman* was hardy in all þat countrey to sette aȝens hem, for
> drede þat *þey* hadde of hem.

> *No one* in the whole country was brave enough to oppose
> them, because *they* were so afraid of them.

Word forms may appear in speech long before they're written down, so it's likely that singular *they* was common in English even before these late-fourteenth-century citations. That makes an old form even older.

But not as old as Old English. Old English didn't have singular *they.* It didn't even have plural *they,* or any kind of *they.* The Old English third-person pronouns all began with *h:* the singular *he* and *heo,* for "he" and "she," along with *hit,* for the Modern English "it." The third-person plural for all the genders was *hi.* The singular pronouns resembled one another when they were written, and they looked like the plural, too, but even more confusing—since most people at the time couldn't read or write—these pronouns tended to sound the same when they were spoken. People would wonder, was Æþelrad talking about a he, a she, or a they? And that confusion, that ambiguity of reference, could have prompted two changes to English that would fix some of the problems: *she,* whose origin is unclear, replaced *heo* as the feminine pronoun, and *they,* borrowed from Old Norse, replaced *hi*. These changes didn't happen overnight, and to some extent the shift from *h-* to *th-* for the plural pronoun has been incomplete: the informal *'em*, so common in speech, is not a reduced form of *them*, but a holdover from the old plural object form, *hem*, with unpronounced *h*.

The important takeaways from this language history lesson:

➤ Ambiguity about gender and number was a feature of the English third-person pronouns pretty much from the start.

➤ When the pronouns caused too much confusion, English speakers tried to clear that up with a new feminine form, *she* (they retained the object form *her* because *her* was not ambiguous).

➤ ... And they borrowed a new set of plural pronouns, *they, them, their*, from Old Norse, the language spoken by Vikings who had invaded and settled in the eastern parts of England in the ninth century CE.

➤ The introduction of these new pronouns was gradual, meaning the ambiguities of the old pronouns didn't clear up right away.

➤ Still, English speakers must have found the pronoun *they* really useful or they wouldn't have borrowed it from the language of their enemies.

And independent of this borrowing process, English speakers have typically adjusted grammatical agreement to fit the sense of what they're saying. Indefinite nouns like *no one, anyone,* and *someone* are technically singular and occur with the singular form of the verb, as in *Nobody is going to remember my instructions*. Not, *Nobody are going to remember*.... But since these indefinites also seem to refer to more than one person, we often link them with plural pronouns: *Nobody is going to forget to bring their grammar books tomorrow, are they?* Maybe if English had developed a third-person singular gender-neutral pronoun on its own, we wouldn't be tempted to use singular *they*. But that didn't happen, and despite the best efforts of earnest wordsmiths, no coined pronoun has gained enough momentum to fill in the blank. Long ago, *they*, like *you*, took on the dual role of singular and plural, and singular *they* has been so well established, for so many centuries, that at this point resistance is futile.

And yet there has been resistance. Singular *they* may have a long and distinguished history, but not everyone's a fan. For the last couple of centuries at least, critics have routinely argued that pairing a singular noun with a plural pronoun is ungrammatical. Writing in 1795 in *English Grammar, Adapted to the Different Classes of Learners*—a textbook used in many American schools—Lindley Murray may have been the first grammarian to imply as much when he gave this example of incorrect pronoun agreement: "Can any one, on their entrance into the world, be fully secure that *they* shall not be deceived." Murray showed how to correct this with generic *he*: that *he* shall not be deceived.[1]

Depending on who's complaining, singular *they* is anything from a minor sin to evidence of complete illiteracy, moral decay, even the end of civilization as we know it. But early on, defenders of the common usage pointed to the well-established singular *you* and asked, if *you* can serve as singular as well as plural, why can't *they* do both as well?

In a sense, singular *you* is even more of a newcomer on the pronoun scene. The plural *you* was applied as a singular pronoun to address royalty as early as the thirteenth century and was used in other situations demanding deference and formality—call the monarch *thy majesty* instead of *your majesty* and it could mean off with your head. But *you* doesn't appear as a singular in all contexts until the 1600s, when it slowly, slowly starts pushing out *thou, thee, thy,* and *thine,* second-person singulars that English speakers had been using since the days of *Beowulf.* The *th-* singulars persist even now in some English dialects, and nineteenth-century grammar books regularly demanded singular *thou* and *thee,* along with *thy* and *thine,* even though these pronouns were no longer considered standard English. They're still familiar to us, to be sure: everyone has heard of *thou, thee,* and *thy*—remember Juliet's "Romeo, Romeo, wherefore art thou Romeo?" Or the King James translation of the Twenty-Third Psalm, "thy rod and thy staff they comfort me." But to the modern ear, forms like *thou* and *thy* sound antique, evoking Shakespeare and the Bible, and when we're not acting or reading scripture, we use them humorously to sound old-fashioned. Given that singular *they* was common by the late 1300s, and singular *you* is a much newer form, *they* should be the model for justifying singular *you,* and not the other way around.

Singular *they* has long been the go-to pronoun to use for words like *someone* and *everyone,* indefinite pronouns which are technically singular—*one* means "one," after all—but which suggest plurality: there are lots of someones and everyones. And singular *they* is used for definite but unnamed persons, too, words like *the reader* or *the writer,* where the reference is to an individual who is a member of a certain group, as when *the writer* refers to writers in general: *The writer may find proofreading their own work to be a challenge.* Even a clearly singular word like *person* can trigger a singular *they,* whether in the eighteenth century, when grammarians strode the earth correcting everybody's English, or much more recently, when the public became more aware of just how complicated gender may be, as in these examples from the *OED:*

> 1759. If a person is born of a . . . gloomy temper . . . they cannot help it.

> 1998. The psychiatric label for a transgender person is that they are suffering Gender Identity Disorder.

That 1998 example of *person . . . they* reflects an earlier negative view of transgender persons. As I mentioned earlier, gender terminology is continually being revised, and it's important to note that the scientific community now rejects the idea that gender nonconformity is a disorder. The most recent edition of the standard reference work used by psychologists and psychiatrists, the *Diagnostic and Statistical Manual of Mental Disorders* (the *DSM-V*) employs the more neutral term *gender dysphoria*. And as if to reinforce the increasing acceptance both of nonbinary gender and of singular *they*, the *OED* adds this example from the *New York Times* in its current entry for *transgender*: "2015 'They' has become an increasingly popular substitute for 'he' or 'she' in the transgender community."

● ● ●

In addition to general references like *a person . . . they*, as we saw in the last chapter, lots of people now use *they* for specific, named individuals, particularly in contexts calling for a nonbinary pronoun: "Alex likes their burger with mustard but not ketchup."

That's not to say that *they* is about to oust *he, she,* and *it.* These pronouns still get plenty of use, and that's not going to change. What's changing is the increasing recognition, and acceptance, of singular *they.*

The fact is that there don't seem to be any other viable options besides singular *they* for that long-sought third-person singular, gender-neutral pronoun. Generic *he* is in deep decline. Relatively few people are opting for invented pronouns. And there's a long-standing dislike of the phrases *he or she, his or her,* and *him or her.* The only choice left is singular *they,* and despite pockets of resistance, an increasing number of respected language authorities, including some major dictionaries, grammars, and usage guides, accept singular *they* as "good usage."

Important, too, is the fact that singular *they* is not an early form that appeared hundreds of years ago and then went dormant, only to pop up again when people started to agitate for women's rights or question the traditional gender binary. It's been common throughout the history of English. The *OED* provides citations from such writers as Lord Chesterfield, Henry Fielding, John Ruskin, Walter Bagehot, and Langston Hughes. Other writers who have used singular *they* include Jane Austen, who used the form seventy-five times in *Pride and Prejudice*,[2] as in this example, where Elizabeth Bennet tells Mr. Darcy, "I always delight in . . . cheating a person of their premeditated contempt." William Shakespeare was a fan: "There's not a man I meet but doth salute me as if I were their well-acquainted friend" (*Comedy of Errors*). Here's a singular *they* (emphasis added) from Virginia Woolf's *A Room of One's Own*, the influential essay about women writing that appeared in 1929, just after Woolf's gender-bending *Orlando*: "It is fatal for anyone who writes to think of their sex."[3] If famous writers use singular *they*, that means ordinary people must be using it too: to put it in modern, nontechnical terms, singular *they* has been part of our normal linguistic landscape since, like, forever.

Singular *they* can serve writers as an important plot device. Here's Charles Dickens using singular *they* intentionally to conceal gender in *The Pickwick Papers*. In one scene, Pickwick has retired to what he presumes to be his bedroom in a tavern, and, changing into his nightclothes while perched on a heavily curtained bed,

[Pickwick] was about to continue the process of undressing, in the best possible humour, when he was suddenly stopped by a most unexpected interruption: to wit, the entrance into the room of *some person* with a candle, who, after locking the door, advanced to the dressing-table, and set down the light upon it.

The smile that played on Mr. Pickwick's features was instantaneously lost in a look of the most unbounded and wonder-stricken surprise. The person, whoever it was, had come in so suddenly and with so little noise, that Mr. Pickwick had had no time to call out, or oppose *their* entrance. Who could it be? A robber? Some evil-minded person who had seen him come upstairs with a handsome watch in his hand, perhaps. What was he to do?[4]

—CHARLES DICKENS, *The Posthumous Papers of the Pickwick Club* (1837)

In this scene, *person* and *they* conceal the gender of the intruder, creating an air of suspense that quickly turns to farce as the "person" turns out to be, not an evil-minded robber, but a lady in "yellow curl-papers" who has just returned to her room, which Pickwick has unwittingly mistaken for his own. This being a Dickens novel, hilarity ensues.

Concealing gender is also the reason why, in 1861, a character in E. D. E. N. Southworth's novel *Eudora* defends her use of singular *they*: "Mamma, when we speak of anyone in the third person without wishing even to divulge their sex, we say 'they' because we have no third person singular of the common gender." That's right: the narrator of a serialized novel is aware that her words are ambiguous and feels compelled to explain that because she used the pronoun "they," her mother "fancied there was more than one."[5]

Singular *they* remains an important technique for concealing someone's identity. In 2018 the *New York Times* published an anonymous op-ed by a high-level White House official asserting that administration insiders felt obliged to thwart President Donald Trump's impulsivity. When *Times* editor James Dao explained the decision to withhold the author's name, he used singular *they* to hide the gender: "It was clear early on that the writer wanted anonymity, but we didn't grant anything until we read it and we were confident that they were who they said they were."[6]

For two centuries, complaints about singular *they* persisted despite its obvious usefulness. In 1839, a writer wishing for a new pronoun charged that singular *they* was "too vulgar to be uttered."[7] Another found singular *they* "a direct violation of the rules of grammar."[8] Richard Whately, an Oxford don before he became archbishop of Dublin, blamed singular *they* on women who don't like *he*. Whately insisted, providing no proof but his own personal bias, "A man will generally say, 'he is'; but women, it would seem, do not like to use the masculine pronoun, and therefore use the pronoun '*they*,' which is of the common gender."[9]

As we've seen, Whately wasn't the only man to blame women for pronoun changes, but most critics admitted that singular *they* was frequently used in speech and writing by everyone. In 1875, the editor of *Appletons' Journal* acknowledged the universal use of singular *they*, but claimed that even when careful writers used it, it was still a mistake.[10] Another editor called for a new gender-neutral pronoun, saying that *one* sounded affected, *he or she* was stilted, generic *he* ignored women altogether—and singular *they* was always incorrect.[11]

The popular nineteenth-century columnist Richard Grant White not only dismissed singular *they* as incorrect, he also denied that people use it all the time.[12] And in 1887 an angry letter writer named Frederick, from Cambridge, Massachusetts, fumed that singular *they* wasn't even English:

> No reputable writer ever put to paper such atrocious violations of syntax as . . . "No 'one' should convict another without giving 'them' a chance to defend 'themselves.'"

These sentences are not English at all. There is no rule of grammar more thoroughly established than the one governing this case, which is that a personal pronoun agrees with its antecedent in number. Another universally recognized rule is that when the antecedent is singular and the gender unknown or doubtful, as above, the pronoun must be masculine. This rule applies to all other languages as far as I know. A singular personal pronoun of common gender is something I never yet found in any tongue.[13]

    —FREDERICK, "A Question of Syntax," *Boston Globe* (1887)

Frederick was wrong on all counts: generic *he* is not a linguistic universal; many languages have gender-neutral pronouns; and the historical record shows that singular *they* is English to the core. But what Frederick's adamant opposition to singular *they* tells us is that it is so much a part of the fabric of English that resistance is, indeed, futile.

The *Atlanta Constitution* came to the defense of singular *they* in 1885. Rejecting *thon,* which had been proposed by "those who find it difficult to get along with the English of the Bible and Shakespeare," the *Constitution* declared,

> There is nothing awkward or ungrammatical in [singular *they*], so far as the construction of English is concerned. It is ungrammatical when measured by the Latin method—but what has Latin grammar to do with the English tongue?[14]
>
>   —"The New Pronoun," *Atlanta Constitution* (1885)

A follow-up by a Chicago grammarian pointed out that variants of singular *they* had "been in the English dialect since Chaucer was a baby."[15] Similarly, an 1888 comment in a Kansas newspaper rejected invented pronouns like *se,* insisting instead that singular *they* was the most natural choice for English speakers:

This usage is very common in conversation, so common that it can hardly be avoided without much painstaking. It is out of common speech that all our language forms have grown, and some of them, long approved and unquestioned, are quite as incongruous as this use of "they" in place of the neglected common gender pronoun. It is perfectly proper, in fact the only proper thing, according to the grammars, to use "he, his and him" to represent the common gender, but the use is awkward, and drives the unlettered people to the use of "they." Really, there is no better reason for "he" than for "they," and as "they" is evidently the most natural, the grammarians should consent to its adoption.[16]

— "The Epicene Pronoun," *Lincoln Republican* (1888)

Writers who should know better

It's not just the masses using singular *they*. When writers "who should know better" used it, the critics got even more exercised. In 1884, the *Boston Globe* greeted Converse's *thon* with skepticism: "The majority of people will continue to say they."[17] But J. E. Pratt, of Sandwich, Massachusetts, lambasted the *Globe* both for approving such an error and for assuming most people to be ignorant.[18] Reactions to *thon* continued to provoke debate over singular *they* in the press. Like the *Boston Globe*, the *New York Commercial Advertiser* declared that singular *they* could not be a mistake because it was used by educated people and respected writers.[19] But the *Chicago Tribune* wasn't having it, calling singular *they* "hideous."[20] The *Commercial Advertiser* then compromised, admitting that even though singular *they* might be wrong, authors like Addison used it freely in the *Spectator*. Instead of wasting time on pronouns made up by "cranks," the paper advised all careful writers to study their Addison.[21]

In 1890, the editor and translator Frederic H. Balfour called singular *they* a grammatical monstrosity.[22] But a columnist writing under the pseudonym Erasmus counseled anyone looking for a gender-neutral pronoun to choose Matthew Arnold's lesser-of-two-evils solution: singular *they* may be a sin, "but it is a venial one."[23]

And in 1916, the *Oxford English Dictionary*, which had finally reached the letter *T*, published its entry for *they*, noting that the third-person plural pronoun is "often used in relation to a singular noun or pronoun denoting a person. . . . Also so used instead of 'his or her', when the gender is inclusive or uncertain." Despite the long and distinguished history of singular *they*, the *OED*'s editors felt compelled to hedge their definition, explaining that singular *they* is "not favoured by grammarians."[24] In 2013, the dictionary scaled back that warning, and the usage note now puts opponents of singular *they* in the minority, observing that "this use has sometimes been considered erroneous."

Not all dictionaries were as accepting as the *OED*. In 1916, the *Funk & Wagnalls* lexicographer James C. Fernald assured his readers that the generic *he* may be used "to refer indifferently to persons of either sex," and he condemned singular *they*, recommending that writers recast their sentences to avoid it.[25] In 1932, another well-known *Funk & Wagnalls* language guru, Dr. Frank H. Vizetelly, argued that singular *they* is always incorrect. "Dr. Viz" told his readers that the best way to refer to two nouns of different genders is to rewrite the sentence.[26] But three years later Vizetelly abruptly reversed himself and okayed singular *they*, citing Samuel Johnson, Byron, and Ruskin as "sufficient literary support" for the pronoun.[27]

The literary use of singular *they* remained a thorny issue. Although authorities like Vizetelly had begun to defend the form, even if it violated the number agreement rule, others argued that a mistake by a great writer was still a mistake. In a multiyear attack on singular *they*, the newspaper columnist Walter Curtis Nicholson warned that it was not used by "good modern authors" or "careful speakers on the public platforms." Despite overwhelming evidence that modern writers and careful speakers did indeed use singular *they*, Nicholson insisted again and again that words like *anyone, everybody, someone, no one,* and *nobody* are always singular—they never take *they*.[28]

Taking on the patriarchy with singular *they*

Language authorities were slow to accept singular *they* as standard English, but that acceptance was inevitable. In her book of advice for writers, the science-fiction writer Ursula K. Le Guin labeled the ban on singular *they* a "fake rule" promulgated by the "grammar bullies" who insist that the pronoun *he* includes both sexes, as in, "If a person needs an abortion, he should be required to tell his parents." For Le Guin, singular *they* was a rejection of the patriarchy:

> My use of *their* is socially motivated and, if you like, politically correct: a deliberate response to the socially and politically significant banning of our genderless pronoun by language legislators enforcing the notion that the male sex is the only one that counts. I consistently break a rule I consider to be not only fake but pernicious. I know what I'm doing and why.[29]
> —URSULA K. LE GUIN, *Steering the Craft* (2015)

And in 2018, Coca Cola implicitly endorsed nonbinary *they* in a Super Bowl ad with the line, "There's a Coke for he, and she, and her, and me, and them."[30] Though Coke placed singular *they* alongside binary *he* and *she,* and some criticized the company for endorsing the nonbinary purely for commercial gain, reaction to this gender-bending foray into the macho world of football was generally favorable, and Coke drew some praise for its inclusive pronoun use.

But the defense of *they* goes back centuries before the Super Bowl, and it doesn't need science fiction or political correctness to back it up. We've seen how the Belle Assembly took on their mansplaining critic, Alonzo, in 1794 when they defended their use of singular *they:* "We wished to conceal the gender." And singular *they* combined social justice with good grammar. In 1879, the Scottish philosopher Alexander Bain wrote one of the few nineteenth-century grammars to approve of singular *they* because it was both inclusive and grammatical:

> When both Genders are implied, it is allowable to use the Plural.... Grammarians frequently call this construction an error: not reflecting that it is equally an error to apply "his" to feminine subjects. The best writers furnish examples of the use of the plural as a mode of getting out of the difficulty.[31]
> —ALEXANDER BAIN, *A Higher English Grammar* (1879)

The case for singular *they* continued to be made in the press, and occasionally, in dictionaries, in writer's guides, and in books like Bain's on grammar and usage. For example, in 1879 a writer in the *Atlantic Monthly* observed that approving singular *they* has the advantage of normalizing what people already do: "It would be easy to adopt this idiom, for we are continually struggling against its use, and how delightful it would be for once to make wrong right!"[32] And in 1896, E. F. Andrews, the librarian at Wesleyan College in Macon, Georgia, defended singular *they,* arguing that "ninety-nine out of a hundred, if they haven't the fear of the schoolmaster before their eyes," will use it too. We've seen that philologists and professors are frequently called on to produce the needed nonbinary pronoun, but Andrews reminded her readers that it's the humble schoolteacher who gets blamed for making everyone afraid to violate the pronoun agreement rule.

Andrews went on to argue that language standards derive from popular usage, not from the whims of monarchs or schoolteachers:

> [Singular *they*] is now so common in conversation that it may almost be said to have become a well-established colloquialism. . . . The queen's English must step down from the throne when the sovereign people take it in hand, as must its queen herself, whether she wield the scepter or the ferrule, and submit to the law of the multitude. Speech is a born democrat; in its realm the voice of the people is supreme.[33]
>
> —ELIZA FRANCES ANDREWS, "Some Grammatical Stumbling Blocks," *The Chautauquan* (1896)

The lesson of singular *you*

Andrews reminded her readers that singular *they* was no different from singular *you*, a pronoun that was originally plural but eventually became singular as well. Today's defenders of singular *they* still point to singular *you* as a precedent, so here's brief digression on how singular *you* became respectable. Originally plural, *you* began to double as a polite or deferential singular in Middle English, but in the seventeenth century it spread as a substitute for *thou* in all contexts. Over the next one hundred years, *you* ousted *thou* and *thee*, along with the nominative plural *ye*. Not surprisingly, some commentators objected that this newfangled singular *you* was ungrammatical. In 1660, George Fox, better known as the founder of the Society of Friends (the Quakers), wrote an entire book devoted to correcting the "error" of singular *you*. Fox argued,

> Is not your own *Original, Thou* to *one* singular, and *You* to *many* plural . . . ? Do not they speak false English . . . that doth

not speak thou to one, and what ever he be, Father, Mother, King, or Judge, is he not a Novice, and Unmannerly, and an Ideot, and a Fool, that speaks You to one, which is not to be spoken to a singular, but to many?[34]

—GEORGE FOX, *A Battle-Door for Teachers and Professors to Learn Singular & Plural* (1660)

Fox lost that battle to the "unmannerly" English of the "idiots" and "fools." Anne Fisher acknowledged this change in the second person in her best-selling 1753 grammar: "As we say *you* for *thou* and *thee*, so we frequently say *your* for *thy*, and *yours* for *thine*."[35]

In 1792, James Anderson, the philosopher whose proposal for thirteen genders we looked at in Chapter 4, also observed that the plural *you* had recently begun "to stand in place of a singular."[36] Both Fisher and Anderson treated singular *you* as a change in progress, but most eighteenth- and nineteenth-century English grammars—the popular schoolbooks of Robert Lowth and Lindley Murray among them—continued to teach *thou* as the exclusive second-person singular, and *you* as the plural, even though speakers and writers of standard English had long abandoned *thou* as quaint or archaic. Well into the nineteenth century, students were required to parse *thou*

		Leading State.	Following State.
1ſt Perſon	Singular	*I*	*Me*
	Plural	*We*	*Us*
2d Perſon	Singular	*Thou* / *You*	*Thee* / *You*
	Plural	*Ye*	*You*
3d Perſon	Singular	*He* / *She*	*Him* / *Her*
	Plural	*They*	*Them*

Anne Fisher's popular school grammar, published as early as 1745, is one of the few to indicate that both *thou* and *you* are singular pronouns. (University of Illinois Library, used by permission.)

on grammar tests and write *thou* in their essays, even though they and their terror-inducing schoolmasters used *you* for everything that wasn't on the test. In 1880 the *Topeka Daily Capital* was one of the few to challenge the grammarians' insistence on keeping *thou* on life support: "The second person singular of the grammar books is obsolete."[37]

It's true that having the same pronoun for both singular and plural can be ambiguous. To remove ambiguity, new colloquial plural forms sprang up—*y'all,* common in the American South; *youse,* an urban form in the United States and Scotland; *you lot* in the United Kingdom; and *yins,* or *you'uns,* in the American Midwest. Most recently, the form *you guys* has transcended regional and dialect variants to

The personal pronouns are thus declined,		
	SINGULAR.	**PLURAL.**
Nom.	I.	We.
Possess.	Mine.	Ours.
Object.	Me.	Us.
	SINGULAR.	PLURAL.
Nom.	Thou.	Ye *or* you.
Possess.	Thine.	Yours.
Obj.	Thee.	You.
	SINGULAR.	PLURAL.
Nom.	He.	They.
Possess.	His.	Theirs.
Obj.	Him.	Them.
	SINGULAR.	PLURAL.
Nom.	She.	They.
Possess.	Hers.	Theirs.
Obj.	Her.	Them.
	SINGULAR.	PLURAL.
Nom.	It.	They.
Possess.	Its.	Theirs.
Obj.	It.	Them.

More than a century after standard English dropped the th- forms of the second-person singular, Lindley Murray continued to include *thou, thee,* and *thy* in his popular 1795 school grammar. Nineteenth-century textbooks continued to enforce the paradigm in teaching standard English to children who never said *thou* or *thee* in class.

become a kind of de facto plural in spoken English. It is paradoxical that this generic use of the masculine *guys* spread as generic masculines like *he* and *man* were in decline, and objections to sexist *guys* and *you guys* still appear.[38] And in yet another stage of the *you*-singular/*you*-plural cycle, some American southerners began to use *y'all* as both singular and plural, prompting the creation of yet another disambiguating regional pronoun, *all y'all.*

Finally, though, *you* became naturalized as the second-person singular pronoun in standard English, conjugated with the plural verb: *you are. You is,* when it occurs, is stigmatized as dialect or nonstandard. Following this pattern, singular *they* typically appears with the plural verb: *they like ketchup on their burger,* not *they likes.* But even here we find variation. This 2015 article quotes the parent of a nonbinary college student using both a singular verb form and the singular reflexive: "This is how they presents themself."[39] And a 2019 *New York Times* article on the growing number of nonbinary bar and bat mitzvahs—or b mitzvahs—quotes one teenager saying, "I have a friend who is nonbinary, gender-fluid and their par-

	2nd. PERSON,	
Nom.	Thou	You
Dat.	To thee	To you
Poss.	Thine	Yours
Obj.	Thee	You

The Leeds newspaper *Northern Star* carried a series of grammar lessons for "the Working Classes" that also preserves the archaic *thou.* Although the Yorkshire farmers and factory workers addressed might still be using a dialect pronoun like *tha* or *ta,* that would hardly have been considered acceptable by the grammarian advising the working classes to choose the "correct" or approved form, *thou.* (Newspaper Image © The British Library Board. All rights reserved. With thanks to The British Newspaper Archive (www.britishnewspaperarchive.co.uk); used by permission.)

ents weren't as accepting. They still had a bar mitzvah even though they doesn't identify as a gender."[40] It's possible that these singular and plural verb forms will remain in flux as singular *they* continues to spread.

Power to the people

Faced with the onslaught of coined pronouns in the 1880s, singular *they* began to seem less and less objectionable, and more observers recognized the old but much-maligned singular *they* as the people's choice. For example, a writer in 1884 recommended *they* as an interim solution to be used while experts pondered *thon* and *lin*.[41] According to another writer, C. K. Maddox, there was no need for invented pronouns because *they* has been singular "for ages" in the writing of standard authors like Dickens. Maddox criticized experts who withheld their approval: "Our grammarians and dictionary makers are very conservative and often positively stupid" for rejecting a term "so natural to the genius of our language that hardly one in a hundred has noticed it as an intrusion."[42]

Sometimes an expert did affirm singular *they* as the people's pronoun. In 1885, Fred Newton Scott, a linguist soon to become president of the National Council of Teachers of English and, later, of the Modern Language Association, argued that the way people talk inevitably becomes the standard recognized by language reference books. Scott observed that pretty much everyone uses singular *they*, both people who care about good grammar, and those who don't: "The word *they* is being used as a pronoun of the common gender every day by millions of persons who are not particular about their language, and every other day by several thousands who are particular." Scott warned purists not to resist the form:

> To the fast-coming objections that the proposed use of [singular *they*] is ungrammatical, inconsistent, illogical, and impracticable, it may be replied, in general, that the English language is full of absurdities and inconsistencies, and with all its faults we love it still.
>
> —FRED NEWTON SCOTT, "The Missing Pronoun,"
> *The Current* (1885)

Furthermore, Scott reminded readers that no one's waiting for the "experts" to choose a pronoun. Quite the opposite, in fact. Language authorities don't establish the rules. Instead, as Scott noted, they take their cues about correctness from popular usage:

> While the critics and philologists are quarreling over the relative advantages of two different modes of expression or pronunciation, the great talking public, which cannot very well suspend communication until the mooted question is decided, goes on talking after its own fashion, and finally talks that fashion into our grammars and dictionaries.

Scott assumed that artificial pronouns like *thon, se,* and *le* didn't stand a chance against singular *they,* which was both natural and common. He even accepted singular *they* with a singular verb: *they was.* Yet Scott couldn't avoid a bit of expert tinkering: to avoid confusion with plural *they,* he suggested respelling *they, their,* and *them* as *tha, thare,* and *tham,* or even Converse's *thon.* And as someone who firmly believed that language charts its own course (with the exception, perhaps, of spelling), he assured readers that his proposal was to be taken as a suggestion, not a mandate.[43]

The philologist Otto Jespersen got into the singular *they* act in 1894, citing writers who struggle with the "cumbrous" *he or she,* as in the following example, when the author wished to conceal a killer's gender:

> "The murderer has written it in his or her own blood."
>
> —ARTHUR CONAN DOYLE,
> *A Study in Scarlet* (1887)

Jespersen concluded that "the substitution of the plural for the singular is not wholly illogical. . . . to supply the missing genderless singular," a convoluted statement that he illustrated with clear examples like these:

> "I never refuse to help anybody, if they've a mind to do themselves justice."
>
> —GEORGE ELIOT, *The Mill on the Floss* (1867)

> "A person can't help their birth."
>
> —WILLIAM MAKEPEACE THACKERAY,
> *Vanity Fair* (1848)[44]

Later, in his seven-volume English grammar, Jespersen confirmed that singular *they* arises from "the lack of a common-number (and common-sex) form in the third-personal pronoun." And he documented instances of plural pronouns with singular noun phrases as antecedents, noting that these noun phrases often have "generic meaning":

> "Unless *a person* takes a deal of exercise, *they* may soon eat more than does them good."
>
> —HERBERT SPENCER, *Autobiography* (1904)

> "Who makes you *their* confidant?"
>
> —JANE AUSTEN, *Emma* (1816)

"As for a doctor . . . what use were *they* except to tell you what you knew?"
—JOHN GALSWORTHY, *The Country House* (1907)[45]

And in 1908, Thomas Lounsbury, a Yale professor and expert in the history of English, defended singular *they* in *Harper's Magazine* because it was good, idiomatic English, and because generic *he* had become offensive. Although we have seen other commentators blaming women for the turn toward gender-neutral language, Lounsbury maintained that, in light of women's positive contribution to language and society, both women and men were justified in their objection to generic *he*:

> One result of the increasingly important part that the female sex plays in life and literature is the growth of a repugnance on the part of the feminine element to have its identity merged in the masculine. Subconsciousness of the injustice of it has now passed over into full consciousness that under this form of expression its claims are not really recognized. Hence, while women may use it, they do not like it; and men have come to share largely in the same feeling.[46]
> —THOMAS R. LOUNSBURY, "The Aristocracy of the Parts of Speech," *Harper's Monthly* (1908)

Like all who comment on the subject, Lounsbury rejected *his or her,* partly because it is cumbersome, but also because it draws attention to gender "where there is neither desire nor occasion to make it prominent." The devotees of grammar may find the phrase acceptable, he said, but it "is usually detested by everybody else." (As we have seen, even the supposed "devotees of grammar" hate *his or her.*) Lounsbury illustrated the popularity of singular *they* among "authors of high reputation" with several examples drawn exclusively from Jane Austen, picking Austen because, "as a general rule, highly cultivated women speak and write the language not only with more naturalness, but with greater scrupulousness and purity than the corresponding class of men. Examples from their works are in consequence more convincing."

When it comes to singular *they,* the people seem continually at odds with "the grammarians"—not linguists like Scott, Jespersen, and Lounsbury, but purists like Lindley Murray and Richard Grant White who dictate rules of usage that are not always in sync with how most people actually use language. In 1886, one writer complained that these grammarians thwarted the natural impulse to use singular *they*:

> There was a strong disposition a few years ago to use the word *"they"* in place of the painfully grammatical expression *"he or she."* The grammarians forbade it, as not consistent with the rules of grammar. If these grammarians had let us alone, *"they"* would have been selected by the people as the pronoun of common gender, third person, singular or plural number, and a great want of the language would have been supplied.[47]
>
> —"We," *Nashville American* (1886)

Another writer took the opposite view, blaming grammarians for not being able to prevent singular *they.*[48] Yet the *Minneapolis Star-Tribune* praised Mrs. Humphrey Ward for using singular *they* in her novels—in an article called "Devious English," they said, "If the best usage approves of a departure from a formerly prescribed rule, the correction will in time become the correct form."[49]

Flash forward now to 1974, when we find a letter to the *Los Angeles Times* defending singular *they* as an error on the brink of becoming standard English:

In spite of the hopes of grammarians, for years we have been substituting the plural for the sex-differentiated singular in any case where ambiguity is desirable (and many where it is not).... This usage is incorrect, as children are still taught, but it has pervaded not only the household and the tavern, but newscasting and even advertising.... and soon must be accepted as the new shape of our language.[50]

—LINDA CRITCHELL, "New Sex-Free Pronouns," *Los Angeles Times* (1974)

Eventually even some of the grammar sticklers started to come around. In 1980, a widely used college textbook, James McCrimmon's *Writing with a Purpose,* acknowledged the prevalence of singular *they* as colloquial, though McCrimmon wasn't ready to approve of it in formal writing.[51] In 1997, James J. Kilpatrick still proclaimed generic *he* the only real solution to the pronoun problem. Like male critics before him, Kilpatrick blamed the current demand for "a neutral referent pronoun" on "feisty" women—apparently men were happy enough to leave their pronouns alone.[52] But in 2009, Kirkpatrick, too, admitted that " 'his' no longer is in common use as a universal pronoun," and he stopped fighting singular *they.*[53]

Experts agree . . . mostly

Although a few serious students of language in the nineteenth and early twentieth centuries recognized that singular *they* was in general use and filled an important need, it's fair to say their pronouncements were ignored by readers and writers, who were taught by schoolteachers, grammarians, and the language gurus of the day to condemn the form. As the journalist H. L. Mencken put it, even though "excellent authors" like Jane Austen and Samuel Johnson routinely used singular *they*, "the schoolma'ams are so hot against it that they have made it infamous."[54]

Henry Fowler, a usage critic whose pronouncements were treated like scripture, recognized that "a perfect language" would have a common-gender pronoun—perhaps that's where A. A. Milne got the idea for *heesh*—but alas, there were no perfect languages. Fowler dismissed the singular *they* of Fielding and Thackeray as decidedly "old fashioned" prose that set "the literary man's teeth on edge"—as if singular *they* had been a misguided Victorian fad and contemporary literary men—not literary women like Woolf, only the men— had finally come to their senses. Fowler backed the grammarians' insistence on *everyone . . . he*, though not without a tongue-in-cheek allusion to the women's rights movement: "Whether that . . . is an arrogant demand on the part of male England, everyone must decide for himself (or for himself or herself, or for themselves)." As for constructions like *everyone . . . they*, repeating Archbishop Whately's claim that women avoid *he*, Fowler sided with the eighteenth-century grammarians who banned singular *they*, and, ignoring evidence to the contrary, he assured his many followers that "few good modern writers would flout the grammarians."[55]

In 1920, William Strunk, whose *Elements of Style* would become an American style bible after it was rediscovered and revised by E. B. White in 1959, found nothing but error in singular *they*:

> A common inaccuracy is the use of the plural pronoun when the antecedent is a distributive expression such as each, each one, everybody, every one, many a man, which, though implying more than one person, requires the pronoun to be in the singular. Similar to this, but with even less justification, is the use of the plural pronoun with the antecedent anybody, any

one, somebody, some one, the intention being either to avoid the awkward "he or she," or to avoid committing oneself to either. Some bashful speakers even say, "A friend of mine told me that they, etc."

Use he with all the above words, unless the antecedent is or must be feminine.[56]

—WILLIAM STRUNK, *Elements of Style* (1920)

But with the increasing stigmatization of generic *he* later in the century, and the continued resistance to the unpopular *he or she,* which even Fowler and Strunk disliked, the authorities on style began to flout those same grammarians by allowing *they* for indefinites like *someone* and *anyone.* In 1932, a usage panel convened by the National Council of Teachers of English concluded that singular *they* was "established in good colloquial usage." A majority of the panelists—teachers, writers, publishers, and business executives—approved *everyone . . . they* constructions, as in, "Everyone was here, but they all went home." Singular *they* with an indefinite antecedent was also found to be well established, as in this brief exchange:

"You just had a telephone call."
"Did they leave any message?"[57]

Even reformers who would make English less sexist could slam singular *they.* Promoting their invented pronoun, *tey,* Casey Miller and Kate Swift, both professional editors as well as crusaders against sexist language, took the opportunity to denounce singular *they* as ungrammatical: "When this patchwork solution begins to appear in print, the language is in trouble."[58] Maybe so, but the "patchwork" singular *they* continues to thrive, while *tey,* Miller and

Swift's gender-neutral alternative, survives as little more than a historical curiosity.

Eventually, the reluctant acceptance of singular *they* shifted to an affirmative recommendation to use the form. Rudolph Flesch, author of the best-selling *Why Johnny Can't Read* (1955), published a style guide in 1964 in which he argued that writers who avoid singular *they* "sound pompous and artificial."[59] And in 1969, the influential *Roberts English Series,* which framed grammar instruction in light of contemporary linguistic insight, taught, "The tendency for the meaning to override . . . syntactic singularity is strongest in the use of *they (them, their)* in reference to an indefinite pronoun: 'Everyone averted their eyes.'" But even the progressive *Roberts* stopped short of endorsing the form: "Conservative usage prefers 'Everyone averted his (or her) eyes.' It's a niggling point but one on which many people niggle."[60] The *Boston Globe* was another defender of singular *they.* A 1983 Boston *Globe* editorial observed that generic *he* is always suspect because it doesn't explicitly mention women, adding, "Anyone still hung up on the traditional *written* usages—the good grammar crowd—may want to insist that 'everyone likes ice cream, doesn't he?' Everybody else will head for the ice cream store, won't they?"[61]

The 1993 version of the influential *Chicago Manual of Style* (*CMOS*) actually advised writers to choose singular *they,* citing "its venerable use by writers from Shakespeare to Austen."[62] But, facing resistance from publishers and editors, *CMOS* walked back that recommendation in 2010: "Many people substitute the plural *they* and *their* for the singular *he* or *she.* Although *they* and *their* have become common in informal usage, neither is considered acceptable in formal writing."[63] The current version of the style manual tersely rejects gender-neutral blends like *s/he* and invented pronouns: "They won't succeed. And those who use them invite credibility problems."[64] But *CMOS* also signals a slight course correction back in the direction of singular *they*. Acknowledging that "*he* is no longer universally accepted," the most recent edition of *The Chicago Manual* allows *they, their, them,* and even *themself* (or *themselves*), or "some other gender-neutral singular pronoun"—that is, an invented form like *xe* or *zie*—if the person referred to prefers it:

> [Singular *they*] is only lately showing signs of gaining acceptance in formal writing, where Chicago recommends avoiding its use. When referring specifically to a person who does not identify with a gender-specific pronoun, however, *they* and its forms are often preferred. . . . In general, a person's stated preference for a specific pronoun should be respected.[65]
>
> —*The Chicago Manual of Style*, 17th ed. (2017)

Which is to say, writers and editors may violate the pronoun agreement rule or use an invented pronoun, not because they see it as the best solution to a long-standing problem, or because it has always fit "the genius of English," but only in order to keep the person they're writing about happy.

Taking a similar approach, the 2019 version of the *Associated Press Stylebook* reversed its previous rejection of singular *they*, labeling it "acceptable in limited cases." The AP warned that "singular *they* is unfamiliar to many readers," though the opposite is true—most readers don't even notice singular *they*. And it advised that "rewording usually is possible and always is preferable," though it grudgingly conceded,

> In stories about people who identify as neither male nor female or ask not to be referred to as *he/she/him/her*: Use the person's name in place of a pronoun, or otherwise reword the sentence, whenever possible. If *they/them/their* use is essential, explain in the text that the person prefers a gender-neutral

pronoun. Be sure that the phrasing does not imply more than one person.[66]

—*The Associated Press Stylebook 2019* (2019)

In his *American Usage,* Bryan Garner—who also wrote the *CMOS* usage note—doesn't like singular *they* but acknowledges that it is "commonplace" and "the most likely solution to the single biggest problem in sexist language . . . the generic masculine pronoun."[67] But the *American Heritage Book of English Usage* is more positive in labeling singular *they* "the alternative to the masculine generic with the longest and most distinguished history."[68] And *Merriam-Webster's Collegiate Dictionary* (11th ed.) accepts singular *they* as "well-established in speech and writing, even in literary and formal contexts."[69] Recently, too, the *Washington Post* approved the limited use of singular *they.* And in a new style guide, Random House copy chief Benjamin Dreyer, who calls himself "too old a dog to embrace" singular *they,* admits that he, too, has begun to use it when referring to a nonbinary colleague whose pronoun is *they:* "One day, when I wasn't even paying attention, the word 'they' slipped out of my mouth, and that was the end of that."[70]

In contrast, although the *Modern Language Association Handbook* is silent on singular *they,* the organization continues to observe the old pronoun number agreement rule in published academic writing. The MLA Style Center does take up the issue of pronoun gender in more detail, suggesting that when gender is ambiguous, pronoun avoidance is the safest option:

If a last name is given, repeat the person's last name on subsequent mentions in your paper. If a last name is not given, continue to use the person's first name. When possible, find a way to vary references by substituting generic nouns. For example, "the author," "the survey respondent," "the speaker," and so on.[71]

—**MODERN LANGUAGE ASSOCIATION STYLE CENTER,**
"What Pronoun Should I Use If I Do Not Know the Gender
of the Person I'm Writing About?" (2018)

Repeating nouns may appease the few purists and self-styled grammarians left who stand by a Latin pronoun agreement rule that never fit comfortably with English, and the fewer still who cling to the doctrine of the worthiness of the genders, but such repetition generates awkward and cumbersome prose full of "the author this" and "the author that," making the much-reviled *he or she* sound simple and direct.

In a separate comment on singular *they,* the MLA permits writers to use it or an invented pronoun when referring to themselves or to others whose pronoun choices are known, and it counsels editors to respect those preferences. The Style Center reminds readers that pronoun advice will change as usage changes, and if in scholarly publishing "a consensus emerges on a singular generic personal pronoun, we'll most likely incorporate it into our usage."[72]

Another influential style guide changed its position on generic *he* and singular *they.* The American Psychological Association (APA) now endorses the use of singular *they,* writing that "singular 'they' . . . is inclusive of all people and helps writers avoid making assumptions about gender. Although usage of the singular 'they' was once discouraged in academic writing, many advocacy groups and publishers have accepted and endorsed it, including *Merriam-Webster's Dictionary.*"[73] The APA advises people to use singular *they* "as a generic third-person singular pronoun to refer to a person whose gender is unknown or irrelevant to the context of the usage," and to always use a person's identified pronoun, whether that's *they* or another nonbinary pronoun such as *ze* or *per.*[74]

Since the 1990s, British reference works have become much more open to singular *they* than their American counterparts. *The Oxford English Grammar* notes that singular *they* is increasingly accepted in Britain, "even in formal style."[75] And R. W. Burchfield, updating the original Fowler's *Modern English Usage,* dismisses objections to singular *they* as unsupported by the historical record. Burchfield further observes that the construction is "passing unnoticed" by speakers of standard English as well as by copy editors, a trend he finds "irreversible."[76] The *New Oxford Dictionary* not only accepts singular *they,* they also use the form in their definitions.[77] And the *New Oxford American Dictionary* calls singular *they* "generally accepted" with indefinites, and "now common but less widely accepted" with definite nouns, especially in formal contexts.[78] Most upbeat of all, *The Cambridge Guide to English Usage* says that singular *they* with indefinites has become "unremarkable—an element of common usage." Even though some people still dislike it, the *Cambridge Guide* announces that "that kind of response . . . is no longer shared by the English-speaking population at large," and it counsels, "Writers who use singular *they/them/their* are not at fault."[79] Of course the insistence by authorities that singular *they* is not wrong also signals that there are still plenty of people around who think that it *is* wrong, and so, even writers who know they're not at fault may have to defend their use of singular *they* if challenged.

So entrenched is *they* as the default third-person singular pronoun that it's starting to crop up in reference to unambiguously male referents, as in this example from a student's paper: "When Robert Frost writes, 'two roads diverged in a wood' they mean . . ."[80] Another sign that singular *they* is no longer controversial is the fact that people are now arguing whether *themself* or *themselves* is the "correct" singular reflexive. In case you're wondering, the jury's still out. In short, resistance to singular *they* seems finally on the verge of collapsing, to the point where it is now possible to imagine a future style guide that is silent on the matter.

The worthiness of *they*

In 2015, the American Dialect Society declared singular *they* its Word of the Year, reflecting a sense among those who voted for it that singular *they* is visible beyond the confines of the academy, or the hushed corridors of the dictionary offices. And so I'd like to conclude this study of the history of gender-neutral and nonbinary pronouns by comparing the pros and cons of invented pronouns with those of singular *they*.

In 1983, UCLA researchers reported that 31% of the people they surveyed thought that English needed a new "sex-neutral" pronoun.[81] But adopting a nonbinary pronoun remains a challenge. Even today, when LGBTQ concerns have once again raised the issue of pronoun inclusivity, there is no single option that everyone agrees on. Some nonbinary speakers select the gendered pronoun, *he* or *she*, that matches their identity. Others, like Florida teacher Chloe Bressack, opt for singular *they*. And some choose *zie, hir,* or one of the other invented pronouns. Even though they are the forms less chosen, invented pronouns still make their presence known across a broad range of users, particularly younger ones, and they have some distinct advantages. These coined words fill a gap in the pronoun paradigm: they supply the "missing word" whose absence has been felt for more than two centuries. As we have seen, pronouns are political, and as they once called attention to women's rights, today coined pronouns call attention as well to the rights of nonbinary and trans persons. In the same way, marriage-neutral titles like *Ms.* once called attention to sexism in language. *Ms.* itself provides a precedent for the current growth of interest in *Mx,* a gender-neutral title that some people are adopting, and that appears as an option on an increasing number of official forms. Many colleges now let students pick their pronouns, and dating apps allow pronoun choice as well, because invented pronouns recognize a person's right to control how they're spoken or written about, always an important element in any linguistic interaction.

But invented pronouns have drawbacks too. They are high profile, calling attention to trans and nonbinary rights. Yes, I've just labeled that a strength, but as Thomas Lounsbury pointed out more than one hundred years ago, focusing on a gender issue may distract from other aspects of a speaker's message, especially if nothing else in the message is gender-related. Politically charged language may also draw a negative response—and that, too, can be a plus or a minus. Sometimes speakers want to get their audience a little bit annoyed or uncomfortable, hoping to raise their consciousness. But sometimes the same language politics can shut down the possibility of discourse and defeat the aim of communication. Another thing about invented pronouns: their usefulness may be time-limited. For now they highlight gender issues, but as gender nonconformity becomes increasingly accepted, it will also become less noticeable, rendering the high-profile invented pronouns less necessary.

On a more practical level, to the uninitiated, invented pronouns appear unfamiliar and are often hard to pronounce. They can be perceived as strident, or, in the case of the Tennessee legislature, a waste of taxpayer dollars. Plus, there are a lot of invented pronouns, not just one. That means too many choices, with no clear mechanism for selecting a finalist, or even a short list of best options.

Singular *they* also has advantages and disadvantages. Surely the strongest advantage is that it's a familiar pronoun with a long history and the clear ability to survive centuries of attacks by grammarians and schoolteachers. Objections to the supposed ungrammaticality of singular *they* are easy to dismiss, since the form is pretty universal, plus there's always the comparison with singular *you*. It's easy to use singular *they* when referring to an unidentified person, or a member of a class of persons (a writer, a grammarian, a language guru). Singular *they* is also becoming more and more common in reference to a specific, named person, particularly if that individual has made their preference known.

And the disadvantages of singular *they*? It drives the grammar sticklers nuts—though that may also be a plus. Critics of singular *they* love to think up contexts where it can be awkward or ambiguous, but you can do that with any pronoun, or any word for that matter, and fixing the problem requires rewording, not banning a word outright. Actually, there don't seem to be too many other reasons to avoid singular *they*.

So getting back to its advantages, singular *they* is used by those who prefer a nonbinary pronoun, or who want to make a point about the politics of gender, and it's used as well by those who don't care about those issues. It's used by people who insist that when it comes to gender, there are only two, and also by those who think of gender as complex, fluid, and idiosyncratic. People who actively oppose singular *they* on grammatical or ideological grounds use it anyway when they're not self-consciously watching their pronouns. As more language authorities signal their acceptance of the form, singular *they* shows every sign of being the missing word that's been hiding in plain sight. And it could be the most common answer to the increasingly common question, "What's your pronoun?"

● ● ●

If we've learned one thing so far, it's that there's no one right answer to "What's your pronoun?" Even with the apparent success of singular *they*, English speakers will go on living with multiple answers to the pronoun question. And that may be the best and most natural solution. It's normal for any language community to display both variable usage and change, even in something as slow to evolve as a pronoun system. But at this point two things do seem sure: generic *he* is stake-through-the-heart dead, and however you answer the question "What's your pronoun?" nobody answers, "My pronoun is actually a phrase, *he or she*." The answer will be, "My pronoun is *she*," or *they*, or *he*, or *zie*, or one of the many other invented pronouns in the chronology that follows.

A Chronology of Gender-Neutral and Nonbinary Pronouns

This chronology focuses on the pronouns suggested, coined, or condemned from 1765 to the present. Where possible, I have supplied specific dates and sources for each entry, along with any rationale provided. For examples treated more thoroughly in the body of this book, I give only brief bibliographic details. Annotations for other entries are more extensive when warranted. Many suggestions for gender-neutral or nonbinary pronouns repeat earlier ones. For example, there are multiple proposals for *heer, um,* and *E.* That's because many enterprising wordsmiths work in a vacuum, unaware of earlier attempts to coin any gender-neutral pronoun at all, let alone the one that they have come up with, and many of them offer more than one paradigm, or pronoun set, hoping that one of their recommendations will catch on. In contrast, sometimes a coinage is mentioned only to condemn it as unnecessary or unlikely to succeed. For a few of the commentators and word coiners, I haven't been able to find out any biographical information beyond their name or location. That's a sign that otherwise ordinary people felt that gender-neutral pronouns were an important issue worth a letter to the editor. Some contributors were anonymous or used a pseudonym, like Peck's Sun, or an initial, like Z. Today's newspapers prefer "name withheld" instead.

I focus this list on invented pronouns, but include as well suggestions for extending the use of existing English words like *it*, *one*, and *she*, along with proposals to borrow words from other languages and new pronouns proposed for languages like Swedish and French. I include passing references to generic *he* and singular *they* when they occur in the context of a coined pronoun. This list is necessarily incomplete, and I welcome additions—the older, the better.

• 1765

lo, zo   Joachim Faiguet de Villeneuve, *trésorier de France*, offers without explanation the pronouns *lo* (sg.) and *zo* (pl.) for his artificial language *Langue Nouvelle*, whose words have no gender. *Langue Nouvelle* went largely ignored. Denis Diderot, *L'Encyclopédie, ou dictionnaire raisonné des sciences, des arts, et des métiers*, vol. 9, p. 271.

• 1770

he; one   Confused by the similarity of Old English third-person pronouns, the eighteenth-century usage critic Robert Baker mistakenly posits that *he* was the first gender-neutral pronoun: "Our Ancestors, in the Infancy of the Language, had but one Word for the Substantives *he, she* and *they*." For Modern English, however, Baker suggests that the pronoun *one* is the only correct way to refer to a man or a woman. Robert Baker, *Reflections on the English Language* (London, 1770), pp. viii, 23–24.

• 1789

ou   William Marshall is critical of the Gloucester dialect use of *ou*, "analogous with the plural *they*,—being applied either in a masculine, a feminine, or a neuter sense. Thus, 'ou wull' expresses either *he* will, *she* will, or *it* will." William Marshall, *The Rural Economy of Glocestershire* (London, 1789), vol. 1, p. 324.

• 1792

ou   The Scottish economist and philosopher James Anderson labels the generic *he* inappropriate because it is "confined to the *male*, which ought equally to include the *female*," arguing instead for the usefulness of an "indeterminate pronoun" like the pronoun *ou*, recently reported in provincial use. James Anderson, "Grammatical Disquisitions," *The Bee*, October 10, 1792, p. 197. Although Marshall was the first to mention *ou*, Anderson is the first to call for a gender-neutral pronoun.

• 1794

singular *they*   A defense of singular *they* accompanied by a suggestion that anyone who doesn't like it is welcome to coin a new pronoun. "Report of a Select Committee from the Belle Assembly," *The Medley, or New Bedford Marine Journal* (MA), March 3, 1794, p. 2; letter, March 17, 1794, p. 2; letter, March 24, 1794, p. 2.

• 1808

it, which   "a neutral pronoun ... instead of, he, she, him, her, who, whom." Samuel Taylor Coleridge, *Anima Poetae*, ed. Ernest Hartley Coleridge (London: Heinemann, 1897), p. 190.

• 1841

E, Es, Em   Francis Augustus Brewster calls these forms "masculor feminine," in his *English Grammar....Simplicity and Conciseness Combined* (Brooklyn: Carter & Foster), p. 19. Brewster, who got his M.D. from Yale in 1840, published a grammar book the next year.

He eventually gave up medicine to sell insurance, announcing that "more than forty years ago" he had published an English grammar "introducing" these common-gender personal pronouns. *The Brooklyn Union-Argus,* November 29, 1878, p. 2.

• **1843**

it Molly Dolan, who writes in Irish dialect, reports, "'IT' is the onely propper pronoun to be applied to an unknown corrispondent—the name being 'neither fish, flesh, nor fowl.'" Molly Dolan, letter, *Ballyshannon Herald,* September 22, 1843, p. 3.

• **ca. 1850**

ne, nis, nim; hiser Note mentioning the coining of these "bastard" words "thirty years ago, or more." *New York Commercial Advertiser,* August 7, 1884, p. 3.

• **1850**

it A racist note defends the use of *it* to refer to slaves in Article XIII of the Kentucky Bill of Rights. "Grammatical Legislators," *New York Evening Post,* January 23, 1850, p. 2.

• **1858**

thon Many sources date Charles C. Converse's pronoun *thon* to 1858, though there is no direct evidence that the word appeared this early; see 1884 for a full discussion of *thon,* one of the best-known gender-neutral coinages. Even if Converse did create the word in 1858, he did not publicize it until 1884.

• **ca. 1860**

heesh, hizzer, himmer In 1900, an anonymous writer, who favors *thon,* reports, "During the '60s another ingenious gentleman proposed . . . Heesh—he or she. Hizzer—his or her. Himmer—him or her. Example. 'The teacher told John and Mary that he would punish himmer if heesh did not learn hizzer lesson.'" "A Common Gender Pronoun," *Princeton Daily Clarion* (IN), June 28, 1900, p. 3.

• 1861

singular *they* A character in a serialized novel explains that *they* is a useful tool for concealing gender. E. D. E. N. Southworth, *Eudora, or, The False Princess, New York Ledger,* September 28, 1861, p. 7.

• 1862

it Writers from the nineteenth century to the present have debated the appropriateness of assigning the masculine pronoun *he* to God. This may lead to gender-neutral translations of scripture, some of them controversial. So far, only one person has recommended a gender-neutral pronoun for the deity: *xe* (see below, 1971). Most discussions concern inclusivity or the problems of accurately translating ancient languages, and some reflect debates over the role of women in religion. Such discussions have been more common since the 1970s, but in this 1862 over-the-top anti-Semitic rant, Robert Gerry writes in the atheist journal *Boston Investigator* that he will refer to the "idol" of the Jews, whom he calls ignorant, violent, and "the most despicable miscreants the earth ever bore up," as *it*. Robert Gerry, "Dr. Syntax," *Boston Investigator,* August 27, 1862, p. 3.

• 1863

er Parenthetical remark: "The monosyllable 'er' is a pronoun of common gender in continual use in rural districts, more especially in the West of England." "Notes Taken at the Worcester Meeting of the Royal Agricultural Society," *The Bucks Herald* (Aylesbury, England), August 15, 1863, p. 8.

• 1864

ve, vis, vim This epicene pronoun is appropriate for "this age of improvement" and will secure, with a little practice, "precision, perspicuity, and brevity" in communication. Philologus, "Notes and Queries," *The Ladies' Repository,* July 1864, p. 439. By "precision" Philologus refers to agreement both in gender and in number. By "perspicuity" he probably means that singular *they* is incorrect. And by "brevity" he surely refers to the *he or she* option of filling in the blank, always dismissed as too wordy.

ze An alternative to *ve*. J. W. L., "An Epicene Pronoun," in "Notes and Queries," *The Ladies' Repository*, September 1864, p. 567.

• 1868

en From the French, suggested by a correspondent, and rejected as unnecessary. Richard Grant White, "Words and Their Uses," *The Galaxy*, August 1868, 241–44.

han, hans, han, hanself The correspondent "L" offers this coinage, admitting that it's easier to incorporate "a hundred new nouns and adjectives, and fifty new verbs," than one new pronoun. L., letter, *Boston Recorder*, October 22, 1868, p. 342.

un, uns; one In a follow-up, "an expert correspondent" finds *han* difficult because "the aspirate is in the way. The English would never accept it; they are plagued enough already with their h's." Instead, they recommend *un*, from the French. In addition, "a missionary pastor at the West" suggests expanding the use of *one*. "The Personal Pronoun," *Boston Recorder*, November 19, 1868, p. 374.

• 1869

in; he, him The summary of a lecture by J. H. Wilson on the history of the city of Reading, UK, reports that Readingites use the pronoun *him*, or its "contracted" form, *in*, for all genders and numbers. "Reading during the Last Thousand Years," *Berkshire Chronicle* (UK), March 13, 1869, p. 6.

um offered in reply to *Appletons'* call for a new pronoun, acknowledging that "it sounds a little odd, but we should get used to it. We have already shown our national capacity for digesting any combination of letters." "Courant Notes," *Hartford Courant* (CT), August 11, 1869, p. 2.

• 1871

[s]he; (s)he; s-he The *Oxford English Dictionary* (under "s/he") reports this blend of the masculine and feminine pronouns, giving a citation from the *American Educational Monthly*: "Some wise body discovered that a meeting was without sex, and at once cried out against the impropriety; chiefly, we suppose, because [s]he did not like the word female, and wished to be rid of it." An 1882 citation offers *(s)he*. And a 1908 variant yields *s-he*. See 1973 for more examples of *s/he*.

hizer, hesh, himer Favorable report in the *New York Sun* that philanthropist Dr. David Parsons Holton coined *hizer* "to take the place of the relative possessive pronoun, 'his or her,' whenever it becomes necessary to use them. It is comprehensive and avoids ambiguity. Such is its nature and significancy. Dr. Holton submits it to the learned and unlearned public. Being a philanthropist, he has not taken out a patent." *New York Sun*, May 3, 1871, p. 2. In a footnote in his subsequent memoir, Holton adds *hesh* and *himer*, with the comment, "one word being used as equivalent to three." "Reminiscences," read before the New York Genealogical and Biographical Society, May 27, 1874. See also *Every Saturday*, August 22, 1874 (vol. 2, no. 8), p. 220.

le A note in the newspaper reports, "A correspondent of the *Philadelphia Star* who has felt the necessity of a pronoun equally applicable to both sexes, proposes 'le' as the word. . . . The additional pronoun is undoubtedly needed and le is just as good as any word if it could be generally adopted." "A New Pronoun," *Wilmington News-Journal* (DE), July 18, 1872, p. 2. Presumably referring to the same coinage, a writer attributes *le* to "a Philadelphia philologist . . . wishing to steer clear of all sexual partiality." The writer provides this example: "Let our Philadelphian keep on, *le* is no doubt in the right, linguistically." "A New Pronoun," *Detroit Free Press*, November 10, 1871, p. 2.

• 1872

hesh, het, shet A correspondent, perhaps unaware of Holton's recent proposal, offers gender-neutral *hesh* for masculine or feminine, rounding out the paradigm with *het* for masculine or neuter, and *shet* for either feminine or neuter. The pronouns *hes, hits, het* are suggested for the possessive case, and *hew, hit, hert* for the objective. And there's a whole set of pronouns to be used when the antecedent may be either plural or singular, covering these possible combinations: *they, thesh, thet* (*they* or *he*; *they* or *she, they* or *it*); *theis, theihe, theits* (*their* or *his, their* or *her, their* or *its*); *thim, ther, thit* (*them* or *him, them* or *her, them* or *it*). "A New Part of Speech," *Daily Louisville Commercial*, September 9, 1872, p. 2 (reprinted from the *American Land and Law Adviser* [Pittsburgh]).

• ca. 1874

se, sis, sim Writing in 1884, Captain J. W. Dozier, head of the West Georgia Agricultural and Mechanical College (Hamilton, GA), claims to have coined this new paradigm about ten years earlier. Dozier took *se* from Latin, and did not offer his coinage to the public until the announcement of *thon* and other pronouns in 1884. John W. Dozier, "A New Pronoun," *Atlanta Constitution*, September 20, 1884, p. 4.

• 1875

it Arguing that "some American should invent a new pronoun to relieve writers of the question which is constantly arising," the writer offers *it,* which for inanimates "flows from the pen as naturally as in . . . other sentences the incorrect word 'they' is so frequently used." "The New Pronoun," *New Hampshire Sentinel* (Keene), May 27, 1875, p. 1.

• 1877

um, um's   According to the report about a local church group, The Monday Evening Literary Club, "language is the servant of the mind and is to do its bidding." The group has found that English is "defective" because it has no gender-neutral personal pronoun. In order to avoid the grammatical blunder of singular *they* or the coordinate *he or she*, "years ago it was suggested that 'um' be used for the common gender." "A Defect in the English Language," *Kansas Weekly Herald* (Hiawatha), September 27, 1877, p. 2.

ita   Reprint of a suggestion by "A Reader" in the *West Salem Monitor* (OH), composed of *it* + *a*, "as a common gender termination," with this example: "Let every teacher and editor give *ita* opinion of the proposed innovation." *Summit County Beacon* (Akron, OH), December 5, 1877, p. 3. It may be the same writer who writes another letter recommending *ita* two days later, to another Ohio paper, and asking, "Let the press and the writers agitate the matter." A Reader, "Let's Invent a Language," *Cincinnati Enquirer*, December 7, 1877, p. 4. The *Enquirer* editor replies dismissively, "Very few persons have thoughts too tremendous to express in the English language. Such as have are at liberty to invent a language of their own—or make signs."

• 1878

e, es, em, emself   Reprint of an article that first appeared in the *Moline Dispatch* (IL), referencing an earlier discussion of pronouns in the *Peoria Daily Tribune* (IL): "Nothing is needed but use to make 'E' just as good a pronoun for the third person as 'I' is for the first." "The Missing Word," *Memphis Daily Appeal*, November 10, 1878, p. 2. F. A. Brewster reminds readers that he had proposed *E, Es,* and *Em* forty years early (see above, 1841).

um   Signing themself "Um," a writer answers the call for a new pronoun with *um,* because "it is the pronoun used in speaking; why not write it, and make it a part of our grammar?" (Presumably a reference to *'em,* which derives from earlier English third-person plural *hem,* but is often presumed to be a form of *them).* "Here's Your Pronoun," *Cincinnati Enquirer,* December 11, 1878, p. 4.

• 1879

singular *they; his or her* The Scottish philosopher Alexander Bain, also known as a rhetorician, grammarian, and psychologist, writes one of the few nineteenth-century grammars to approve of singular *they.* Alexander Bain, *A Higher English Grammar* (New York: Holt, 1879), p. 310.

hesh, hiser, himer; e, es, em;* singular *they Alice Heath, identifying herself as "a progressive teacher," thinks *e* is "less harsh" than another gender-neutral pronoun, *hesh,* adding, "We wouldn't conscientiously use *them* as we know it would be incorrect." Alice L. Heath, "The New Pronoun," *Holt County Sentinel* (MO), January 31, 1879, p. 3.

um An unsigned article says, "It is nothing more nor less than the creation, or discovery, of a *new sex,* or a no sex, answering to the new pronoun 'um' that is proposed when you want to say 'he' or 'she' but can't." "Contributors' Club," *The Atlantic Monthly,* March 1879 (vol. 43, no. 257), p. 397.

• 1881

se, sis, sin C. M. Arnold claims in 1884 that he invented this paradigm three years earlier. (Arnold is apparently unaware of Dozier's coinage of the similar *se, sis, sim* in 1874.) C. M. Arnold, "A New Word Needed," *Frank Leslie's Illustrated Newspaper* (New York), December 27, 1884, p. 315.

• 1883

who, whose The writer suggests *who* as a gender-neutral pronoun, for example, "I hope each member of the congregation will give liberally according to whose several ability." The writer notes, "In the eye of the law, of course, 'his' and 'their' include both sexes, irrespective of race, color, or previous condition, but in the colloquies of everyday life a new combination pronoun is required, and the sooner the philologists come to the rescue the better it will be for all concerned." "Something for Grammarians to Consider," *The Republic* (Columbus, IN), May 15, 1883, p. 2.

hisern   A short note declares that "*hisern* is the new personal pronoun of the common gender. A long felt want is supplied and one can tell a story without any of the agonies of 'he or she,' 'his or her.'" "Current Notes," *Boston Daily Journal*, July 14, 1883, p. 2.

• 1884

thon, thons [1858?]   The composer and attorney Charles C. Converse offers this signed contribution, dated July 23, 1884, at Erie, Pennsylvania. Converse says he came up with *thon* after trying and rejecting other coinages. *Funk & Wagnalls Standard Dictionary* dates *thon* to 1858, possibly based on correspondence between Converse and the editor, Isaac K. Funk. Whatever the date, Converse's announcement sparks an extended discussion of the missing word. Charles Crozat Converse, "A New Pronoun," *The Critic*, August 2, 1884, p. 55.

one; singular they   A writer who dislikes *thon* and refers to earlier failed coinages (see above, ca. 1850), recommends the generic *he*, the existing pronoun *one*, or singular *they*, which is not an error, at least in spoken English: "Many persons who are by no means ignorant accept, in conversation at least, the plan of using the plural common gender pronouns, 'they, their, theirs,' etc., indifferently as singular or plural. And in this they are not without authority of good usage." *New York Commercial Advertiser*, August 7, 1884, p. 3.

hi, hes, hem   Francis H. Williams suggests this alternative to *thon*, but the editor points out that *hi* is too easily confused with *he*. Francis H. Williams, "The New Pronoun," *The Critic*, August 16, 1884, pp. 79–80.

that'n, they'uns Rejecting *thon* because it is "impracticable to introduce a new pronoun into a language whose whole literature exists without it," the writer suggests the colloquial *that'n* or the Southern *they'uns,* but prefers the generic masculine: "With all their faults we cannot get along well without the precision of He, She and It." "The New Pronoun," *St. Louis Post-Dispatch,* August 20, 1884, p. 4.

le, lis, lim (from the French)***; unus; talis; it*** Picking up on the *thon* discussion, Edgar Alfred Stevens recognizes the need for a gender-neutral pronoun and suggests that the pronoun *it* may have been created for that purpose, though it has proved unsuccessful. Stevens faults *thon* for its obscure etymology and its lack of case endings, instead deriving a new pronoun from the French *le* and patterning it after the masculine *he, his, him.* He further suggests that word coiners submit their creations and let writers adopt the one they like best. Edgar Alfred Stevens, "The Missing Word," *The Current,* August 30, 1884, p. 137.

hiser, himer (hyser, hymer); one Charles Sherman coins a pronoun "composed of parts of 'his' and 'her.'" As for the pronoun *one,* Sherman questions the grammaticality of a sentence like "Every man or woman is the architect of one's own fortune," adding, "It would hardly run smoothly in usage." Charles P. Sherman, "Wanted—A New Pronoun," *The Literary World,* September 6, 1884, p. 294.

twen, twens, twem; twon Charles Dietz joins the fray with a paradigm based on *twen,* giving this example: "If any man or woman breaks this rule twen shall be fined $5." Dietz adds, "The syllable twon, suggesting two and one, might be used instead of twen." Charles Dietz, "Application in Behalf of a New Pronoun," *New York Sun,* September 8, 1884, p. 2.

hersh, herm The writer reports that some years ago, *New York Tribune* editor Horace Greeley "offered a reward for a new word . . . of common, or no, or both genders," yielding *hersh,* "a compound of his or her," along with *herm,* from *him or her.* Hersh also approves of *thon* and *le* instead of the phrase *his or her:* "Speaking of both sexes disjunctively is destructive of all that is poetic in a sentence." Hersh adds, "Legislatures get over the difficulty by writing the laws in the masculine gender and then, by a sweeping statute, declaring that wherever in the law the masculine pronoun is used it shall be deemed to include the feminine." Hersh finds that such a workaround is inappropriate for nonlegal English. "Wanted, a Word," *Daily Record Union* (Sacramento, CA), September 10, 1884, p. 1. Greeley, a well-known political figure and founding editor of the *New York Tribune,* died in 1872; a search of the *Tribune* database turns up no reference to the call for a pronoun, and no earlier record of *hersh.*

hisern, hisen   An anonymous, blatantly antifeminist article calls the recent inventions of *hisern, hisen, thon,* and *lin* "barbarous" and insists that generic *he* includes both men and women. *Atlanta Constitution,* September 13, 1884, p. 4.

ip, ips   Responding to the earlier call in *The Current* for a new gender-neutral pronoun, Emma Carleton offers *ip* and laments that "no man [has] risen to supply the missing word." Emma Carleton, "The Missing Word," *The Current,* September 20, 1884, p. 186.

um   "Double Z" suggests *um* as preferable to *thon* and *le:* "If John or Jane wants this book, tell um (either one of them) I will return it to-morrow." ZZ adds, "We already use 'em in the objective plural in rapid speaking, and um will be no harsh intrusion on the ear." Double Z, letter, "An Esthetic Language," *Inter-Ocean* (Chicago), September 22, 1884, p. 5.

hae, haes/hais, haim   Clearly pronouns are in the air, for "Suggester" refers to "the new personal pronoun," assuming readers will be familiar with the issue, as hae offers haes new words. Suggester, "The New Pronoun," *Atlanta Constitution,* September 24, 1884, p. 4.

gosh (jocular)   Rejecting coined pronouns, the *New York Sun* observes, "Hundreds of millions or more of English speaking people manage to worry through the ordinary requirements of polite and impolite conversation without using thon or lin. It seems to us inappropriate that the English language, after waiting five centuries for somebody to supply it with a personal pronoun of common gender, should be put off with so awkward a fabric as thon or one so feeble as le, lis or lin. How would gosh do?" *New York Sun*, September 2, 1884, p. 2.

• 1885

tha, thare, them (thon); singular *they* The linguist Fred Newton Scott favors singular *they*, but recommends respelling according to his new paradigm, with *thon* as a possible replacement for *them*. Scott reminds readers that singular *they* is used by millions in speech, and by large numbers of careful and well-educated writers. Fred Newton Scott, "The Missing Pronoun," *The Current*, January 17, 1885, pp. 43–44.

thon; thar The *Atlanta Constitution* disapproves of *thon*, "which has been proposed by those who find it difficult to get along with the English of the Bible and Shakespeare." According to the *Constitution*, *thon* "fills no long-felt want. It is simply the haphazard outgrowth of an attempt to fit the English language to the precise and invariable methods of Latin and Greek grammar." The paper prefers singular *they*: "There is nothing awkward or ungrammatical in this, so far as the construction of English is concerned. It is ungrammatical when measured by the Latin method—but what has Latin grammar to do with the English tongue?" "The New Pronoun," *Atlanta Constitution*, February 25, 1885, p. 4.

The *Chicago Times* accuses the *Constitution* of southern ignorance for supporting singular *they*. In reply, the *Constitution* ridicules the *Times* for condemning *thar*, a Southern pronunciation of *their*, "which has been in the English dialect since Chaucer was a baby." The paper then repeats its attack on school grammar: "There are a number of little boys and girls who are undergoing the agony of trying to learn so-called English grammar [from some] 'professor' who . . . knows less about the English language for all practical purposes than the ten year old boy who has had access to such books as Robinson Crusoe, Gulliver's Travels, and the Pilgrims Progress." "A Chicago Grammarian," *Atlanta Constitution,* March 21, 1885, p. 4. The *Constitution* is silent on how ten-year-old girls learn about pronouns.

thon "Peck's Sun" finds *thon* unnecessary. Its adoption will drastically increase the cost of already overpriced schoolbooks. Peck's Sun goes on, "If the inventor of 'thon' wants to place a pronoun where it will do the most good, let him introduce it in France, where they have no neuter gender, everything being either 'he' or 'she.' " The writer's final recommendation? "Shoot the thon." Peck's Sun, "Tinkering the English Language," *Springfield Globe-Republic* (OH), March 25, 1885, p. 2.

zyhe, zyhe's, zyhem The writer summarizes previous coinages and offers *zyhe,* consisting of Anglo-Saxon *he* combined with *zy,* "the Danish for *she.* . . . Pronounce zah-e, zah-e's (*s* having the sound z), zah-e-m." George Washington Eveleth, "The Lacking Word," *The Current,* March 28, 1885, p. 199. Eveleth was wrong: the Danish feminine pronoun is *hun.*

• 1886

one The writer says that using two pronouns, *he or she,* to represent one noun, is "cumbrous and in a degree destructive of the convenience to serve which pronouns have been invented," and that singular *they* is an error highlighting the absence of a pronoun. They would like to extend the use of *one* to fill the gap. "Wanted, a Pronoun," *Blackwood's Magazine,* reprinted in the *Sheffield and Rotherham Independent* (Sheffield, England), March 6, 1886, p. 4.

hom; ho, hus, hum (jocular?)   A report on the state teacher's institute held at Florence, Alabama, observes that a Prof. Davis, of Court-
land, proposed *hom* as the common-gender noun, "and 'Ho,' nom.,
'Hus,' poss., and 'Hum,' obj, should be the pronoun." Given that this
paradigm yields *ho-hum*, it is possible that the suggestion was not
entirely serious. *Montgomery Advertiser* (AL), June 11, 1886, p. 2.

his-her, him-her   Cites a reference by a correspondent in the
New York Evening Post to a coinage by "a Maryland lady sojourning in New Haven" of a "hermaphroditic pronoun to represent both
sexes . . . a word which has the advantage of being free from fantastic
form or unfamiliar sound." According to the proposer, once the form
becomes familiar, the hyphen can be dropped. "A New Pronoun Suggested," *Baltimore Sun*, December 13, 1886, p. 6.

• 1887

id, ids   *The Gate City Journal* "recommends 'id' with a possessive
'ids.' Such a pronoun is certainly a much needed addition to our language. . . . Start the word out and we will all be glad enough to adopt
it." *The New Era* (Humeston, IA), February 24, 1887, p. 3.

• 1888

ir, iro, im (sing.); tha, thar, them (pl.)   Language reformer Elias
Molee creates an "Amerikan Grammar" by restoring the Germanic
roots of English; as part of his nativist project, Molee adds gender-
neutral singular pronouns. Elias Molee, *Plea for an American Language* (Chicago: John Anderson, 1888), pp. 200–201.

te, tes, tim   A correspondent offers this paradigm instead
of J. W. Dozier's *se* (see ca. 1874, above). "Current Notes," *Boston
Morning Journal*, March 20, 1888, p. 2.

ze, zis, zim   J. W. Leeds reports that Joshua Hoopes, a botanist and
Latin scholar from West Chester, PA, had coined this paradigm a few
years earlier, likening it to the *se, sis, sim* paradigm coined by Dozier. Leeds argues that since English is becoming global, and other

languages already have gender-neutral pronouns, "there is no reason why we should not possess the same convenience." Josiah W. Leeds, "The Unsupplied Common Gender Pronoun," *Philadelphia Ledger*, rpt. in the *Macon Telegraph* (GA), March 30, 1888, p. 4.

de, der, dem An anonymous writer in the *Richmond Dispatch* suggests this paradigm from African American English. The proposal is racist and stereotypical, expressing an attitude that is unfortunately all too common in nineteenth-century periodicals. *Atlanta Constitution*, April 7, 1888, p. 6.

e, es, em A writer proposes, "In advance of the Volapük reformation of all languages, let us devise a pronoun of common gender 'e,' 'es,' 'em'.... [It] would be a positive addition both to the force and grace of English, if we were used to it. We never will be, apparently, however." Volapük, developed in 1879, is an artificial international language like Esperanto. *Indianapolis News*, July 10, 1888, p. 2.

generic *he* The writer apologizes for having to refer to women stenographers with the masculine pronoun: "It is the misfortune of the English language that it has no pronoun capable of expressing in the singular number a substantive of either the masculine or feminine gender.... Let it not be supposed, however, that we are unmindful of the very large element of women in the shorthand profession." "Women Stenographers," *New York Evening World*, July 7, 1888, p. 2.

generic *she* Another writer complains of just the opposite, the fact that, "in the education journals of the day, how often the teacher is spoken of as 'she.'" He asks whether this is meant to diminish male teachers, "or does it arise from the fact that a large majority of the teachers in the North and West are ladies?" The writer suggests that generic *she* "violates the well-known principle in English grammar that the masculine, being the stronger, etc., may be used when reference is made to one of a class including both males and females." In an age of "woman's rights, woman suffrages, etc.," the writer urges men to "assert our rights while yet there is hope." *The Standard* (Concord, NC), October 12, 1888, p. 3.

en, ens   The temperance reformer Frances E. Willard suggests this pair, and the *Wilkes-Barre Record* finds that *en* is a better solution than *thon* because it is briefer and easier to pronounce. The paper concludes, "If we who read this adopt it and make its use known it is probable that its use would soon become general." But *en* did not become general. "Pronoun Suggested for Adoption," *Wilkes-Barre Record,* July 7, 1888, p. 3.

• 1889

ons (from one)   In proposing *ons*, C.R.B. asks, "What has become of that impersonal pronoun which was to be evolved before now for the economy of writers' brain-power?" The reply by the editor, William H. Hills, proved correct: "People will readily agree that such a word would be a useful addition to the language, but they will not agree upon a word, and without common consent no word can ever come into general use." C.R.B., *Writer* 3 (1889): 231.

• 1890

ith, iths   Coined in 1890 by the writer George Winslow Pierce. *The Life-Romance of an Algebraist* (Boston: J. G. Cupples, 1891), p. 35.

e (from he), es, em (from them)   James Rogers, of Crestview, Florida, objects to *thon* because "every one has to be told how to pronounce it" and "it is more than twice as long as *e*." To be exact, so far as spelling is concerned, *thon* is four times longer than *e*, though both forms take about the same time to pronounce. James Rogers, "That Impersonal Pronoun," *Writer* 4 (1890): 12–13.

ta, tas, tan   Ebenezer Lakin Brown, of Schoolcraft, Michigan, former regent of the University of Michigan and father of a Michigan senator, finds that *thon* is "heavy and seems scarcely capable of the inflections." Brown would prefer to revive *ta*, as used by Shakespeare (*ta* is still a colloquial second-person pronoun in British English).

The retired Brown, with time on his hands, set his recommendation in verse. The final quatrain of the poem illustrates the paradigm:

> Ta will deserve a meed of fame,
> Honors will cluster 'round tas name.
> And all shall long remember tan,
> Be it woman, or be it man.
>
> —EBENEZER L. BROWN, "To Restore an Ancient
> Pronoun," *New York Tribune,* December 8, 1890,
> p. 10.

hi, hes, hem The writer recommends the paradigm for its brevity; its resemblance to the masculine and feminine pronouns; and its preservation of the endings—though these are the endings of the masculine, not the feminine. As for acceptance, "Of course the eye and ear experience a shock at first, but this will be the same for any word which can be coined." "The Needed Common Pronoun," *Weekly Irish Times,* July 26, 1890, p. 3. Rpt. in *The Rocky Mountain News* (Denver), August 3, 1890, p. 19; also, *Pearson's Weekly* (UK), April 15, 1893, p. 15.

hor, hors, horself; zie A writer signing "X," from Pittsfield, Massachusetts, noting that the Colorado school code contains many coordinate *his or her* phrases, submits a proposal for *hor,* pronounced "like the first syllable of the word horror." The editor adds *zie* to round out the paradigm: *zie, hor, hors.* "To Indicate the Common Gender," *Chicago Daily Tribune,* September 27, 1890, p. 7. Replying belatedly to this suggestion, another writer objects to *zie* but recognizes the need for a new word: "If the college professor of philology and grammar would recommend a new common pronoun it would start out with some show of authority, and might then stand a chance of growth into the pronoun family." *Chicago Daily Tribune,* December 14, 1890, p. 12.

•1891

hizer; singular they Forrest Morgan argues that singular *they* is grammatically correct because good writers use it, like the perfectly acceptable *your* for *thine*. Morgan finds singular *they* better than "such atrocious inventions as 'thon' or 'hizer.'" It's not clear that *thine* was used seriously in 1891. Forrest Morgan, "An Indeterminate Pronoun," *Writer* 5 (1891): 260–62.

zie The *zie* debate continues (see above, December 1890), as a *Chicago Tribune* editorial complains that schools are teaching children to capitalize every word: "The great majority of these writers need to be told when *not* to capitalize, and it would seem superfluous to increase the amount of this unlearning to be done by the pupil if 'Zie' would write correctly." Presumably the pronoun *Zie* mocks German pronouns and capitalization practices, as the teaching of German in the schools was a controversial issue in Illinois at the time. *Chicago Daily Tribune,* January 15, 1891, p. 4.

zie; ha, har And speaking of German, "An Old Educator" responds to the *Tribune,* taking the pronoun seriously: "I do not like your invention of 'Zie' for the common gender. It is the same in sound and almost the same in form as the German word for *they*. It omits the one letter which is found in all our pronouns of this class—viz.: the letter h." The Old Educator prefers *ha* and *har,* saying, "Thus we should present the uniformity of this class of words and avoid perplexing the student by a very wide departure in both sound and form." Since this would produce the paradigm *ha, har, har,* the suggestion is likely to be facetious. An Old Educator, "Agrees with 'The Tribune' in the Main," *Chicago Daily Tribune,* January 23, 1891, p. 5.

heh, hes, hem Proposal in the *New York World* for "the three pronouns much needed." Rpt. *Spokane Review,* June 18, 1891, p. 11.

•1892

tu, tum, tus Indirect pronouns invented by Robert Louis Stevenson. Not gender neutral, but intended for use to avoid confusion when more than one person is being referenced. Stevenson's example of two men fighting: "*He* seized *tum* by *tus* throat, but *tu* at the same moment caught *him* by *his* hair." Robert Louis Stevenson, *Letters of Robert Louis Stevenson*, ed. Sidney Colvin (New York: Charles Scribner's Sons, 1911), vol. 4, p. 39.

• 1893

e, es, en   The Rev. James Rogers, a spelling reformer, writes in the *Phonographic Magazine* (a magazine about phonetic spelling, not about musical recordings) that a common-gender pronoun "would be such a relief that few would care whether it were scientific or not." Rogers proposes *e, es,* and *en* as short, easy to pronounce, and derived from the masculine and feminine forms. James Rogers, "The Much Needed Pronoun," *Garden City Tribune* (KS), February 9, 1893, p. 3.

• 1894

shee; hesher, hiser, himer   The presence of women in the Colorado legislature prompts one letter writer from Fort Logan to offer *hesher, hiser,* and *himer*. And another, Charles G. Warden, suggests *shee*. "A Bi-Personal Pronoun," *Rocky Mountain News,* December 17, 1894, p. 4.

• 1895

sit, sis, sim   The *Philadelphia Times* writes that neither generic *he* nor generic *she* covers a context where both genders are included. The *Times* finds *he or she* acceptable, but a single word would be better. Singular *they* is always wrong, even though it remedies a defect in the language. The editor remembers seeing a proposal for *sit, sis,* and *sim*. But until a new pronoun can be chosen, they recommend *he or she* instead of the "verbal abomination," singular *they*. "What the Editor Has to Say to Our Boys and Girls," *Philadelphia Times,* June 16, 1895, p. 24.

hoo   Brief discussion of this Lancashire dialect pronoun. Although usually thought to be feminine, the writer asserts that *hoo* is "a pronoun of indifferent personality," used for both masculine and feminine, but not neuter. *Weekly Standard and Express* (Blackburn, England), August 10, 1895, p. 8.

en, ens, enself, generic *woman*   A radical feminist essay by the social reformer Moses Harman proclaims the lack of a gender-neutral pronoun as one of the "discriminations as to words" to which "women writers, teachers, lecturers acquiesce." Generic masculines make women "a lower class, a primary or a minor class, and therefore, rightfully, a subject class." Harman advises women that "they have rights who dare to take them," and calls on them to be aware of the defects of vocabulary that are "the causes that enslave themselves and their sisters." He considers designating *woman* as the generic term for human beings instead of *man,* but in the end he recommends *homo.* Harman also calls for the adoption of *en, ens,* and *enself* as gender-neutral pronouns. Moses Harman, "Our Editor's Bi-weekly Letter," *Lucifer The Light-Bearer* (Topeka, Kansas), November 15, 1895, p. 2.

• 1896

hin; ta, tas, tan   The writer objects to the new constitution of the Young People's League of Trinity Episcopal Church, in Albany, NY, which "recently printed an edition of its constitution with 'hin' used for a personal pronoun of common gender. . . . There is no call for any such word, there is no philological warrant for the word proposed. A genius in Michigan some time ago proposed the word 'ta,' declined 'ta, tas, tan,' for the same purpose. . . . The English language is ample enough in its present form for all uses and the Young People's league of Trinity church would do well to suppress the last edition of its constitution." "Neither Good for the Constitution Nor the Bylaws," *Brooklyn Daily Eagle,* March 9, 1896, p. 6. (For *ta,* see above, 1890.)

E, ez, en   Journalist J. L. Merriman rejects compound *he or she* as "lame," and generic *he* as "not at all true," offering *E* because all of the other vowels also double as words: *a,* an article, *O,* an interjection, *I,* often called "the vertical pronoun," and *U,* for *you.* Merriman argues that *E* would make a good gender-neutral pronoun, but he undercuts his own suggestion by treating all the vowels as masculine: "E is just as good as any of them, and much more frequently used, but I don't think it is quite fair to continually associate *him* with vulgar consonants while his kinsmen each have a space to himself." Note that Merriman treats *each* and *himself* as singulars, but deploys the plural verb, *have.* J. L. Merriman, "Round About Town," *Dallas Morning News,* April 19, 1896, p. 3.

• 1899

un, un's Responding to a complaint about singular *they,* a writer signing unself Kokni (as in Cockney) offers *un,* "pronounced like unaccented *an,*" a pronoun found in the Dorset dialect that could be brought into general use by "upstart authorities." Kokni, "Who Is the Authority on Grammar?" *Pall Mall Gazette,* February 21, 1899, p. 3.

• 1900

heesh, hizzer, himmer* (ca. 1865); singular *they The writer says that *heesh, hizzer,* and *himmer* were coined thirty or forty years earlier, possibly a reference to the earlier *hiser* mentioned above. They also discuss singular *they,* still regarded as ungrammatical but common in speech and even found in careful writing, "though generally by oversight." They complain that grammarians have not been able to halt singular *they,* and "usage may ultimately force a recognition of the plural pronouns as singular pronouns also when the common gender is used." The writer concludes, "At all events, an epicene pronoun will have to be developed in some way; one made to order is not likely to be accepted. That is not the law of language, except, possibly, in the case of the names of new inventions, such as the telegraph, telephone, and the like." "An Epicene Pronoun," *Louisville Courier Journal,* May 10, 1900, p. 4. A transatlantic recommendation for *heesh* appears the next month in *The Warder and Dublin Weekly Mail*, June 2, 1900, p. 4.

• 1901

mun; heesh, himmer, hizzer   A correspondent identified as "a Lancashire Lad" suggests filling the pronoun gap in English with the dialect word *mun*, from Devon. *Western Times* (Exeter), October 12, 1901, p. 2. Picking up on this theme, a woman identified only by the initials L. M. writes to the *London Daily Chronicle* to insist that the lack of a "bisexual pronoun . . . is one of the great evils of our time." "Wanted—a Bi-sexual Pronoun," *London Daily Chronicle*, rpt. *St. James Chronicle*, October 25, 1901, p. 6. The *Chronicle* replies by noting that "some time ago" it pointed out this gap, and that a correspondent suggested *heesh, himmer,* and *hizzer*. Rpt. *Sunderland Daily Echo*, October 10, 1901, p. 2.

• 1903

hesh, hish, hush, hoosh, hash (jocular)   Report on the *New York Sun*'s thirty-year battle to endorse a gender-neutral pronoun "in the battle for justice to women" (see *hizer*, 1871). The writer rejects alternating generic *he* and generic *she*, and finds *thon* unworkable: "it made the proofreader 'atrabilious,'" resulting in the following damage in the editorial department: "7 chairs, 11 transom windows, 17 yards of plaster, three dozen electric light bulbs and the serious abridgment of the covers and pages of the dictionaries . . . 13 Mergenthalers disabled . . . three proofreaders Sing-Singed," and so on (the Mergenthaler was a Linotype machine; Sing Sing is a notorious New York State prison). The writer claims that *The Sun* coined *hesh, hish, hush, hesh,* and *hoosh,* with the plural *hash,* but to no avail. *St. Paul Globe,* January 28, 1903, p. 4.

hem, hirm   A writer objects to the use of singular *they* and the pair *he or she* in a new statute, and offers these blends as improvements. "In My Armchair," *The Wa-Keeney Tregonian* (KS), May 15, 1903, p. 2.

• 1908

thon, e, es   *The St. Paul Pioneer Press* reports the revival of *thon*, a much-needed "pronoun of dual gender," by the *Brooklyn Eagle*. The writer notes that new words are entering the language in areas as diverse as electrical science, golf, and "tiddledewinks," and quotes the *Rochester Democrat-Chronicle* on how to get a new pronoun adopted: "If a few high class newspapers, philologists and educators were to start such a movement . . . there would be a rapid falling into line and . . . the dictionaries would soon be compelled to recognize the new word." But the writer prefers the pronouns *e, es* instead: "No lack of euphony there, no harsh consonant sound as in 'thon.'" "'Thon' or 'E' or Either," *Kansas City Times*, December 8, 1908, p. 6.

• 1909

e, es, em   With no reference to the discussion of *e* the year before, H. C. W., of Baltimore, suggests the paradigm based on *e* invented "many years ago," the logical extension of the pronoun *I*, the interjection *O*, and the pronoun and substantive *you* and *ewe*. H. C. W., letter, *New York Sun*, June 25, 1909, p. 8.

• 1910

hier (or heir), hierself   E. P. Jots, of New Decatur, Alabama, responds to an earlier *Sun* editorial on *thon* with the suggestion that *hier* is preferable, since it combines *his* and *her*. E. P. Jots, "Let Each One Choose for H-i-e-r-self," *Baltimore Sun*, February 12, 1910, p. 5.

um   Walter Scott Priest, a pastor, proposed *um, um's*, deployed when a parishioner gave a generous donation to the church fund but did not want um's gender to be revealed in the announcement. The congregation laughed at the announcement, but Priest persisted, offering plural forms *ums, ums'*. "'Um' New Personal Pronoun to Denote Either of Genders," *Wichita Daily Eagle*, March 20, 1910, p. 11.

• 1911

he-er, his-er, him-er; hisers, himerself (**also written as,** *heer, hiser,* *himer*)   Fred Pond, of Chicago, offers these pronouns in a letter to an Ohio newspaper. Some months later, Chicago Superintendent of Schools Ella Flagg Young would take credit for them (see below, 1912). Pond argues that *he or she* is too awkward, and so he proposes his blend of masculine and feminine. The disjunctive is *hisers,* the reflexive, *himerself.* Pond acknowledges that the forms "sound strange and perchance ludicrous," but he feels that people would get used to them, as they have gotten used to other new words. They "would enable the speaker—whoever heer may be—to be correct and intelligible." Fred S. Pond, "The Personal Pronoun," *Mansfield News-Journal* (OH), March 21, 1911, p. 4.

E, es, em   E. Fennell suggests that, "just as we have a capital 'I' for the first person," *E* would work for the third-person common-gender pronoun. "Wanted—A Pronoun," *Irish Independent,* September 13, 1911, p. 8.

• 1912

he'er, him'er, his'er, his'er's   Ella Flagg Young, Superintendent of the Chicago Public Schools and the first woman president of the National Education Association, says she had long felt the need for such a word and that she had just invented the paradigm on the way to a meeting with school principals (but see above for Pond's invention of the words the previous year). "Mrs. Ella Young Invents Pronoun," *Chicago Tribune,* January 7, 1912, sec. 1, p. 7.

she'er, her'er   Responding to *heer, himer,* and *hiser,* St. Louis Superintendent of Schools Ben Blewett tells local reporters that he prefers the generic masculine to Young's new pronouns. "Blewett Not in Favor of He'er, His'er or Him'er," *St. Louis Post-Dispatch,* January 8, 1912, p. 14.

heris, herim　An editorial comment on Young's pronoun says, perhaps dismissively, "In this age of feminism, if we must have such a word wouldn't it be better to change the order and make it 'heris' [her-his] and 'herim' [her-him]? Besides, it would be more euphonious." *New York Tribune,* January 8, 1912, p. 6.

It-er　A hometown-paper report on the pronouns invented by Buffalo native Ella Flagg Young "to fill the long felt want of our language for the third person singular common gender pronoun.—that's all," adding, without comment, "How do you like 'It-er?'" *Buffalo Enquirer,* February 2, 1912, p. 4.

Mss.　The writer rejects coined pronouns like Young's *hiser:* "The need for such a pronoun is not very great; it is felt mainly in regard to a few things which, like teaching, for instance, are nearly but not quite a monopoly of women." However, the author does see a need for a marriage-neutral title, combining *Miss* and *Mrs.* to produce *Mss.,* which he finds particularly useful, and ambiguous, in reference to authors. "Those New Pronouns," *Minneapolis Tribune,* March 20, 1912, p. 4.

hisen, hern　Critical of Ella Flagg Young's attempt "to revive the proposed system brought out and laughed down a number of years ago," this writer sneers, "There were those that went farther and recommended 'hisen' and 'hern.'" "Stands by the Laughed At Method," *Salem Statesman Journal* (OR), May 26, 1912, p. 15.

e　This short notice appears without comment: "At a meeting of the Delaware County Teachers' Association...the president, Prof. W. C. Joslin, principal of the Media High school, proposed 'e' as a third person, singular number, common gender pronoun." "Suggests 'E' as Pronoun," *Wilkes-Barre Times Leader,* February 20, 1912, p. 13. Later reports quote Joslin as repeating the 'every vowel a pronoun' mantra: "If 'a' and 'I' and 'o' are words, then there can be no objection to 'e.'" Example: "If any person in the room wishes a copy of this let e raise e's hand." *Philadelphia Press,* reprinted as "E Is Now Suggested as the Needed New Pronoun," *The Buffalo Morning Express and Illustrated Buffalo Express,* April 6, 1912, p. 10.

heor, hisor, himor A. E. Schuyler, of Edison Park (IL), proposes this paradigm, whose forms will not "conflict, in sound if not in spelling, with other words already in use." They may be hyphenated *he-or, his-or, him-or.* "Another Common Gender Pronoun Offered," *Meade County News* (KS), April 11, 1912, p. 3.

• 1914

hie, hiez, hie (phonetic spellings of he, hes, he); ov hie Language reformer Mont Follick, D. Phil. (Sorbonne), British spelling reformer, and member of Parliament, prefers to reduce all third-person singular pronouns to this simplified version of the masculine paradigm. Follick further suggests discarding the possessive altogether in favor of the prepositional phrase, *ov hie,* "of he." Mont Follick, *The Influence of English* (London: Williams & Norgate, 1934), pp. 198–99.

• 1917

hes During World War I, a writer signing herself Josephine finds the phrase *his or her* wasteful. In looking for a "sexless pronoun" as a necessary piece of the "war-economy," she asks, "How would 'hes' do? It looks a little funny, but new words generally do. They have to pay their footing before they can be accepted by the other words. And it's most expensive to get into the dictionary." "Woman's World of Today," *Gloucester Journal* (UK), October 6, 1917, p. 5.

• 1919

hesh, shis, shim Thomas W. Gilmer rejects the generic masculine and claims that "in view of the nineteenth amendment . . . she is more likely to include him." He offers *hesh, shis,* and *shim,* assuring readers that the words "would sound natural after a little usage." Thomas W.

Gilmer, "New Pronouns Needed," *Sunday Star* (Washington, DC), November 23, 1919, p. 3.

The next day, Francis de Sales Ryan quotes James C. Fernald, editor of *Funk & Wagnalls New Standard Dictionary*, who insists that "the masculine has always stood as the representative gender and still stands 'even in this period of militant feminism.'" Francis de Sales Ryan, "A Genderless Pronoun," *Evening Star*, November 24, 1919, p. 2. James C. Fernald, *Expressive English* (New York: Funk & Wagnalls, 1919), pp. 255–57. *Funk & Wagnalls Standard Dictionary* had added *heer, himer,* and *hiser* in 1913.

• 1920

vey The American social activist Warren Edwin Brokaw prints this notice on the first page of each edition of his journal, *The Equitist*: "'Vey' is a common pronoun, meaning EITHER 'he' OR 'she'— necessary for accurate, precise and grammatical expression." *The Equitist*, January 2, 1920 (no. 96), p. 1. Brokaw, who uses *vey* and *veys* regularly in the text, is credited with inventing the pronoun (see below, 1929). He implies that generic *he* is not generic, and that singular *they* is not "grammatical." The "combination pronoun" *vey* was picked up by the *Canadian Railroad Employees Magazine,* which explained that the pronoun "avoids the assumption of the inferiority of the feminine sex." "The Influence of Feminism on Grammar," *The Leader-Post* (Regina, Saskatchewan), July 10, 1924, p. 4.

it Hilda Finnemore, a writer of children's books and local guide-books, proposes making *it* the pronoun of the common gender, not the neuter gender, and applying it to humans in place of the less commodious *he or she*: "No doubt the effect at first would be slightly ludicrous, like children in their first spectacles. . . . but there are few things that time and custom cannot stale." And if not *it,* then "surely great big men who can invent such fine words as 'radioactinium' and 'spectroheliograph' should be able to devise a little useful pronoun like that!" "Wanted: A Word," *Daily Gazette* (Birmingham, UK), July 30, 1920, p. 4.

hir   In August 1920, the *Sacramento Bee* offers *hir*, explaining, "All writers and most readers, in fact, have felt the need for some single pronoun which would take the place of the words 'he or she'.... In these days of a super-abundance of verbiage, such short-cuts to brevity and clearness as can logically be taken, should be. Therefore, 'hir.'" " 'Hir' Will Be the Bee's Word for 'He or She," *Sacramento Bee*, August 14, 1920, p. 28. The *Bee* continued to use *hir* intermittently up to the 1940s.

Remembering the failure of *thon*, the *Klamath Falls Evening Herald* rejects the *Bee*'s coinage: "Enthusiastic word reformers who believed in Converse and his 'thon' died of senile debility while watching and waiting for somebody with the courage to use it.... The generic use of the masculine covers every possible case with sufficient accuracy." The *Herald* quotes the *Stockton Record* as well: "[Hir] looks as if the one using it doesn't know how to spell." "A New Word," *Klamath Falls Evening Herald* (OR), September 2, 1920, p. 4. The *Oakland Tribune* is a little more optimistic about the *Bee*'s venture, though it worries that *hir* "will attract the startled attention from the unwary visitor to Sacramento." "Now as a Reformer!" *Oakland Tribune*, August 20, 1920, p. 16.

• 1921

su   The writer derives *su* from Spanish, observing that since the passage of the Nineteenth Amendment, "some women ... are insisting that the grammatical or historically approved use of man, he, his or him to refer to both man and woman, be subjected to the amendment—and this they consider fundamental, constitutional and foundational.... The modern woman feels that man is 'putting something over' by use of the words he, him, his, although they are of common gender when used with reference to a class and used as a collective noun." "A Common Pronoun," *Gulfport Daily Herald* (MS), February 11, 1921, p. 2.

• **1922**

hesh, himer, hiser Mississippi state senator W. A. Ellis proposes S. B. 423, "An Act creating, pronouncing, defining and legalizing three new English words, arising out of the exigencies of the times on account of woman's new political freedom." The Ellis pronoun bill failed by a vote of 14–15. *Journal of the Senate of the State of Mississippi*, 1922, pp. 889, 1175. The text of the Ellis bill appears not in the journal, but in a Jackson newspaper: "Senator Proposes New Word Factory," *Clarion-Ledger* (Jackson, MS), March 15, 1922, p. 8.

thon, thone The writer refers to the failed attempt by Senator W. A. Ellis to have the state legislature adopt a gender-neutral pronoun, and wrongly attributes *thon* to an Ohio school superintendent named White, ca. 1894–95, adding the form *thone,* a contraction of *that one.* Thon also notes its usefulness in the context of votes for women: "When the word was first proposed, we saw no real need of another personal pronoun as the language was fairly well expressive without its use. Now, however, since woman's sphere is so widened that she takes part in matters which were then considered wholly within the province of the sterner sex, such a word is needed and should come into use to lessen the burden on the language." "A New Pronoun," *Okolona Messenger* (MS), April 6, 1922, p. 1.

he-she, his-her, him-her The Reverend G. A. Kratzer comments on the lack of a neutral pronoun for God: "No really spiritual religionist would speak of God by any pronoun implying sex, if the English language had a pronoun of common gender.... The writer avoids the difficulty in his own writings by always using the compound pronouns 'He-She,' 'His-Her,' and 'Him-Her' in referring to God." "Important Truth," *Llano Colonist* (Leesville, LA), August 26, 1922, p. 6.

idn Independently of W. A. Ellis in Mississippi, Kansas City judge A. N. Gossett, a delegate to the Missouri Constitutional Convention in 1922–23, proposes an amendment to the state's constitution recognizing the common-gender *idn*, a word useful for drafting bills. The amendment did not pass. The text of his proposal appears in the *Journal and Debates 1st–266th Day* (Jefferson City, MO: Hugh Stephens Press, 1922–23, v. 4, November 1, 1922), pp. 3–5.

le, lis, lim O. C. Ludwig recommends this paradigm, explaining, "The 'L' in connection with vowels has long been used in various languages to indicate gender." O. C. Ludwig, *Arizona Republic,* December 25, 1922, p. 4.

• 1924

hos The *Lincoln Journal Star* (some editions published as *Nebraska State Journal*) alludes to a discussion of the need for a new pronoun in the *Portland Express,* but warns that pundits don't decree or prescribe words. The *Journal Star* offers this analysis from its correspondent "Phil Ology": a new pronoun "cannot be forced. It must come spontaneously. Perhaps some maker of slang will pick up a word that will mean both he and she. That is the most feasible way to secure its general adoption." "A Common Gender Pronoun," *Lincoln Journal Star* (NE), June 25, 1924, p. 12.

hizzer Two years later, the *Nebraska State Journal* recommends *hizzer* because "the women vote now." "A Grammatical Dilemma," *Nebraska State Journal* (Lincoln, NE), November 2, 1926, p. 4.

• 1927

ha, hez, hem A writer responding to the *Forum*'s call for new words to be included in a hypothetical dictionary of future American English, to be published a decade hence, calls for a "bisexual pronoun" and recommends this paradigm. *The Forum* 77 (1927): 265–68. Later, the paradigm is attributed to Lincoln King, of

Primghar, Iowa. H. L. Mencken, *The American Language,* 4th ed. (New York: Alfred A. Knopf, 1936), 460n.

hesh (heesh), hizzer, himmer; on   Linguist and educator Fred Newton Scott responds to King's suggestion of *ha, hez, hem* by mentioning the earlier creation of *on. The Forum* 77 (1927): 754. Mencken adds, "In 1934 James F. Morton, of the Paterson (NJ) Museum, proposed to change *hesh* to *heesh* and to restore *hiser* and *himer.*" H. L. Mencken, *The American Language,* supplement 2 (New York: Alfred A. Knopf, 1948), p. 370.

•1929

shim; hes, shes   Charles W. Bush writes that English needs a neutral pronoun and mentions that these forms have been suggested. *Wilmington News Journal* (DE), March 16, 1929, p. 7.

pronoun wanted   In the United Kingdom, the prominent suffragist Lady Annette E. Matthews writes to *The Times* to argue that a "bi-sex pronoun . . . would remove from the newly enfranchised woman elector the absurd position of being left to the imagination, or appearing as an afterthought in parenthesis." Annette Matthews, "His or Her," *The Times* (London, UK), April 25, 1929, p. 17. Matthews's letter sparks a flurry of follow-up letters to *The Times*—most from men—recommending common-gender coinages, although one woman defends singular *they* and another notes the occurrence of generic *she* and *un* in Devon. These are the responses to Lady Matthews:

    vey   F. W. Garrison reminds *Times* readers of F. E. Brokaw's use of *vey* (see above, 1920). "His or Her," April 27, p. 8.

    singular *they*   Agnes Carter argues not for an invented pronoun, but for singular *they,* analogous to singular *you.* (April 29, p. 10.)

    su; tu, tum, tus   Ulric Gantillon champions *su,* which fits "the monosyllabic genius of English," but he is resigned that "we shall continue to say 'they' just as 'you' is also singular." And the Rev. H. J. recalls Robert Louis Stevenson's fanciful coinage of *tu, tum, tus* as the "indirect" pronouns of an invented language. (April 30, p. 12.)

oo A. F. Walker recommends a form "commonly used by agricultural and industrial workers in the North," though he is skeptical that *oo* would thrive in the South. (May 1, p. 12.)

heshe, himmer, hisser, hissers W. Snow reminds readers that hisser late brother, Thomas C. Snow, an Oxford classicist, coined and used these "necessary words." (May 1, p. 12.)

generic *he, she, it* Col. A. de B. V. Paget notes that Dorset workers use the third-person singular pronouns interchangeably. (May 2, p. 12.)

generic *her, un; hes* A Mrs. Mathews, of Devon, also reports on alternatives current in dialect speech: "In the West Country we shall probably continue to say 'her' instead of 'he,' and 'un' indiscriminately. Mr. A. J. Jacobs writes to support *hes*, "which is obtained either by a transposition of the vowels or of the final consonants." (May 4, p. 8.)

hes; mun, muns Major-General Sir Reginald Pinney offers indeclinable *hes* for the third-person pronouns of either or both sexes, both singular and plural; and Mr. R. L. Wason picks the Somerset dialect forms *mun, muns,* used locally not just for the third-person singular, but sometimes for all persons and numbers. (May 6, p. 12.)

lu, lua Gilbert H. Richardson reminds *Times* readers that the constructed international language Ido has these forms for *he or she* and *his or her.* (May 7, p. 12.)

hesh, hier, hiers; her Richard Temple, who writes, "New words are adopted, not for reasons pleasing to purists, but solely if the public likes them," seconds the earlier suggestion of *hesh* and *hier,* adding *hiers.* Temple also notes that a generic, indeclinable *her* was universal in the South Worcestershire dialect. (May 8, p. 12.)

heoshe, himoher, hisoher   In the last of this series in *The Times,* Reginald Sayers would blend masculine and feminine. (May 13, p. 12.)

Referring to Matthews's letter, a Yorkshire writer seeks a new "bisexual" pronoun to placate "what is known as the woman's movement" to avoid the "ignominy of a mere it." The need for such a word exists "apart altogether from questions of sex equality," though such a word must arise spontaneously. "Wanted, a New Pronoun," *Yorkshire Evening Post,* April 25, 1929, p. 6.

ot   Homer Brett, of Nottingham (UK), proposes *ot,* which he coined along with other needed words while returning on a twenty-day ship voyage from Italy. "Mr. Homer Brett's Happy Inspiration," *Nottingham Journal,* June 3, 1929, p. 4.

• ca. 1930

thir   Proposed by Sir John Adams; cited by Philip Howard, *New Words for Old* (New York: Oxford University Press, 1977), p. 95.

se, sem, serself, semself   Coined in the early 1930s by Alfred Speltz when he taught English and music at Winona High School, in Minnesota. "The proposal drew favor from language experts, including the chairman of the English Department at the University of Minnesota, but efforts to enlist such national publications as Readers Digest and the Saturday Evening Post in the crusade proved futile." "Determinedly Tilting without Success," *Winona Daily News* (MN), April 6, 1975, p. 14.

• 1930

female he   The linguist and philosopher C. K. Ogden creates Basic, a simplified international English with a vocabulary of 850 words which can be combined to represent complex ideas. Although Basic has the nouns *man* and *woman,* the only third-person pronoun is *he.*

The feminine is constructed by pairing *he* with *female,* a word listed under the category "opposite." C. K. Ogden, *Basic English, A General Introduction with Rules and Grammar* (London: Paul Treber, 1930). In subsequent versions of Basic English, Ogden added *she*.

che, chis, chim   W. E. Fohl, of Pittsburgh, offers his coinage, first printed in a local newspaper and subsequently receiving national coverage in *Time* magazine. Like many inconsistent pronoun reformers, Fohl employs generic *his* alongside *che* and *chim* in his example: "Should a married pedagog's tribe increase while che is serving the college, an increase in tuition may necessarily be made, in order to cover and give chim a raise in his salary." W. E. Fohl, *Time,* March 10, 1930, p. 6.

heesh   A. A. Milne writes in the preface to the *Christopher Robin Birthday Book*, "If the English Language had been properly organized . . . then there would be a word which meant both 'he' and 'she', and I could write, 'If John or Mary comes, heesh will want to play tennis', which would save a lot of trouble." A. A. Milne, *The Christopher Robin Birthday Book* (London: Methuen, 1930) New York: Dutton, 1931, pp. vi–vii.

fe, fem, fer   Proposal in the *Christian Science Monitor* for a long-needed common gender pronoun set. If not this paradigm, then perhaps some other? "At any rate, down with 'they.'" Rpt. in *Hanford Sentinel* (CA), March 26, 1930, p. 2.

• 1932

ha, ham, shas; tra, trem, tres   In its "Saturday Competition," the *Guardian* offered a two guinea prize for the best list of ten most-needed words. *Ha, hem, shas,* proposed by Arthur L. Dakyns, of Manchester, took second prize of one guinea. The other paradigm did not win. "New Words," *Manchester Guardian,* October 26, 1932, p. 18.

• 1934
she, shis, shim (**gender-specific, tripartite parallel to** *he, his,* *him*)   Philip B. Ballard recalls this proposal at a woman's conference some time ago. Phillip B. Ballard, *Thought and Language* (London: Univ. of London Press, 1934), pp. 7–8.

• 1935
himorher; hes (**pron.** [his]), *hir* (**pron.** [hir]), *hem; his'n, her'n*   "The Post Impressionist," *Washington Post,* August 20, 1935, p. 6.

• 1938
se, sim, sis   Gregory Hynes, "See?" *Liverpool Echo,* Sept. 21, 1938; cited by H. L. Mencken, *American Language,* supplement 2 (New York: Alfred A. Knopf, 1948), p. 370.

• 1945
hse   Modeled on Chinese. Buwei Yang Chao, *How to Cook and Eat in Chinese,* 3rd ed. (New York: Vintage, Random House, 1972 [rep. of 1963 ed.]), p. xxiv.

• 1951
che, chis, chim   The columnist Frank Colby cites W. E. Fohl's coinage (see above, 1930) reminding readers that *thon* is already in the dictionary. Frank Colby, "Take My Word for It," *Washington Evening Star* (DC), January 29, 1951, p. 33.

• 1958
hesh, hirs, herm   Coined as early as 1958 by the microbiologist Max S. Marshall, of the University of California Medical Center. Marshall subsequently suggests that simply using the pronouns, as he does, in a letter in the journal of the College English Association, "should be enough to make these words official." Max S. Marshall, "Those Missing Pronouns," *CEA Critic* 25 (November 1962): 9.

• 1963

he/she   Mary Norris reports finding this in a 1963 dictionary. Mary Norris, *Between You and Me: Confessions of a Comma Queen* (New York: W. W. Norton, 2015), Chapter 3.

• 1966

hen   A new Swedish gender-neutral pronoun, proposed by Rolf Dunås as the alternative for Swedish generic masculine *han*, "he," on the grounds that women should not be linguistically subordinate to men. Dunås rejects the compound *han eller hon*, "he or she," as pedantic and clumsy. He likens *hen* to the Finnish pronoun *hän* (Finnish pronouns do not express gender). A school board member may have tried to popularize *hen*, but the pronoun was not successful at the time. Rolf Dunås, "He or She," *Upsala Nya Tidning*, November 30, 1966. See below, 1994.

• ca. 1969

jhe   Milton R. Stern, Dean of Continuing Education at the University of California at Berkeley, coins or recommends *jhe*, according to later reports. William A. Caldwell, "Jhe, Is Tey a Person?" *The Record* (Hackensack, NJ), March 31, 1972, p. 16. Paul Dickson, *Words* (New York: Delacorte, 1982), p. 113, would also attribute *jhe*, pronounced "gee," to Stern, who had since moved to the University of Michigan.

• 1969

kin   All-purpose pronoun in the language of the fictional people of Ata. Dorothy Bryant, *The Comforter*; reprinted 1971 as *The Kin of Ata Are Waiting for You* (New York: Random House/Moon Books), p. 51.

• 1970

she (contains *he*), *heris*, *herim*   Dana Densmore, "Speech is the Form of Thought," *No More Fun and Games: A Journal of Female Liberation* (April 1970); cited in *Media Report to Women* vol. 3, no. 1 (January 1975): 12.

co **(from IE **ko*), *cos***   Mary Orovan, *Humanizing English* (New York [1975]: self-published). Reported in wide but not exclusive use since at least 1970 in the Twin Oaks Community in Virginia. Jolane Flanagin, "The Use and Evolution of Gender-Neutral Language in an Intentional Community," *Women and Language* vol. 3, no. 1 (2013): 27–41.

ve, vis, ver   Varda (Murrell) One. *Everywoman*, May 8, p. 2.

• 1971

xe, xen, xes   Don Rickter, of Arlington, MA, coined *xe* as the singular form of *they* in November 1971, and recommends *xe, xen,* and *xes* in a letter to the editor of *UU World,* the journal of the Unitarian Universalist Church, on May 1, 1973. According to Rickter, "*xe* is *not* sexless" and should be used for God to avoid "a patriarchal hierarchy." This may be the only gender-neutral pronoun proposed for the deity. Rickter also coins the masculine *Mrr.* to parallel feminine *Ms.* "Unisex Pronoun," *UU World,* May 1, 1973, p. 2. The coinage date of 1971 is given by Jan Freeman, "He Said, Xe Said," *Boston Globe,* March 28, 2004, p. 43.

tey, ter (ters), tem   In the preview issue of *Ms. Magazine,* Casey Miller and Kate Swift argue that "the problem of the generic personal pronoun is a problem of the status of women." Miller and Swift propose this paradigm, based on the plural *they, them, their,* as a way for people to "kick the habit of using *he* when they mean anyone, male or female." They find *he or she* "awkward," and they disapprove of singular *they:* "When this patchwork solution begins to appear in print, the language is in trouble." In their view, earlier invented pronouns lack "the transparently logical relationship to existing pronouns that is necessary if a new word is to gain wide acceptance." In contrast, "*they, their,* and *them* suggest *tey, ter,* and *tem.*" Casey Miller and Kate Swift, "Desexing the Language," *Ms. Magazine,* preview issue, spring 1972; appearing as an insert in *New York Magazine,* December 21, 1971, pp. 103–4. (The first stand-alone issue of *Ms.* appeared in the spring of 1972.) See also Casey Miller and Kate Swift, "What about New Human Pronouns?" *Current* 138 (1972): 43–45.

***ta, ta-men* (pl.)**   Leslie Blumenson, a biostatistician from Buffalo, suggests borrowing this neutral pronoun from Mandarin Chinese: "What a gesture it would be if President Nixon were to proclaim before his China visit that 'ta' would now be part of the official American legal language. It would clearly demonstrate our readiness to recognize the superiority of the Chinese in some matters without jeopardizing our defensive posture in the least." Blumenson adds that the plural form is *ta-men*. Leslie E. Blumenson, "And Now, a Unisex Pronoun," *New York Times*, December 30, 1971.

• 1972

person;* generic *she   In an insensitive parody of a quiz on feminism in the *New York Times Magazine,* the sociologist Amitai Etzioni asks, "To help redress some of the exaggerations built into the Women's Liberation proclamations, would you wince [at] substituting the pronoun 'she' for the universal 'he'?" Amitai Etzioni, "A Test for the Female Liberationist," *New York Times,* February 27, 1972, p. SM23.

fm   Paul Kay, *Newsletter of the American Anthropological Association* 13 (April 1972): 3.

it; z   Abigail Cringle of Edgerton, Maryland, rejects epicene *it* in favor of "a new pronoun, 'z,'" and calls for "a committee of enlightened and impartial individuals be established to ... determine the best method for initiating the use of our new pronoun." Abigail Cringle, "Drop Sexist Pronouns," *Washington Post,* May 2, 1972, sec. A, p. 19.

shis, shim, shims, shimself   Robert B. Kaplan, *Newsletter of the American Anthropological Association* 13 (June 1972): 4.

ze* (from Ger. *sie*), *zim, zees, zeeself; per* (from *person*), *pers   Steven Polgar of Chapel Hill, North Carolina, proposes the *ze* paradigm; John Clark offers *per. Newsletter of the American Anthropological Association* 13 (September 1972): 17–18. Cited in the *OED*.

• 1973

na, nan, naself June Arnold, *The Cook and the Carpenter* (Plainfield, VT: Daughters, Inc., 1973).

it; s/he Norma Wilson et al., editors, "A Woman's New World Dictionary," *51%: A Paper of Joyful Noise for the Majority Sex*, 1973, pp. 3–4. *S/he* is recorded in *Merriam-Webster's Unabridged,* defined as "she or he—used in writing as a pronoun of common gender." Three pronunciations are listed: she-he, she-or-he, she-slash-he.

s/he; him/er; his-or-her Cited and rejected by Gordon Wood, "The Forewho—Neither a He, a She, Nor an It," *American Speech* 48 (1973): 158–59.

humit Revising the rape statute "so either a male or female could commit rape and either a male or female could be the victim," Representative Midge Miller, chair of the Wisconsin State Legislative Council's special committee on equal rights, offers *humit* as an alternative to generic *he.* "When 'His' Means 'Her' an Image Problem Occurs," *The Capital Times* (Madison, WI), August 21, 1973, p. 6.

tey, ter, tem The University of Tennessee's *Daily Beacon* begins using these gender-neutral pronouns, originally proposed by Miller and Swift (see above, 1971): "A September 1973 issue of The Daily Beacon offered an example for the usage of the pronouns: 'Tey will take English 110, but does not know ter section number which has not yet been assigned to tem yet.' The experiment was eventually discontinued." Tanner Hancock and Heidi Hill, "1973 Beacon Used Genderless Pronouns," *Daily Beacon* (Knoxville), September 14, 2015.

shem; herm Quidnunc, "Thon—That's the Forewho," *American Speech* 48 (1973): 300–302.

heshe, shehe In a piece about nonsexist language, the *Los Angeles Times* columnist Art Seidenbaum mentions that a friend is promoting *heshe,* though "his girlfriend . . . insists that 'shehe' is the fairer sexlessness after centuries of male precedence." Art Seidenbaum, "Unsex to Untitle," *Los Angeles Times,* February 6, 1973, p. 29.

se (pron. [si]), *ser* (pron. [sir]), *sim* (pron. [sim]), *simself*   William Cowan, of the department of linguistics, Carleton University (Ottawa), *Times Two* 6 (May 24, 1973). (See also 1979.)

j/e, m/a, m/e, m/es, m/oi; jee, jeue   A set of French coined pronouns. Monique Wittig employs the slashed pronouns as feminines, and cites *jee* and *jeue,* which employ the more traditional feminine *e; Le corps lesbien* (Paris: Editions de Minuit); *The Lesbian Body,* trans. David LeVay (London: Peter Owen, 1975).

heesh, heesh's, heeshself   The pronouns are used in a science fiction novel to refer to a "triune" species, the Didonians, but only halfheartedly; *he* is used as well. Poul Anderson, *The Day of Their Return* (New York: Nelson Doubleday/New American Library, 1973).

• 1974

ne, nis, ner   Mildred Fenner attributes this to the educator Fred Wilhelms, former secretary of the Association for Supervision and Curriculum, writing in the October issue of the NEA journal. *Today's Education* 4 (1974): 110. UPI humor columnist Dick West rejects Wilhelms's "unisex pronouns," attributing them to the women's liberation movement. "Writer Deplores Unisex." *Leader-Telegram* (Eau Claire, WI), October 23, 1974, p. 35.

she (**includes** *he*)   Gena Corea, "Frankly Feminist," rpt. as "How to Eliminate the Clumsy 'He,'" *Media Report to Women* vol. 3, no. 1 (January 1975): 12.

en, es, ar   David H. Stern, of Pasadena, California, writes that the *n* in *en* echoes *someone;* the *s* in *es* suggests *his;* the *r* in *ar* recalls *hers.* Stern also coins *emman* for "man or woman," and *Masir* as a gender-neutral title (suggestive of *master*) instead of *sir* or *madam.* David H. Stern, "We Need a Sex-Free Pronoun," *Los Angeles Times,* January 19, 1974, sec. 2, p. 4.

ve, vis, vim; **singular** *they*   Amanda Smith writes to ask the *Washington Post* to adopt singular *they*. She argues that the form is so prevalent, "English teachers exert themselves to stop students from saying 'Everyone should hang up their coat.' The prevalence of this usage, incidentally, shows that plain folks as well as the feminists feel a need for an impersonal pronoun." Smith mentions the coinages *ve, vis, vim,* but finds them humorous because they derive "from the Latin *vir,* meaning man!" Amanda Smith, "Revising the Language," *Washington Post,* April 11, 1974, A29.

E   Suggesting that "women's lib has now liberated us from" singular *they* and the cumbersome *his or her,* Harriet Kelley recommends this single vowel and compares *E* with *I, a, o,* and *u*—a truncation of *you*—as vowels common to almost all the personal pronouns, singular and plural, that *E* would replace. Harriet Stovall Kelley, "E Is for Everybody," *Atlanta Constitution,* June 9, 1974, p. 270.

shit   In November 1974, California voters passed Proposition 11, a referendum amending the state constitution to make its language gender neutral. John Abraham, of Fullerton, adds his own sexist formula by combining *she, he,* and *it* in that order to create a scatological gender-neutral pronoun. John Abraham, "Proposition 11," *Los Angeles Times,* November 2, 1974, p. 30.

shem, hem, hes   Child psychologist Paul Silverman, of Rockville, MD, proposes to "purge the language of unnecessary references to persons by sex" with this paradigm. He adds, "Hopefully, however, grammarians can operate with some restraint in generating neuter alternatives lest children's comprehension of language be retarded indefinitely." Paul L. Silverman, "Purging the Language," *Washington Post,* December 17, 1974, A17.

• 1975

hesh, himer, hiser, hermself   Jan Verley Archer, "Use New Pronouns," *Media Report to Women* 3.1 (January 1975): 12.

singular *they; han; nogen*   Dr. Patricia Wells, of the Oregon State University School of Business, suggests that the binary honorifics *sir* and *madam* should be replaced by *nogen,* which stands for "no gender," and that singular *they* should replace the traditional binary pronouns. If that doesn't work, then English should borrow the gender-neutral pronoun *han* from Finnish. "Dear Nogen: Professor Has an Idea for New Gender Ender," *Los Angeles Times,* June 30, 1975, p. 3.

se **(pron.** [si])   H. R. Lee of Alexandria, Virginia, *Forbes* 116 (August 15, 1975): 86.

shim   "The apostles of asexuality.... want to purge, not so much society of its inequities, as language of its substance. It has been advocated, quite seriously, that the pronouns of gender be stripped from our language and be replaced with a neutered makeshift like *shim.*" Peter A. Jay, " 'Ms.' Can Be Misused, Too, as in 'Mr. and Ms.' " *Baltimore Sun,* August 15, 1975, p. A13.

ey, eir, em; uh   Christine Elverson of Skokie, IL, editor of the G. D. Searle employee newsletter, offers *ey, eir,* and *em* to win the Chicago Association of Business Communicators' contest for a new "transgender" pronoun, to be used for addressing mixed audiences. Another contestant facetiously suggests *uh:* "If it isn't a he or a she, it's uh, something else." Judie Black, "Ey Has a Word for It," *Chicago Tribune,* August 23, 1975, sec. 1, p. 12.

h'orsh'it **(facetious scatological blend** *of he, or, she,* **and** *it***)**   Joel Weiss of Northbrook, Illinois, *Forbes* 116 (September 15, 1975): 12.

hir, herim **(facetious)**   Milton Mayer, "On the Siblinghood of Persons," *The Progressive* 39 (September 1975): 20–21.

• ca. 1976

il, ils, ilself   Suggested by the linguist Dwight L. Bolinger in correspondence with Ralph B. Long. Bolinger apparently selected *il* because the phoneme /l/ was not used in other English pronouns (he does not mention the French masculine pronoun *il*). *Il* takes the same form for subject, object, and possessive, and it is to be pronounced like *ill*. Ralph B. Long, "Problems in English Grammar," *TESOL Quarterly* 10 (March 1976): 123–24.

• 1976

ho, hom, hos, homself (from Lat. *homo*, "man," and prefix *homo-*, "the same, equal, like") Donald K. Darnell invents this paradigm. Donald K. Darnell and Wayne Brockriede, *Persons Communicating* (Englewood Cliffs, NJ: Prentice-Hall, 1976), 148.

he or she;* to be written as *(s)he Elizabeth Lane Beardsley, "Referential Genderization," in Carol C. Gould and Marx W. Wartofsky, eds., *Women and Philosophy* (New York: G. P. Putnam's Sons, 1976), 285–93.

***she, herm, hs* (facetious; pron. "zzz")** Paul B. Horton, "A Sexless Vocabulary for a Sexist Society," *Intellect* 105 (December 1976): 159–60.

it Millicent Rutherford, "One Man in Two Is a Woman," *English Journal*, December 1976, p. 11.

• ca. 1977

po, xe, jhe Cited as recent and ephemeral by Casey Miller and Kate Swift, *Words and Women: New Language in New Times* (1976; rpt. New York: Anchor Press, 1991), p. 130.

E, E's, Em; one *E* was created independently once again, this time by psychologist Donald G. MacKay of the University of California at Los Angeles.

• 1977

s/he Edward Devol, a former editor, writes an op-ed in the *Washington Post* discussing the absence of a gender-neutral pronoun in English: "The He/She Dilemma," *Washington Post*, February 6, 1977, p. 36. In response, David Bollier, of Washington, argues "that *s/he* would, in one stroke, resolve the contrived impasse posed by he/she; silence our overzealous grammatical guardians; and spare beleaguered *Post* readers from the bushwah produced by writers-in-search-of-a-topic." David Bollier, "The 'He/She Dilemma,'" *Washington Post,* February 13, 1977, p. 34.

e, ris, rim   Werner Low, of Bethesda, MD, offers *e,* which parallels the first-person *I* and which is, "after all, what he and she, men and women, have in common." Alternatively, he offers *ris* and *rim* as "a trade-off: the lady gets the first letter, the gentleman the other two. Nothing could be more equitable." Werner Low, "A Solution to the 'He/She Dilemma,'" *Washington Post,* February 20, 1977, C6.

sheme, shis, shem; heshe, hisher, himmer   The *sheme* paradigm is proposed by Thomas S. Jackson of Washington, DC; Middleton also refers to the coinages *heshe, hisher, himmer.* Thomas H. Middleton, "Pondering the Personal Pronoun Problem," *Saturday Review,* March 9, 1977.

O;* generic *she   Writing in the *Wall Street Journal,* former *WSJ* editor Vermont Royster reports two suggestions from readers, *O,* from Hungarian, via Barbara Hazlett, and generic *she,* recommended by Carolyn Aggarwal. Vermont C. Royster, "Sex and the Single Pronoun—a Dilemma," *Sunbury Daily Item* (PA), April 22, 1977, p. 4.

hei, heis   Eldon F. Gunter, of the Bill Sandy Corp., specialist in communications services for the automobile industry, coined these blends of *he* and *she,* "as the bisexual possessive," to avoid the "never-ending 'his or her,'" with *heis* pronounced to rhyme with "sighs." Cited in "Merry Mix-up of Sexist Words," by the King Features Syndicate columnist Phyllis Battelle, *Coshocton Tribune* (OH), March 24, 1977, p. 4. Although in this column Battelle seems to approve of the coinage, the following year she rejects new pronouns: "These ideas are too complex, requiring mental sorting, confusion—possibly even drunkenness." Phyllis Battelle, "To Each His or Her Own," *Coshocton Tribune,* May 5, 1978, p. 4.

em, ems   Jeffrey J. Smith (using pseudonym TINTAJL jefry), *Em Institute Newsletter,* June 1977.

generic *he*   In 1977, the Texas State Textbook Committee, as part of a back-to-basics initiative, calls for gender-neutral language to be used in all approved schoolbooks. This would include getting rid of generic *he,* though no alternative word is offered. Although the *Austin American-Statesman* prefers generic *he* to the cumbersome *he or she* and the ungrammatical singular *they,* it notes in an editorial, "If somebody can think of [a gender-neutral pronoun], he/she will qualify for a Nobel Peace Prize for bringing an end to the eternal squabbling over one of the shortest words in the English language." "The Generic 'He,'" *Austin American-Statesman,* September 17, 1977, p. 8.

hee, hea, hi, hie, hio, heo; ke, kos, kem   In a follow-up op-ed to the *Statesman* comment, Lois Parker, an English professor at Southwestern University, runs through and rejects *hee, hea, hi, hie, hio, heo* before settling on *ke, kos, kem,* "three little words [that] add grace to the language." How they are more graceful than the rejected forms is not clear. Lois Parker, "At a Loss for Words," *Austin American-Statesman,* September 25, 1977, p. 29.

• 1978

ae   Cited as occurring in fiction, especially science fiction. Cheris Kramer(ae), Barrie Thorne, and Nancy Henley, "Perspectives on Language and Communication," *Signs* 3 (1978): 638–51.

hir   Ray A. Killian, *Managers Must Lead!* (AMACOM) press release; cited in "The Epicene Pronoun Yet Again," *American Speech* 54 (1979): 157–58. An article on the coinage appears the next year: Muriel Lederer, "Just Call Me 'Hir,'" *Wilkes-Barre Times Leader* (PA), March 21, 1979, p. 8.

hesh, hizer, hirm; sheehy; sap (from *homo sapiens*)   The *hesh* paradigm is proposed by Prof. Robert Longwell of the University of Northern Colorado; *sheehy* by David Kraus of Bell Harbor, NY; *sap* (facetiously) by Dr. Lawrence S. Ross, of Huntington, NY; several readers offer blends of *he, she,* and *it.* Tom Wicker, "More about He/ She and Thon," *New York Times,* May 14, 1978, p. E19.

e, ir   UPI reports that the Broward County (FL) School Board's new "Program Guide for Gifted Education" uses these pronouns, containing common elements from the masculine and feminine forms, in order to comply with federal regulations that ban non-gender-neutral language in educational publications. "He and She Headed, Ir, for Trouble," *Arizona Republic,* May 29, 1978, pp. 1, 14.

heesh, hiser(s), herm, hermself   Leonora A. Timm, "Not Mere Tongue in Cheek: The Case for a Common Gender Pronoun in English," *International Journal of Women's Studies* 1 (1978): 555–65.

þe (the), im, ir(s); þane   Reviving the Old English letter called thorn, þ, to be used for the unvoiced th sound of *think.* þe rhymes with "he" and contrasts with the old second-person singular pronoun *thee.* þane ('thane') will be used for a person of unspecified sex: man, woman, þane. John Newmeyer, Ph.D., of San Francisco. David Wallechinsky and Irving Wallace, *The People's Almanac #2* (New York: William Morrow, 1978), pp. 1374–75.

•1979

one   Lillian E. Carleton, "An Epicene Suggestion," *American Speech* 54 (1979): 156–57.

et, ets, etself   Aline Hoffman of Sarnia, Ontario; cited by William Sherk, *Brave New Words* (Toronto: Doubleday Canada, 1979).

hir, hires, hirem, hirself   Jerome Ch'en, professor of history at York University, suggests reviving the "obsolete" *hir.* Jerome Ch'en, " 'Hir' Tomorrow?" *New York Times,* January 6, 1979, p. 18.

shey, sheir, sheirs; hey, heir, heirs   Paul Encimer favors the first over the second paradigm. *The Peacemaker* 32 (February 1979): 2–3.

ey, eir, em   Roszel Thomsen suggests this paradigm, made from the plural pronouns without the initial *th-,* as easy to understand and remember. "Proposal," *Baltimore Evening Sun,* February 6, 1979, p. 8.

se, sim, sine; Ct   William Cowan, a linguist specializing in Algonquian languages, first proposed the pronoun set in 1973 (see above), with "a monumental lack of success." This time Cowan comes up with the gender-neutral honorific *Ct,* for citizen, to replace the traditional gendered *Miss, Mrs, Ms,* and *Mr.* He argues that it works just as well in French as in English, making it suitable for use in bilingual Canadian contexts. Geoff Johnson, "New Master Plan Just Can't Miss," *Ottawa Citizen,* March 8, 1979, p. 41.

it   Herman Arthur, "To Err Is Huperson; to Forgive, Divine," *American Educator* 4 (Winter 1979): 30–32.

• 1980

hes   Letitia (Tish) Baldrige, former social secretary to Jacqueline Kennedy Onassis, writes in her syndicated etiquette column, "I am no word specialist and maybe 100 people have come up with a better solution, but I have a word candidate: hes" (combining *he* and *she,* and pronounced *hess*). According to Baldrige, the pronoun *hes* will prepare the way for a woman president. Letitia Baldrige, "Helping Out the Dictionary," *Los Angeles Times,* January 4, 1980, p. 57. Still waiting for both the pronoun and the president.

• 1981

ha, hom, hos   Edward Barry, a retired *Chicago Tribune* editor, recommends this paradigm as superior to previous coinages, adding that if *he* is gender neutral, "then it is manifestly unfair to deny a like privilege to 'she' and 'her.' Yet no grammarian will rise to defend a sentence such as this: 'Each driver must keep her own cab clean.'" Edward Barry, "Don't Emasculate English Language," *Chicago Tribune,* January 5, 1981, p. 34.

heshe, hes, hem   Ronald C. Corbyn, "Getting Around Sexist Pronouns," *Anthropology Newsletter* 22 (October 1979): 10–11.

• 1982

shey, shem, sheir   Mauritz Johnson; cited by William Safire, *What's the Good Word?* (New York: Times Books, 1982), 30. Also attributed to Mary Jane Hawley, of Kirkland, WA. Fran Wallace, "Let's Talk Language," Twin Falls, ID, *Times-News*, April 18, 1982, p. 18.

se, sis, sim, simself; sey, seir, sem, semself; um, ums; ti   Reporting on the gender-neutral options proposed by Temple University physicist W. Kenneth McFarlane, columnist Clark DeLeon snarks that it's "apparent why McFarlane teaches physics and not English." DeLeon prefers singular *they*, on the analogy of singular *you*. Clark DeLeon, "Language: As he/she was saying to him/her." *Philadelphia Inquirer*, March 16, 1982, p. 2B. Responding to DeLeon's column, Dessa Ewing, of Delaware County Community College, offers *um, ums*. Clark DeLeon, "Language: How about he/she/se/um?" *Philadelphia Inquirer*, March 28, 1982, p. 2-B. And another report adds McFarlane's proposal to transpose the two letters of *it* to form *ti*. "Speech Without Sex," *Wausau Daily Herald* (WI), March 23, 1982, p. 4.

• 1984

ghaH (pronounced [ɣɑx])   The structured version of the Klingon language, created by the linguist Marc Okrand for *Star Trek III: The Search for Spock*, includes gender-neutral *ghaH* as the sole "animate third-person singular pronoun in Klingon." "It" is rendered by the Klingon *'oH* [ʔox]. There are no gender-neutral pronouns in Vulcan. Mark Mandel, personal emails, July 16 and 19, 2017.

hiser   McClain B. Smith, *Ann Arbor News*, January 20, 1984, p. A6.

hes   Ernie Permentier, *Ms.*, May 1984, p. 22.

hann   Steven Schaufele, of the University of Illinois Linguistics Department, takes *hann* from Old Norse, the language that is also the source of English *they*; analogous to Finnish *han*. (See Swedish invented common-gender *hen*, 1994.) *Colorless Green Newsflashes* 4 (November 9, 1984): 3.

• 1985

zhe Cited by the *Oxford English Dictionary* (under "ze"). "*Re: Non-sexist Lang. (Hist.)* in *net.nlang* (Usenet newsgroup), June 14, 1985. 'My nomination? Zhe. (The zh is pronounced like the z in azure.)'"

herm Attributed to the magazine *Lysistrata*. Jenny Cheshire, "A Question of Masculine Bias," *Today's English* 1 (1985): 26.

a, un, a's Although she prefers singular *they,* science fiction writer Ursula K. Le Guin used this paradigm, based on British dialect, in a 1985 screenplay for her novel *The Left Hand of Darkness* (1969); in the novel, Le Guin uses conventional *he/his/him.* "Is Gender Necessary? Redux" (1976, revised, 1987), in Ursula K. Le Guin, *Dancing at the Edge of the World: Thoughts on Words, Women, Places* (New York: Grove Press, 1989), p. 15.

gee, hem, hes; they Ian Thornton, of South Yarra, Australia, offers *gee, hem, hes,* and J. R. Taylor opts for singular *they.* Ian Thornton, "Gee, Hem or Hes?" *The Age* (Melbourne), July 5, 1985, p. 12.

che, chim, chis, chimself David Throop, of Austin, TX, writes in support of this paradigm: "The idea is not to force a new convention on anyone. We need not rework our literature to make it gender neutral. We should browbeat no one into learning new words. . . . It's easier to deal with than the stilted phrases and minor slights over which we've been stumbling. And don't you think [*che*] has kind of a ring to it?" David Throop, "A Sex Problem," *St. Louis Post-Dispatch*, November 16, 1985, p. 17.

• 1987

re, hos, hov The copy editor William Drennan coins these pronouns, along with some 1,000 other new words, or, as he calls them, "neonyms," in an attempt to improve the English language. Dan Oldenburg, "Wordsmith Struggles to Expand the Language by Coining 'Neonyms,'" *Minneapolis Star and Tribune*, August 17, 1987, pp. 1c–2c (rpt. from *Washington Post*).

• 1988

han, hans A. M. Stratford, of Norfolk, England, creates this form to resemble other British initialisms (HM, HRH, HMS, HE, HMSO). *English Today* 14 (1988): 5–6.

Hs. Roy M. Fish, of Springhill, LA, offers this abbreviation of *he/ she* to use "when gender is unknown or inconclusive, and one [*sic*] is unwilling to use the masculine, he, to include both sexes, and does not choose to use he/she or he or she, yet refuses to speak of one person as 'they.' " Roy M. Fish, "The English Language Is Worth Preserving," *Shreveport Times* (LA), June 7, 1988, p. 6.

e, e's The ever-popular *e* reappears, this time coined by Eugene Wine, of Miami-Dade Community College. Wine is hardly the first to note that *e* is the common letter in *he* and *she*, and that *I* and *you* "have already been reduced to a single vowel sound." *Chronicle of Higher Education*, September 21, 1988, p. 2.

• 1989

ala, alum, alis Michael Knab, of Goodwin, Knab and Co., Chicago, derives these from Latin *al*, "other," and feels they resemble the Hawaiian sex-neutral pronouns *oia, ia*. Press release and personal communication.

le, les Ron Sebring, of Independence, MO, would like to submit his coinage to a contest for best gender-neutral pronoun. Sebring suggests *le* would be useful to refer to God as well as to personified inanimates, for example, a speaking tree or a singing wind. Ron Sebring, "Language and Gender," *Philadelphia Daily News*, January 28, 1989, p. 13.

generic *she* Andrew Sullivan finds the "she rule" to be common "here in politically correct land," otherwise known as Boston, but he objects to generic *she* as "silly" and asks for alternative suggestions. Andrew Sullivan, "Boston Diarist," *The New Republic*, July 3, 1989, p. 42.

se, hir, hirself   Offered by the syndicated columnist Sarah Overstreet in response to Sullivan's discussion of generic *she*. Sarah Overstreet, "Pronoun Gender," *Orangeburg Times and Democrat* (SC), July 13, 1989, p. 20.

e, e's, emself, em   Victor J. Stone, professor of law at the University of Illinois at Urbana, reinvents this paradigm, which first appears in 1841, in the Chicago Bar Association's *CBA Record* 3 (July/August 1989): 12.

ne, nis, nim   James K. Rohan, of Agoura, California, solves "the missing-word puzzle" by coining this paradigm to help those users of singular *they* "who would rather be illiterate than sexist." Rohan smugly says, "By emasculating the pronoun 'he' while retaining the singular form I titillate the feminists and provide a sane alternative to their solecism." Rohan then challenges writers, editors, broadcasters, teachers, and scholars to promote his word. "At Last! The Missing Bisexual Pronoun Supplied," *Baltimore Sun*, August 7, 1989, p. 7.

• 1990

fe, hod, hods; 'a, 'as   G. C. Tjepkema suggests the first set as clearer, fairer, and more grammatical than generic *he* or singular *they*. Tjepkema, a member of the CANAL Club, a group "promoting gender equality through language," would also consider reviving the obsolete *'a, 'as*. G. C. Tjepkema, "Hung for Wrong Reason," *Ottawa Citizen*, November 27, 1990, p. 8.

glug, glum, hes   Dick Mercer facetiously suggests these forms, with *glug* serving both as a pronoun and as a noun meaning "adult human being." Dick Mercer, "Moving toward a Kinder, Gentler Language," *Morristown Daily Record* (NJ), December 5, 1990, p. 9.

shet   Used jocularly with the warning, "Be careful of the spelling." Henrietta Hay, "English Language Badly Needs Bisexual Singular Pronouns," *Daily Sentinel* (CO), December 31, 1990, p. 9.

• 1991

de, deis; den, din   Richard Strand, Keith Roberson, Dan Fisher, BLAST (Computer) Support Office, Department of Mechanical Engineering, University of Illinois, create *de, deis* (rhymes with "dee, dyes") based on some Germanic influence; *den* and *din* created on a similar "root," both to replace *man/woman* and *men/women*.

s/he   In her column in the syndicated Sunday supplement *Parade,* Marilyn Mos Savant offers this form, pronounced "se-HEE," in response to a reader's question about "the apparent conflict between women's rights and the lack of gender-free singular third-person pronouns." Marilyn Mos Savant, "Ask Marilyn," *Baltimore Sun,* November 17, 1991, p. 375.

• 1992

se, hir   According to John Cowan (email communication, 1992), this paradigm is regularly used on the electronic newsgroup alt.sex .bondage. I have taken hir word for it.

E, e, es, eself   Qing Guo proposed this on the computer network newsgroup alt.usage.english (1992); the uppercase *E* is the subject form, the lowercase *e* the object form; also proposed are *U, u, ur, urs, urself, urselves* for the second-person paradigm (and this before the age of texting).

han; hey; mef; ws, wself; ze, zon   These coinages appear in *The Oxford Companion to the English Language,* edited by Tom McArthur (Oxford: Oxford Univ. Press, 1992), under "generic pronoun":

han	Business writer Audrie Stratford, King's Lynn, England.
hey	Ronald Gill, Derby, England.
mef	George Wardell, Reading, England.
ws, wself	Dr. John B. Sykes, editor, *Concise Oxford Dictionary,* 7th ed.
ze, zon	Don Manley, Oxford, England.

E, herm   Proposed by Bruce Ketron, an attorney, who adds that if the forms sound strange, they're no stranger "than a $7.1 million settlement for sexual harassment." Bruce Ketron, "Strange Verdict," *Napa Valley Register*, October 4, 1994, p. 12.

• 1993
heesh, hirm, hizzer   Abigail "Dear Abby" Van Buren advises reader Ruth Gurry, of Florida, who asks about this paradigm, "Better to bear the ills we have than to fly to others we know not of." Abigail Van Buren, "Dear Abby," *Fremont News-Messenger* (OH), September 23, 1993, p. 20.

ey, em   Pronouns to be used in Oceania, a floating city-state in the Caribbean being planned as a libertarian refuge by a Las Vegas developer. "Booby Traps Are OK—As Long As It's in Your Own Country," *Daily Sentinel* (CO), November 26, 1993, p. 24.

zie, zir   These forms, cited in an update to the *OED* in March 2019, and presumably related to the base form *ze* (1864), appear in the Usenet newsgroup soc.bi, December 29, 1993.

• 1994
hen   (See above, 1966.) Swedish gender-neutral pronoun, revived by the linguist Hans Karlgren, who proposes it for cases where gender is unknown or distracting. Karlgren asserts, without proof, that generic *he* works well enough to satisfy "even the most militant feminists," yet he offers *hen* as a way to make Swedish pronouns more inclusive. *Hen* would ultimately receive official approval in 2015, when it was added to the dictionary of the Swedish Academy, the *Svenska Akademiens Ordbok*. Hans Karlgren, "Politiska ord: hen," *Svenska Dagbladet*, August 28, 1994; rpt. in Anders Q. Björkman, "'Hen' was suggested by language researchers before, in 1994," *Svenska Dagbladet*, October 3, 2012. See also Nick Noack, "Sweden Adopts 'Hen' as Neutral Pronoun," *Montreal Gazette*, April 2, 2016, p. 12. While not universal, and not to everyone's liking, *hen* is com-

mon enough that Swedish media no longer feel the need to explain the word every time it appears. In the Swedish-Danish television hit *Bron/Broen* (*The Bridge*) shown on British and US TV, a Danish detective, who has to have *hen* explained to her, teases her Swedish counterpart for being politically correct (series 3, episode 1). And in the 2017 Swedish series *Rebecka Martinsson,* a male detective just back from a gender-training course chides a superior because she did not refer to an unknown killer as *hen* (series 1, episode 7).

• 1995

se, hem, hes   Responding to a referendum to remove unnecessary masculine pronouns from the Wisconsin Constitution, Bruce Marsh suggests this paradigm. The referendum failed. Bruce Marsh, "Who Wants a Sexless Society?" *Wisconsin State Journal,* March 4, 1995, p. 7.

• 1997

ey, em   These pronouns appear in Usenet discussion groups online. J. M. Hirsch, "Hey, Netizens, Writing Can Be Kewl," *Rutland Daily Herald* (VT), December 2, 1997, p. 5.

• 1999

shhe, shim, shis   J. M., of Cornwall, PA, suggests this to etiquette columnist Ann Landers. Landers replies, "Gimme a break." *Elko Daily Free Press* (NV), February 19, 1999, p. 6.

hu, hus, hum   Report that Bandana Books, of Santa Barbara, CA, issued a revised version of Walt Whitman's poems changing masculine pronouns to these neutral versions. "What Hu Meant to Say," *Wisconsin State Journal,* August 3, 1999, p. 9. I have not been able to locate a copy of this updated Whitman edition.

• 2001

generic *she; herm*   The syndicated columnist James J. Kilpatrick notes that Justice John Paul Stevens has used generic *she* and alternating *he or she* in some of his Supreme Court opinions, and that Justice Ruth Bader Ginsburg has used a generic feminine in an opinion as well. Kilpatrick adds that Bill Hallock, of Rochester, WA, suggested *herm*. James J. Kilpatrick, "Pronouns Cause Debate over Gender," *Northwest Herald* (Woodstock, IL), September 16, 2001, p. 9. Kilpatrick later goes on record opposing singular *they*, though he then softens that position.

• 2002

ree, hurm Michael Newdow, an attorney and physician who is best known for his failed lawsuit to remove "under God" from the pledge of allegiance, also proposes these gender-neutral pronouns. Jeff Gottlieb, "An Irreverent Look at Law and Politics," *Los Angeles Times*, October 14, 2002, p. 23.

• 2003

het, hes, hem New Mexico writer and teacher Andrew Schmookler says he cringes when the rules of grammar are broken. Yet he offers this paradigm, saying, "Language is ours to make. (This is not France!) This sorely needed innovation can become a part of the language, if enough of us implement the change. Power to the people." Andrew Bard Schmookler, "New Pronouns for a New Year," *Baltimore Sun*, January 2, 2003, p. A15.

xe, xem, xers Adele Wick proposes this paradigm, with *xe* pronounced as in *Xerox*, and where *x* represents the common chromosome shared by men and women, as well as the mathematical unknown. Jan Freeman, "An X-treme Proposal," *Boston Globe*, January 5, 2003, p. 59.

gender-neutral pronouns The syndicated "News of the Weird" reports that Smith, historically a women's college, will replace the feminine pronoun with gender-neutral pronouns, since some students after being admitted as female subsequently identify as transgender. (By 2014 this news would no longer be filed under "weird" by most of the media.) "P.C. Overload," *Munster Times* (IA), May 20, 2003, p. 45.

• 2004

yo Working with her students, Elaine Stotko, chair of the Johns Hopkins University Department of Teacher Preparation, discovers this naturally occurring pronoun in use in Baltimore middle and high schools, announcing the find in 2007. Elaine Stotko and Margaret Troyer, "A New Gender-Neutral Pronoun in Baltimore, Maryland: A Preliminary Study," *American Speech* 82 (Fall 2007): 261–79.

nekom, wiin; **singular** *they* The columnist Barbara Wallraff reports that MIT linguistics professor Norvin Richards has found gender-neutral pronouns in about 40% of the world's languages. Wallraff asks whether *nekom* or *wiin,* from Passamquoddy and Ojibwa, respectively, might "tide you over while we wait for 'they' to become standard?" Wallraff's suggestion that we adopt these Native American words is clearly not a serious one, though her support of singular *they* probably is. Barbara Wallraff, "Word Court," *Detroit Free Press,* September 5, 2004, p. 64.

• 2006

hu, hu's The *Los Angeles Times* cites DeAnn (aka D. N.) DeLuna, of Johns Hopkins University, who uses this coinage in her edited book on the historian J. G. A. Pocock. The pronoun *hu* rhymes with "duh," and the *Times* asks, "Do the egalitarian principles of hu outweigh the fact that it looks like a Vulcan vocabulary word?" (Vulcan does not have gender-neutral pronouns—see above, 1992.) "He Said, She Said, Hu Said," *Los Angeles Times,* October 1, 2006, p. 112.

• 2009

ze, zir, zim, hir The Society for the Study of Social Problems calls on editors and publishers to let stand writers' gender-neutral pronouns and to respect people's pronoun choices. The SSSP's letter is no longer on the society's website, but columnist Rex Smith writes that these are the pronouns the society has chosen to endorse as a way to end gender bias in society. Smith points to languages like Chinese that lack gendered pronouns to ask whether people who speak them are less biased. Rex Smith, "This Should Concern Everyone, No Matter What Their Sex," *Montreal Gazette,* October 27, 2009, p. 17.

• 2010

ze, hir Johnny Blazes, a burlesque performer and artists' model (and in 2011, founder of the band Johnny Blazes and the Pretty Boys), writes to protest the *Boston Globe*'s refusal to use hir gender-neutral pronouns of choice in a recent review of hir work. Of the pronouns, Blazes says, "This has nothing to do with the biology of my body, but instead with my gender expression." Johnny Blazes, "Gender-Neutral Pronouns Would Be a Positive Step," *Boston Globe,* July 13, 2010, A10. The review refers to Blazes as *she:* Cate McQuaid, "Drawing Attention: Dr. Sketchy's Combines Art with Spirit of Burlesque," *Boston Globe,* July 9, 2010, G18–19. (Johnny Blazes and the Pretty Boys currently identifies the band's leaders as a "father-kid duo.")

• 2014

ee, eet; herim, herimt; herimself, herimtself; hiser(s), hiserts C. Marshall Thatcher proposes these inclusive pronouns for legal contexts. *Ee* and the other forms without *t* represent males and females; *eet* and the other forms with *t* encompass animates and inanimates. Unwieldy, to be sure, this proposal drew little support, but to be fair, it's not as complex as James Anderson's system of multiple gender reference proposed in 1792. C. Marshall Thatcher, "What Is *Eet?* A Proposal to Add a Series of Referent-Inclusive Third Person Singular Pronouns and Adjectives to the English Language for Use in Legal Drafting," *South Dakota Law Review* 59 (2014): 79–89.

hir; judy   *Hir* is the title of a play by MacArthur Fellow Taylor Mac, about "a semi-mad housewife . . . with a transgender son," and other family members. Taylor Mac, *Hir: A Play* (Evanston, IL: Northwestern Univ. Press, 2015). According to Mac's website (http://www .taylormac.org/about/), "Taylor Mac . . . uses "judy", lowercase *sic,* not as a name but as a gender pronoun."

• 2017
iel, ille; iels, illes; celleux, ceulles   Suggested French inclusive pronouns. The High Council on the Equality between Women and Men, a division of the French Ministry of Families, Children, and Women's Rights, publishes a guide recommending "inclusive writing" that does not silence or demean women. The guide cites these egalitarian pronouns, coined by "certain usage experts." Le haut conseil à l'égalité entre les femmes et les homme, *Pour une communication publique sans stéréotype de sexe: Guide pratique* (*Practical Guide for Nonsexist Writing*), Paris: 2017, http://www.ecriture-inclusive.fr.

The French Academy immediately condemns these innovations and warns that their adoption would signal the death of French and allow other languages to win the race for world domination. "Déclaration de l'Académie française sur l'écriture dite 'inclusive,'" October 26, 2017, http://www.academie-francaise.fr/actualites/ declaration-de-lacademie-francaise-sur-lecriture-dite-inclusive.

• 2018
singular *them*   Coca-Cola runs an ad during Super Bowl LII (February 4) with the line "There's a Coke for he . . . and she . . . and her . . . and me . . . and them." The company is praised by LGBTQ supporters for its inclusive pronoun use, though the singular *they* is used alongside the traditional binary pronouns *he* and *she*. Reaction is generally highly favorable. Lexy Perez, "Super Bowl: Coca-Cola

Represents 'Them' in Non-Binary Ad," *Hollywood Reporter,* February 5, 2018.

• 2019

what's your pronoun?   At a concert for the 50th anniversary of the Stonewall uprising, Lady Gaga tells the audience, "Ask the question: What is your pronoun? . . . For a lot of people, it's really hard, and their pronouns aren't respected or they're not asked." Alexander Kacala, "Lady Gaga Honors Pride Month, Stonewall Uprising, at NYC Concert," NBC News, June 25, 2019, https://www.nbcnews.com/feature/nbc-out/lady-gaga-honors-pride-month-stonewall-uprising-nyc-concert-n1021551.

Acknowledgments

I have been studying gender-neutral pronouns for so many years that it's going to be hard to thank everyone who has helped and supported me along the way. There's the long-ago librarian in the New York Public Library's newspaper archive who showed me how to make a photostat of an early number of the *New York Commercial Advertiser,* and the creators of the website that let me replace that out-of-focus copy with a hi-res image of that same article in just a few clicks on my laptop. John Algeo, editor of *American Speech* back in 1981, saw fit to publish my pronoun article and encouraged my research on usage. With the kind but firm guidance of Ellen Graham at the Yale University Press, I later expanded that work as part of my book, *Grammar and Gender.* With the coming of the internet, the University of Illinois kindly hosted my pronoun page, allowing me to record additions to the pronoun study and make them available to the public. That online presence brought many reporters' queries, and their stories prompted readers to send me pronouns they had found or coined. And of course I thank my students: all I ever had to do was ask, "What's your pronoun?" and they filled the rest of the hour with animated, reasoned, and impassioned thoughts.

My editors at Liveright, Marilyn Moller along with associate editor Claire Wallace and copy editor Jodi Beder, offered tactful but perceptive comments that helped me focus my ideas and root out errors. Many others at Liveright and elsewhere have helped make this book what it is, including Steve Attardo, Cordelia Calvert, Nick Curley, Lily Gellman, Becky Homiski, Gabriel Kachuck, Nat Kent, Rev. Mak Kneebone, Peter Miller, Anna Oler, Jared Oriel, Emma Peters, Jordan Wannemacher, and, especially, publisher Bob Weil, who supported this book from the beginning. My wife, Iryce Baron, to whom I dedicate this book, suggested what was missing from my historical investigation. Any coherence this account displays I owe to her.

As Norris, the butler, tells Philip Marlowe in *The Big Sleep*, "I make many mistakes." It's a commonplace of publishing that, despite a writer's best efforts, no book is ever finished unless it has a mistake. Of course, those mistakes and failures to correct are all my own.

Notes

INTRODUCTION

1. *Silent Witness*, series 22, episode 1, "Two Spirits, pt. 1," at 40:50. bbc.co.uk, 2019.
2. A. W. Geiger and Nikki Graf, "About one-in-five U.S. adults know someone who goes by a gender-neutral pronoun," *FactTank*, Pew Research Center, Sept. 5, 2019, https://www.pewresearch.org/fact-tank/2019/09/05/gender-neutral-pronouns/.
3. Lindsey Bever, "Students Were Told to Select Gender Pronouns. One Chose 'His Majesty' to Protest Absurdity," *Washington Post*, Oct. 7, 2016, https://www.washingtonpost.com/news/education/wp/2016/10/07/a-university-told-students-to-select-their-gender-pronouns-one-chose-his-majesty/?utm_term=.69ffb462bf91.
4. Rachel N. Levin, "The Problem with Pronouns," *Inside Higher Education*, Sept. 19, 2018, https://www.insidehighered.com/views/2018/09/19/why-asking-students-their-preferred-pronoun-not-good-idea-opinion?utm_source=Inside+Higher+Ed&utm_campaign=e539882f5b-DNU_COPY_02&utm_medium=email&utm_term=0_1fcbc04421-e539882f5b-199719493&mc_cid.=e539882f5b&mc_eid=384cfe9fdd.
5. Monica Hesse, "Was Their Child a Boy or a Girl? Naya's Parents Wanted to Let Naya Decide," *Washington Post*, Sept. 19, 2018, https://www.washingtonpost.com/lifestyle/style/what-does-it-mean-to-be-a-boy-or-a-girl-the-parents-of-one-young-child-let-the-child-decide/2018/09/18/18c0ec68-b6a4-11e8-a7b5-adaaa5b2a57f_story.html?utm_term=.ac6c2da3a555.
6. Ted Thornton, "'I identify as a suitcase. Can I fly for free now?' United Airlines is mocked after becoming first in the world to allow passengers to identify as gender neutral Mx," DailyMail.com, April 1, 2019, accessed July 22, 2019, https://www.dailymail.co.uk/travel/travel_news/article-6872355/United-Airlines-mocked-Twitter-introducing-non-binary-gender-ticketing-options.html.

7. "To Restrict Kissing by Law," *New York Tribune,* Jan. 31, 1903, p. 7; emphasis added.

8. "Can 'She' Be 'He', a Congressman, and Be Woman?" *Minneapolis Star Tribune,* Nov. 13, 1916, p. 1. Montana, Colorado, and a number of other states had universal suffrage before the passage of the Nineteenth Amendment ensured that all American women could vote.

9. *San Antonio Evening News,* Oct. 5, 1922, p. 4. Wilmans easily won that seat—with the support of the Texas Ku Klux Klan. After the passage of the Nineteenth Amendment, women's suffrage, particularly in the American South, was often leveraged to dilute the African American vote.

10. "A New Treatise on Everyday English," *Springfield Republican* (MA), Jan. 5, 1896, p. 6.

CHAPTER 1 • THE MISSING WORD

1. "Gender-Neutral Teacher Transferred," *USA Today,* Sept. 26, 2017, https://www.usatoday.com/story/news/nation-now/2017/09/26/gender-neutral-teacher-transferred/706944001/.

2. Tom Quimby, "Fifth-grade Teacher Gets Schooled by Parents after Gender-Neutral Grammar Lessons," *Washington Times,* Sept. 28, 2017, https://www.washingtontimes.com/news/2017/sep/28/chloe-bressack-florida-teacher-gives-gender-neutra/.

3. Abby Walton, "Gender-Neutral Student Speaks Out about Controversy," WCTV, Oct. 17, 2015, updated Dec. 10, 2015, http://www.wctv.tv/home/headlines/Controversy-Over-Schools-Response-333116711.html.

4. Leon County Schools, "Transgender and Gender Nonconforming Students," Teacher Training, 2015, slide 18, https://www.scribd.com/document/287596644/Transgender-and-Gender-Nonconforming-Students#full screen&from_embed.

5. Eric Miller, "Gender-Neutral Pronoun Use Offers a Teachable Moment," *Tallahassee Democrat,* Sept. 23, 2017, p. A4.

6. Associated Press, "Tennessee Students Asked to Use Gender-Neutral Pronouns," *Tennessean,* Aug. 30, 2015, http://www.tennessean.com/story/news/education/2015/08/30/university-tennessee-gender-neutral-pronouns/71416632/.

7. Peter Schworm, "Colleges' Final Frontier: Mixed-Gender Housing," *Boston Globe,* Apr. 2, 2008, p. 7.

8. Casey Miller and Kate Swift, "Desexing the Language," *Ms. Magazine,* preview issue, Spring, 1972; appearing as an insert in *New York Magazine,* Dec. 21,

1971, pp. 103–4; Tanner Hancock and Heidi Hill, "1973 Beacon Used Genderless Pronouns," *Daily Beacon* (Knoxville, TN), Sept. 14, 2015.

9. Collin Binkley, "Colleges Try Gender-Free Pronouns," *Daily Item* (Sunbury, PA), Sept. 20, 2015, p. F9.

10. Maura Lerner, "He, She or Ze? Pronouns Could Pose Trouble under University of Minnesota Campus Policy," *Minneapolis Star-Tribune*, July 14, 2018, http://www.startribune.com/maura-lerner/10645281/; https://www.documentcloud.org/documents/4598811-Updated-Draft-Gender-Identity-Policy.html.

11. *Newton Daily Republican* (KS), Dec. 31, 1892, p. 4.

12. William Lily, *A Short Introduction of Grammar,* London, 1549; Lily, who wrote *the* Latin grammar for English schools, actually lists seven Latin genders, but fortunately that's got nothing to do with English pronouns. This idea of gender worthiness first appears in Latin grammars around the sixth century BCE, and it's reiterated in sixteenth-century Latin textbooks like the one William Lily wrote for English schoolchildren.

13. For example, 120 years later in *Priscianus Embryo et Nascens, Being a Key to the Grammar-School, in Two Parts* (London, 1670), Part 2, p. 2.

14. Anne Fisher, *A New Grammar, with Exercises of Bad English: Or, An Easy Guide to Speaking and Writing the English Language Properly and Correctly* (London, 1753), p. 114n.

15. Robert Baker, *Reflections on the English Language* (London, 1770), pp. viii–x.

16. U.S. Constitution, Art II, sec. 1; emphasis added.

17. Eliza Frances Andrews, "Some Grammatical Stumbling Blocks," *The Chautauquan,* June 1896 (vol. 23, no. 3), pp. 339–43.

18. Alexander Bain, *A Higher English Grammar* (New York: Holt, 1879), p. 310.

19. Ursula K. Le Guin, *Steering the Craft* (Boston: Houghton Mifflin, 2015), p. 17. An earlier printing (Portland, OR: Eighth Mountain Press, 1998), p. 33, has a slightly different version.

20. "Instability," *Leavenworth Times,* Feb. 18, 1866, p. 4.

21. *Newton Daily Republican* (KS), Dec. 31, 1892, p. 4.

22. Andrew Sullivan, "Boston Diarist," *The New Republic,* July 3, 1989, p. 42.

23. Jeanne Holub, "Dr. Spock Pulls Switch in Generic Pronoun Use," *The Courier* (Waterloo, IA), Jan. 27, 1974, p. 30.

24. *Palazzolo v. Rhode Island et al.,* 533 U.S. 606 (2001) at 638.

25. James J. Kilpatrick, "Pronouns cause debate over gender," *Northwest Herald* (Woodstock, IL) Sept. 16, 2001, p. 9.

26. The case is *Taylor v. Sturgell* (128 S.C. 2161, 2174 [2008]), cited in Leslie M. Rose, "The Supreme Court and Gender-Neutral Language: Setting the Stan-

dard or Lagging Behind?" *Duke Journal of Gender Law and Policy.* 17 (2010): 81–129, https://digitalcommons.law.ggu.edu/cgi/viewcontent.cgi?referer=& httpsredir=1&article=1010&context=pubs, accessed June 5, 2018.

27. Jan Freeman, "A Girl Called 'It,'" *Boston Globe,* Sept. 28, 2008, p. 50. *It* may be more common for infants in Britain than the United States. For example, in her 1992 novel *The Choir,* Joanna Trollope repeatedly refers to the Chancellor infant as *it.*

28. James Anderson, "Grammatical Disquisitions," *The Bee,* Sept. 26, 1792, p. 124.

29. Third Constitution of Kentucky, 1850, Article XIII, Bill of Rights, sec. 3, http://www.courts.ky.gov/NR/rdonlyres/514E219E-9A7A-4D29-A862 -0C9BD00A3EC1/0/3rdKYConstitution.pdf.

30. "Grammatical Legislators," *New York Evening Post,* Jan. 23, 1850, p. 2; emphasis added.

31. "Dr. Syntax," *Boston Investigator,* Aug. 27, 1862, p. 3. The *Investigator* did not express its anti-Christian views with this sort of venom.

32. Dorothy Sayers, *Strong Poison* (London: Gollancz, 1958, rpt. of 1930 ed.), p. 82.

33. Bruce Montgomery, writing as Edmund Crispin, *The Case of the Gilded Fly* (New York: London House and Maxwell, 1970, rpt. of 1944 ed.), p. 55; emphasis added.

34. Miscellaneous Language Changes Regarding Gender, California Proposition 11 (1974), http://repository.uchastings.edu/ca_ballot_props/797.

35. "Gender-Neutral Standard Gets Senate Approval," *St. Cloud Times,* Mar. 13, 1986, p. 16.

36. "Taking 'She' out of Smith," *Boston Globe,* June 15, 2003, p. 58; see also Adrian Brune, "When She Graduates As He," *Boston Globe,* Apr. 8, 2007, p. 243.

37. Baker, *Reflections on the English Language,* pp. viii–x.

38. William Marshall, *The Rural Economy of Glocestershire* (London, 1789), vol. 1, p. 324.

39. James Anderson, "Grammatical Disquisitions," *The Bee* 11, Oct 10, 1792, pp. 195–97.

40. "Notes taken at the Worcester meeting of the Royal Agricultural Society," *The Bucks Herald* (Aylesbury, England), August 15, 1863, p. 8.

41. Kokni, "Who Is the Authority on Grammar?" letter, *Pall Mall Gazette,* Feb. 21, 1899, p. 3.

42. "Report of a Select Committee from the Belle Assembly," *The Medley, or New Bedford Marine Journal,* Mar. 3, 1794, p. 2; emphasis added.

43. Letter, *The Medley,* Mar. 24, 1794, p. 2.

44. Daphne, "The Women's own corner," *Luton Reporter,* May 27, 1909, p. 5.

45. Samuel Taylor Coleridge, *Anima Poetae,* ed. Ernest Hartley Coleridge (London: Heinemann, 1897), p. 190.

46. "Something for Grammarians to Consider," *The Republic* (Columbus, IN), May 15, 1883, p. 2.

47. "New Words," the *Mercury and Weekly Journal of Commerce* (New York), Jan. 31, 1839, p. 4.

48. John Stuart Mill, *A System of Logic, Ratiocinative and Inductive,* 3rd ed., vol. 2 (London, 1851), p. 406n. Mill's *Logic* was first published in 1846; the note on generic *he* does not appear in the first edition.

CHAPTER 2 • THE POLITICS OF *HE*

1. Jacob Bright, Bill to Remove the Electoral Disabilities of Women, first introduced in Parliament 1870. Rpt. in Helen Blackburn, ed., *Handbook for Women Engaged in Social and Political Work* (Bristol, 1881), p. 10.

2. "Mr. Jacob Bright's Bill to Remove the Electoral Disabilities of Women," *The Times* (London), Apr. 30, 1873, p. 9; emphasis added.

3. Vermont C. Royster, "A Writer's Problems with 'He' and 'Man,'" *Des Moines Tribune,* Mar. 30, 1977, p. 15.

4. William Strunk and E. B. White, *The Elements of Style,* 3rd ed. (New York: Macmillan, 1979), pp. 60–61.

5. William Strunk and E. B. White, *The Elements of Style,* 4th ed. (Needham Heights, MA: Allyn and Bacon, 2000), p. 60.

6. Representation of the People Act, 1832 2 & 3 Will. IV c. 45; emphasis added.

7. Representation of the People Act, 1867 30 & 31 Vict. c. 102.

8. An act to shorten the language of bills used in Parliament, 1850, 13 Victoria ch. 21, sec. 4, also called Lord Brougham's Act, or the Act of Interpretation. For twenty years or more, a number of individual British laws had included a "*man* means 'woman' too" provision, and the goal of the Interpretation Act was to eliminate the need for such specific definition in future bills. A 1978 revision made the gendered pronouns reciprocal: masculines would include feminines, and feminines, masculines. Interpretation Act of 1978, ch. 30, sec. 6, https://www.legislation.gov.uk/ukpga/1978/30/section/6.

9. Hansard, *House of Commons Debates,* May 20, 1867, vol. 187 cc. 779–852.

10. Hansard, *House of Commons Debates,* Mar. 25, 1867, vol. 186 c. 467, http://hansard.millbanksystems.com/commons/1867/mar/25/question; emphasis added.

11. Chisolm Anstey, "Women Voters," Revising Barrister's Court for the Borough of Finsbury, Sept. 23, 1868, in *Law Magazine and Law Review* 26 (1869): 121–

40. The revising barrister was appointed by a judge to review cases involving voter qualifications.

12. *Chorlton v. Lings, Court of Common Pleas Law Reports,* Nov. 9, 1868, p. 388.

13. "Prohibitory Liquor Law," *Buffalo Morning Express,* Jan. 27, 1854, p. 2. This instance of legal reciprocity in pronoun reference, where the masculine includes the feminine, and the feminine, the masculine, is rarely found before the revised British Interpretation Act of 1978. https://www.legislation.gov .uk/ukpga/1978/30.

14. "An Act Imposing Taxes on Distilled Spirits and Tobacco, and for Other Purposes," U.S. Statutes at Large, Ch. CLXXXVI § 104. 40th Congress, July 20, 1868.

15. "An Act prescribing the Form of the Enacting and Resolving Clauses of Acts and Resolutions of Congress, and Rules for the Construction Thereof," 41st Congress, Session III, ch. 71, sec. 2; now part of 1 U.S.C. 1.1.

16. "Woman's Eligibility to Office," *Chicago Tribune,* Apr. 4, 1869, p. 2.

17. *North-Eastern Daily Gazette,* May 23, 1889, p. 2.

18. *Woodhull and Claflin's Weekly,* Apr. 8, 1871, pp. 6–7.

19. Susan B. Anthony, "Is it a Crime for a Citizen of the United States to Vote?" Apr. 3, 1873, http://voicesofdemocracy.umd.edu/anthony-is-it-a-crime -speech-text/, from Ann D. Gordon, ed., *The Selected Papers of Elizabeth Cady Stanton and Susan B. Anthony, Volume II: An Aristocracy of Sex, 1866–1873* (New Brunswick, NJ: Rutgers Univ. Press, 2000).

20. "Woman Suffrage," Annual Meeting of the Illinois Woman Suffrage Association, *Bloomington Pantograph,* Feb. 14, 1872, p. 4.

21. Elizabeth Cady Stanton, *The Woman's Bible* (New York, 1895), p. 74. Stanton made similar comments in explaining Deuteronomy, p. 127: "We are tried in the courts, imprisoned and hung as 'he,' 'him' or 'his,' though denied the privileges of citizenship, because the masculine pronouns apply only to disabilities."

22. Anna Johnson, "The Last Day of Registry," *New York Tribune,* Oct. 26, 1888, p. 4.

23. "Address of the President," *Boston Investigator,* Oct. 5, 1881, p. 3.

24. Equal Franchise Act, 1928, 18 & 19 George 5 c. 12.

25. William Cunningham Glen, *The Summary Jurisdiction Acts, 1848–1884* (1887), p. 325.

26. "A Salutary Prosecution," *Portsmouth Times and Naval Gazette,* November 9, 1867, p. 7.

27. Agatha Christie, *The A.B.C. Murders* (London: Collins, and New York: Dodd, Mead, 1936; rpt. New York: Berkley, 1991, p. 115). Poirot uses singular *they* in this scene in the 2018 BBC production, which takes many liberties with Christie's language and her plot.

28. "The Citation Was Correct," *Boston Daily Advertiser,* Mar. 4, 1896, p. 2.

29. "Discrimination," *Iola Daily Index* (KS), May 3, 1909, p. 5.

30. *The Lincoln, Rutland and Stamford Mercury* (Stamford, England), Oct. 4, 1867, p. 3.

31. "Justice Frederickson: Can't Sit in My Court," *Los Angeles Times,* Oct. 24, 1911, p. 26.

32. "Illinois Women Declared Eligible for Jury Service," *Atlanta Constitution,* July 12, 1925, p. 16.

33. *Carrow v. State,* in *Reports of Cases Argued before the Supreme Court of New Jersey,* vol. 96, Mar. 1921, p. 155.

34. Texas Constitution of 1876, art. 5, sec. 13, https://tarltonapps.law.utexas.edu/constitutions/texas1876/a5; emphasis added.

35. "Women, Seeking Jury Service, Must Amend U.S. [*sic*] Constitution, Judge Rules," *El Paso Times,* Nov. 3, 1921, p. 12. The body of the article makes clear that the ruling concerned the *state* constitution.

36. Chris Daniel, "Women Were Kept Off Texas Juries until 1954," *Houston Chronicle,* July 31, 2014.

37. "Strive to Save Mrs. Nitti by Legal Loophole: Statute Says 'He,' not Woman," *Chicago Daily Tribune,* July 28, 1923, p. 3. Nitti was also known as Sabella Nitti Crudelle. A similar defense in a 1931 New Jersey murder case also failed, though defendant Hattie Evans's death sentence was eventually commuted to life imprisonment. "Pronoun to Save Mrs. Evans' Life, Counsel Believes," *Asbury Park Press* (NJ), June 27, 1931, pp. 1, 2.

38. Elizabeth A. Hall, "Grammar and Law," *Indianapolis News,* Feb. 14, 1934, p. 6.

39. "Women Priests Sympathizer Guilty," *Baltimore Sun,* June 21, 1975, p. 5.

40. Lysander Spooner, *The Unconstitutionality of Slavery* (Boston, 1845), p. 117n.

41. Wendell Phillips, "The Constitution and Slavery," *The Liberator,* Aug. 29, 1845, p. 139. The US Supreme Court later formalized this in *United States v. Verdugo-Urquidez,* 494 U.S. 259 (1990), ruling that a word in the Constitution must have the same meaning throughout the document.

42. Lysander Spooner, "Reply to Wendell Phillips," *The Liberator,* Sept. 5, 1845, p. 36.

43. Hansard, House of Commons Debate, June 16, 1870, vol. 202, ch. 259, https://api.parliament.uk/historic-hansard/commons/1870/jun/16/question.

44. "Is She Eligible?" *Topeka Daily Capital,* Apr. 20, 1888, p. 8.

45. *Idaho Daily Statesman* (Boise), Feb. 8, 1897, p. 2.

46. "Women Stenographers," *New York Evening World,* July 7, 1888, p. 2.

47. Hollis W. Field, "Paper Box Makers Become Human Machines," *Chicago Tribune,* May 23, 1909, p. 3.

48. "Women as Lawyers," *Wisconsin State Journal,* Apr. 22, 1879, p. 4. This time, Ryan was not involved in Goodell's admission.
49. "Mrs. Lockwood in Maryland," *New York Times,* May 11, 1881, p. 1. Sec. 6 of the Maryland code contained the *he*-means-*she* provision.
50. "Woman Not a Person," *The Inter-Ocean,* Apr. 18, 1885, p. 11.
51. "Barred from the Bar: Women Cannot Practice Law in Maryland," *Frederick News* (MD), Nov. 22, 1901, p. 3. New Jersey courts had made a similar ruling, and in 1895 the New Jersey legislature passed a law permitting women to be lawyers. But the pronoun *he* kept them ineligible to serve on school boards. "Women Are Not Eligible," *Montclair Times* (NJ), Apr. 6, 1895, p. 3.
52. "Women Chosen Truant Officers," Chicago *Daily Tribune,* June 21, 1903, p. 38.
53. *Bebb v. Law Society,* Division of the Chancery, 1913 B. 305 (1914), pp. 286–99, http://ww3.lawschool.cornell.edu/AvonResources/Bebb-v-Law-Society.pdf.
54. L. F. Nettlefold, "Women and Aviation," *The Common Cause,* Jan. 3, 1919, pp. 453–54.
55. "Science of Teaching," *Lewisburg Chronicle* (PA), Sept. 26, 1873, p. 1.
56. "She," *The Standard* (Concord, NC), Oct. 12, 1888, p. 3.
57. "Why Men Do Not Study Music," *Springfield Sunday Republican* (MA), Jan. 24, 1897, p. 13.
58. Texas Revised Statutes, 1879, Title LIX, ch. 4, p. 455.
59. "The Abolition of Grammar," *New York Times,* Feb. 25, 1879, p. 4.
60. "Mrs. Baxter's Eligibility," *St. Louis Post-Dispatch,* Nov. 17, 1890, p. 4.
61. "Wyoming. A New Star Will Soon be Added to the Old Flag of the Nation," *Boston Daily Journal,* June 28, 1890, p. 6.
62. "The Constitution Says 'He,'" *New Orleans Daily Picayune,* Nov. 25, 1892, p. 4. Male writers commonly invoked the worthiness of the grammatical genders by smirking that the masculine pronoun "embraces" the feminine.
63. "No Such Restrictions," *Pittsburgh Dispatch,* Nov. 24, 1892, p. 4.
64. *Nebraska State Journal,* Nov. 19, 1893, p. 12.
65. *Cincinnati Enquirer,* July 17, 1906, p. 3.
66. "A Woman Representative," *Davenport Daily Times* (IA), July 24, 1909, p. 3. The Constitution also requires representatives to be at least twenty-five years old.
67. "A Congresswoman?" *Des Moines Daily Tribune,* July 27, 1909, p. 4.
68. "Women's Eligibility as Candidates for Legislature," *Baltimore Sun,* Oct. 11, 1909, p. 4.
69. "Thinks Her Ineligible," *Baltimore Sun,* Oct. 11, 1909, p. 14.
70. "Can 'She' Be 'He', a Congressman, and Be Woman?" *Minneapolis Star Tribune,* Nov. 13, 1916, p. 1.

71. Constitutionalist, "Ineligibility of Miss Rankin," *Philadelphia Evening Public Ledger,* Dec. 20, 1916, p. 12.

72. "Argue That 'He' in Constitution Might Bar Miss Rankin from House," *Washington Post,* Nov. 12, 1916, p. 6.

73. "The Woman Congressman," *Oakland Tribune* (CA), Dec. 2, 1916, p. 8.

74. "Dutton Says 'He' Takes Congress out of Congresswoman," *Woodland Daily Democrat* (CA), Nov. 21, 1916. Dutton's objection to women in Congress might be connected to the fact that, in 1891, Mrs. J. W. Dutton, of the Oakland Nationalist Club, petitioned the state legislature "to grant equal rights in suffrage, irrespective of sex."

75. "Miss Jeanette Rankin's Seat in Congress Does Not Appear to Be In Jeopardy," *Woodland Daily Democrat,* Nov. 21, 1916, p. 2.

76. "A Common Gender," *Marshalltown Evening Times-Republican* (IA), Nov. 23, 1916, p. 6, citing the *Minneapolis Journal.*

77. *Nebraska State Journal,* Dec. 1, 1916, p. 8.

78. "His Dilemma about Her," *Morning Oregonian* (Portland), Nov. 26, 1916, p. 12. We'll consider the pronoun *thon* in more detail in the next chapter.

79. "Colorado's Woman Solons," *Centralia Enterprise and Tribune* (WI), Jan. 26, 1895, p. 4.

80. "Deny Law Bars Office to Women," *Washington Post,* Feb. 26, 1921, p. 3.

81. "Women 'as Good' as Men—Officially," *Baltimore Sun,* Aug. 30, 1937, p. 30.

82. "The Pronouns Mixed," *Jeffersonian Democrat* (Clarendon, OH), July 15, 1864, p. 4; rpt. from the *Springfield Republican.*

83. "Wanted—a Pronoun," *Somerset Herald* (PA), Dec. 29, 1875, p. 1.

84. Fogy, "Hotch-Potch," *Freemont Weekly Journal* (OH), Dec. 29, 1871, p. 1. In some jurisdictions, people who could not pay their poll tax could opt to work it off repairing local highways.

85. Moses Harman, "Our Editor's Bi-weekly Letter," *Lucifer The Light-Bearer* (Topeka, KS), Nov. 15, 1895, p. 2.

86. Bertha Moore, "Influence of Language," *Lucifer The Light Bearer* (Chicago, IL), Sept. 25, 1902, p. 290.

87. William T. Miller, "Some Words Our Language Needs," *Boston Globe,* Oct. 5, 1913, p. 46.

88. "The Position of Women," *Church League for Women's Suffrage,* Sept. 1, 1914, p. 9n.

89. "A Common Pronoun," *Gulfport Daily Herald* (MS), Feb. 11, 1921, p. 2.

90. "Our Changing Language," *Arizona Republic,* Dec. 23, 1922, p. 4.

91. Philip B. Ballard, *Thought and Language* (London: Univ. of London Press, 1934), pp. 7–8; emphasis added. Ballard uses *he* to refer to grammarians, even

though his example concerns a woman coining a new pronoun. We've already seen that in 1770, Robert Baker noted the same defect in the feminine pronoun.

92. Stephen Leacock, "My Particular Aversions," *American Bookman* 1:1 (Winter 1944): 39–40.

93. W. Worthington Wells, "Word Stories," *Atlanta Constitution*, Aug. 13, 1941, p. 6.

94. Richard Albert, "Rewrite the Constitution," *Boston Globe*, Sept. 25, 2016, p. K6.

95. "Drive On for Gender-Neutral State Constitutions," *Wilkes-Barre Times Leader* (PA), May 22, 2003, p. 4.

96. James McCrimmon, *Writing with a Purpose*, 7th ed. (Boston: Houghton Mifflin, 1980), p. 455.

CHAPTER 3 • THE WORDS THAT FAILED

1. *The Semi-Weekly Eagle* (Brattleboro, VT) Jan. 1, 1852, p. 3, quoting the *Lowell Morning News*.

2. "Coin a Word," *Rocky Mountain News*, Dec. 13, 1894, p. 4.

3. "Three Women Solons," *Chicago Daily Tribune*, Jan. 12, 1895, p. 16.

4. Charles G. Worden, "A Bi-Personal Pronoun," *Rocky Mountain News*, Dec. 17, 1894, p. 4.

5. S. B. 423. *Journal of the Senate of the State of Mississippi*, 1922, pp. 889 (Mar. 14, 1922), 1175 (Mar. 24, 1922).

6. "Senator Proposes New Word Factory," *Clarion-Ledger* (Jackson, MS), Mar. 15, 1922, p. 8. See also "Senate Passes Insurance Tax Exemption Bill," *Clarion-Ledger* (Jackson, MS), Mar. 15, 1922, pp. 1, 5; "A New Pronoun," *Okolona Messenger* (MS), Apr. 6, 1922, p. 1. Ellis's suffrage bill, S. B. 115, also failed, though the state's women were already enfranchised by the 19th Amendment. Although Northern suffragists were often abolitionists as well, women's suffrage in Mississippi and other southern states was a white supremacist tactic intended to dilute and suppress the African American vote.

7. "A New Pronoun," *Okolona Messenger*, Apr. 6, 1922, p. 1.

8. *Journal and Debates 1st–266th Day* (Jefferson City, MO: Hugh Stephens Press, 1922–23), vol. 4, Nov. 1, 1922, pp. 3–5. See also " 'Idn' Is Proposed as New Legal Word," *The Christian Science Monitor*, Dec. 6, 1922, p. 11.

9. "Folk Lore," *Nebraska State Journal*, Dec. 12, 1922, p. 6.

10. A. N. Gossett, "That Word *Idn*," *Christian Science Monitor*, Feb. 8, 1923, p. 12.

11. Francis Augustus Brewster, *English Grammar . . . Simplicity and Conciseness Combined* (Brooklyn: Carter & Foster, 1841), p. 19.

12. "The Missing Word," *Memphis Daily Appeal,* Nov. 10, 1878, p. 2, referencing an earlier pronoun discussion in the *Peoria Daily Tribune.*

13. *Brooklyn Union,* Nov. 29, 1878, p. 2.

14. "Suggests 'E' as Pronoun," *Wilkes-Barre Times Leader,* Feb. 20, 1912, p. 13.

15. Donald G. MacKay, "Psychology, Prescriptive Grammar and the Pronoun Problem," *American Psychologist,* 35(5): 444–49. In addition to studying whether test subjects recognized the gender reference when using generic *he, they, E,* and *tey,* MacKay used *E, Es,* and *Eself* in a ten-week class at UCLA (personal communication). See also Werner Low, "A Solution to the He/She Dilemma," *Washington Post,* Feb. 20, 1977, p. C6.

16. "He and She Headed, Ir, for Trouble," *Arizona Republic* May 29, 1978, pp. 1, 14. Versions of this UPI story ran in other newspapers in May and June.

17. *New York Commercial Advertiser,* Aug. 7, 1884, p. 3.

18. Philologus, "An Epicene Personal Pronoun Needed," in "Notes and Queries," *The Ladies' Repository,* July 1864), p. 439. The grammar mongers bestriding education might have failed "Philologus," whose name means 'word lover,' for linking *neither* with *three* pronouns, since technically *neither* should only refer to *two.*

19. J. W. L., "An Epicene Pronoun," *The Ladies' Repository,* Sept. 1864 (vol. 24, no. 9), p. 567.

20. Richard Grant White, "Words and Their Uses," *The Galaxy,* Aug. 1868, pp. 241–44.

21. "Careless Use of Pronouns," *Boston Recorder,* Sept. 24, 1868, p. 310.

22. "Various," *Boston Recorder,* Oct. 22, 1868, p. 342.

23. "Table Talk," *Appletons' Journal,* Aug. 21, 1869, p. 26. *Appletons'* comments are only implicitly antifeminist, but suggesting that if women want a pronoun, they should coin it, implies that gender-neutral language is women's work, not men's.

24. "Editor's Table," *Appletons' Journal,* Apr. 10, 1875 (vol. 13, no. 316), pp. 468–69.

25. "Courant Notes," *Hartford Daily Courant,* Aug. 8, 1869, p. 2. (The date appears out of sync with the *Appletons'* article because *Appletons'* published in advance.)

26. "Here's Your Pronoun," *Cincinnati Enquirer,* Dec. 11, 1878, p. 4.

27. "Contributors' Club," *The Atlantic Monthly,* Mar. 1879 (vol. 43, no. 257), p. 397.

28. Double Z, letter, "An Esthetic Language," *The Inter-Ocean* (Chicago), Sept. 22, 1884, p. 5.

29. "'Um' New Personal Pronoun to Denote Either of Genders," *Wichita Daily Eagle,* Mar. 20, 1910, p. 11.

30. "Let's Invent a Language," *Cincinnati Enquirer,* Dec. 7, 1877, p. 4.

31. Unsigned article, *Atlanta Constitution,* Sept. 13, 1884, p. 4.

32. John W. Dozier, "A New Pronoun," letter, *Atlanta Constitution*, Sept. 20, 1884, p. 4.

33. C. M. Arnold, "A New Word Needed," *Frank Leslie's Illustrated Newspaper* (New York), Dec. 27, 1884, p. 315.

34. Gregory Hynes, "See?" *Liverpool Echo*, Sept. 21, 1948; cited by H. L. Mencken (*American Language*, supplement 2, 1948, p. 370).

35. William Cowan, of the Department of Linguistics, Carleton University (Ottawa), *Times Two* 6 (May 24, 1973).

36. H. R. Lee of Alexandria, Virginia, *Forbes*, Aug. 15, 1975 (116), p. 86.

37. "Speech Without Sex," *Wausau Daily Herald* (WI), Mar. 23, 1982, p. 4.

38. "Contributors' Club: We Want a New Pronoun," *The Atlantic Monthly*, Nov. 1878, pp. 260–62.

39. Alice M. Heath, "The New Pronoun," *Holt County* (MO) *Sentinel*, Jan. 31, 1879, p. 3.

40. Ibid.; emphasis added.

41. "The Needed common pronoun," *Weekly Irish Times*, July 26, 1890, p. 3.

42. William D. Armes, "Wanted—a New Pronoun," *The Literary World*, June 14, 1884, p. 199.

43. Charles Crozat Converse, "A New Pronoun," *The Critic*, Aug. 2, 1884, p. 55.

44. *Boston Globe*, Aug. 7, 1884, p. 2.

45. H. L. Mencken, *The American Language*, 2nd ed. (New York: Knopf, 1921), p. 192n.

46. *Winfield Courier* (KS), Mar. 12, 1885, p. 1. Presumably, the teachers taught *thon*, and either the reporter or an editor got it wrong.

47. B. D. W., "Answers to Questions," *Nebraska State-Journal* (Lincoln), Aug. 6, 1927, p. 4.

48. O. P. Hurford, *The Critic*, Aug. 16, 1884, p. 79.

49. Francis H. Williams, *The Critic*, Aug. 16, 1884, p. 80.

50. J. H. W., *The Critic*, Sept. 13, 1884, p. 131.

51. "Thon," *The Critic*, Nov. 1, 1884, p. 210.

52. Peck's Sun, "Tinkering the English Language," *Springfield Globe-Republic* (OH), Mar. 25, 1885 p. 2.

53. "New Pronoun for the New Woman," *Des Moines Register*, Apr. 19, 1900, p. 4.

54. "Proposing a New Gender," *Baltimore Sun*, Jan. 10, 1910, p. 4.

55. "Personal and General Notes," *The Daily Picayune* (New Orleans, LA), May 26, 1884, p. 1.

56. Z., "Questions, no. 824," *The Critic*, Nov. 8, 1884, p. 228.

57. *Ms.* is first recorded in the *Springfield Republican* (MA), Nov. 10, 1901, p. 4.

58. Edgar A. Stevens, "The Missing Word," *The Current*, Aug. 30, 1884, p. 137. For more on legislating pronouns, see Chapter 3, "The Politics of *He*."

59. Emma Carleton, "The Missing Word," *The Current*, Sept. 20, 1884, p. 186.

60. *The New Era* (Humeston, IA), Feb 24, 1887, p. 3.

61. "How Thon Would Work," *Bristol Herald* (VT), Nov. 17, 1910, p. 7, citing an article in Lippincott's.

62. Henry G. Williams, *Outlines of Psychology*, 3rd ed. (Syracuse, NY: C. W. Bardeen), p. 5n. Williams did not credit Converse with the new word, prompting some readers to assume that Williams coined the word thonself.

63. Eugene O. Lewis, "The New Pronoun," *Hillsboro News-Herald* (OH), June 20, 1895, p. 1; emphasis added.

64. *Funk & Wagnalls Standard Dictionary of the English Language,* vol. 2, 1897.

65. *Century Dictionary,* vol. 12 (New York: The Century Co., 1909), supplement, pt. 2. The citation for *thon* is from W. J. McGee, "Primitive Numbers," *Report of the Bureau of American Ethnology,* 1897–98, pt. 2, p. 831.

66. Caldwell Titcomb, "He, She, and Thon," *New York Times Magazine*, Oct. 2, 1955, p. SM6; letter, *New York Magazine*, Jan. 24, 1972, p. 6; see also Tom Wicker, "More about He/She and Thon," *New York Times*, May 14, 1978, p. E19. A prolific writer, Titcomb also championed US civil rights and actively opposed South African apartheid.

67. M. S. R., *The Current,* Nov. 22, 1884, p. 334.

68. Wolstan Dixey, "Wanted—a New Pronoun?" *The Literary World*, June 28, 1884, p. 213.

69. Charles P. Sherman, "Wanted—a New Pronoun," *The Literary World*, Sept. 6, 1884, p. 294.

70. Charles Dietz, "Application in Behalf of a New Pronoun," *New York Sun,* Sept. 8, 1884, p. 2.

71. "Wanted, a Word," *Sacramento Record-Union* (CA), Sept. 10, 1884, p. 2. Most blenders put the masculine part of the pronoun first.

72. Suggester, "The New Pronoun," *Atlanta Constitution*, Sept. 24, 1884, p. 4.

73. George Washington Eveleth, "The Lacking Word," *The Current,* Mar. 28, 1885, p. 199.

74. *Montgomery Advertiser,* June 11, 1886, p. 2. Some pronoun coinages were intended as jokes; since this one yields the paradigm *ho, hum,* it could have been suggested in fun.

75. "A New Pronoun Suggested," *Baltimore Sun*, Dec. 13, 1886, p. 6.

76. "The Needed Common Pronoun," *Weekly Irish Times*, July 26, 1890, p. 3; rpt. in *The Rocky Mountain News* (Denver, CO), Aug. 3, 1890, p. 19.

77. "To Indicate the Common Gender," *Chicago Daily Tribune,* Sept. 27, 1890, p. 7.

78. "An Epicene Pronoun," *Louisville Courier Journal,* May 10, 1900, p. 4.

79. "Chivalry and the Pronoun," *The St. Paul Globe,* Jan. 28, 1903, p. 4.

80. E. P. Jots, "Let Each One Choose for H-i-e-r-self," *Baltimore Sun,* Feb. 12, 1910, p. 5.

81. "Mrs. Ella Young Invents Pronoun," *Chicago Tribune,* Jan. 7, 1912, sec. 1, p. 7.

82. Fred S. Pond, "The Personal Pronoun," *Mansfield News-Journal* (OH), Mar. 21, 1911, p. 4. Pond used the dash in presenting his new paradigm, but not in the sample sentences he gave to illustrate the new forms. As mentioned in the note above, Young used apostrophes instead, and that may be her only real contribution to the invented words, which were printed in *Funk & Wagnalls* solid, with no internal punctuation.

83. "Wanted: A Duo-Personal Pronoun," *New York Sun,* Feb. 11, 1912, p. 15; emphasis added. Young's use of *and myself* suggests that she herself was not comfortable with the existing pronoun paradigm.

84. Isaac K. Funk, "Use of 'Himer' and 'Hiser,'" *New York Times,* Jan. 12, 1912, p. 12.

85. "Opposes 'Him'er' Pronoun," *St. Louis Globe-Democrat,* Jan. 9, 1912, p. 6.

86. "Blewett Not in Favor of He'er, His'er or Him'er," *St. Louis Post-Dispatch,* Jan 8, 1912, p. 14.

87. "An Enlargement of English," *St. Louis Globe-Democrat,* Jan. 9, 1912, p. 8.

88. *New York Tribune,* Jan. 8, 1912, p. 6.

89. *Topeka State Journal* (KS), Jan. 10, 1912, p. 4.

90. Reprinted as "Views with Alarm," *University Daily Kansan,* Jan. 17, 1912, p. 2. Indiana University was one of the first public colleges to admit women, in 1867, but in this *Daily Student* complaint, *we* included only men.

91. "Aristocratic Pronouns," *University Missourian,* Feb. 1, 1912, p. 4.

92. Thomas W. Gilmer, "New Pronoun Needed," *Sunday Star* (Washington, DC), Nov. 23, 1919, p. 3.

93. George Harvey, "'Man' Includes Women," *Harper's Weekly,* Jan. 27, 1912, p. 5.

94. Frank H. Vizetelly, 1915, *Essentials of English Speech and Literature* (New York and London: Funk & Wagnalls), p. 154.

95. James C. Fernald, *Expressive English,* 2nd ed. (New York: Funk & Wagnalls, 1919), pp. 255–57.

96. A. E. Schuyler, "Another Common Gender Pronoun Offered," *Charlevoix (Michigan) County Herald,* Apr. 27, 1912, p. 2.

97. "'Hir' Will Be the Bee's Word for 'He or She,'" *Sacramento Bee,* Aug. 14, 1920, p. 28.

98. "Now as a Reformer!" *Oakland Tribune* (CA), Aug. 20, 1920, p. 16.

99. "A Grammatical Dilemma," *Nebraska State Journal* (Lincoln, NE), Nov. 2, 1926, p. 4.

100. Thomas W. Gilmer, "New Pronouns Needed," *Sunday Star* (Washington, DC), Nov. 23, 1919, p. 3.

101. G. A. Kratzer, "Important Truth," *The Llano Colonist* (Leesville, LA), Aug. 26, 1922, p. 6. Kratzer uses these compound forms to refer to God.

102. "A Common Gender Pronoun," *Lincoln Journal Star*, June 25, 1924, p. 12, attributes the suggestion to a correspondent named Phil Ology.

103. "The New American Language," *The Forum* 77 (1927): 754.

104. Credited to James F. Morton, of the Paterson, New Jersey, Museum, 1934; H. L. Mencken, *American Language,* supplement 2 (New York: Knopf, 1948), p. 370.

105. Charles W. Bush, "Likings and Aversions," *Wilmington News Journal* (DE), Mar. 16, 1929, p. 7.

106. W. E. Fohl, "Che, Chis, Chim," *Time Magazine*, Mar. 10, 1930, p. 6.

107. "The Post Impressionist," *Washington Post*, Aug. 20, 1935, p. 6.

108. Jan Verley Archer, "Use New Pronouns," *Media Report to Women* vol. 3, no. 1 (Jan. 1975): 12.

109. Buwei Yang Chao, *How to Cook and Eat in Chinese* (New York: Vintage, Random House, 3rd ed., 1963, rpt. 1972), xxiv.

110. Annette A. Matthews, "His or Her," *The Times* (London), Apr. 25, 1929, p. 17.

111. A. A. Milne, *The Christopher Robin Birthday Book* (London: Methuen, 1930; New York: Dutton, 1931), pp. vi–vii.

112. "New Words," *Manchester Guardian,* Oct. 26, 1932, p. 18.

113. H. L. Mencken, *The American Language*, 4th ed. (New York: Knopf, 1936), p. 460n.

114. Mont Follick, *The Influence of English* (London: Williams and Norgate, 1934), pp. 198–99. Follick revised all the pronouns with an equal lack of success.

115. Donald K. Darnell and Wayne Brockriede, *Persons Communicating* (Englewood Cliffs, NJ: Prentice-Hall, 1976), 148.

116. See the Chronology of Gender-Neutral and Nonbinary Pronouns for citations documenting these and other pronouns mentioned only in passing.

117. Casey Miller and Kate Swift, "Desexing the Language," *Ms. Magazine,* preview issue, Spring, 1972; *Ms.* appeared as an insert in *New York Magazine*, Dec. 21, 1971, pp. 103–4, and began publishing independently in mid-1972.

118. Don Rickter, "Unisex Pronoun," *UU World,* May 1, 1973, p. 2. The coinage date of 1971 is given by Jan Freeman, "He Said, Xe Said," *Boston Globe,* Mar. 28, 2004, p. 43. In 1989 Ron Sebring (see Chronology of Gender-Neutral and Nonbinary Pronouns) suggested *le* for God as well as for personified inanimates.

119. Dudley Glass, "Trip in Installments," *Atlanta Constitution,* Sept. 5, 1942, p. 7.

120. "Cross Word Puzzle," *Brooklyn Daily Eagle,* Dec. 29, 1930, p. 14.

CHAPTER 4 • QUEERING THE PRONOUN

1. Riki Anne Wilchins, *Read My Lips: Sexual Subversion and the End of Gender* (Ithaca, NY: Firebrand Books, 1993), p. 112.
2. Taylor Mac, *Hir* (Evanston, IL: Northwestern Univ. Press, 2015), p. 21. (First performance San Francisco, 2014.) Text in square brackets is a stage direction.
3. http://www.taylormac.org/about/.
4. Kory Stamper, "The Long, Long History—and Bright Future—of the Genderless 'They,'" *Boston Globe,* Sept. 5, 2018, https://www.bostonglobe.com/ideas/2018/09/05/the-long-long-history-and-bright-future-genderless-they/LhGIzOTm6PPKMKws8cE2SN/story.html.
5. James Anderson, "Grammatical Disquisitions," *The Bee,* Oct 10, 1792 (11), pp. 195–97.
6. Ruth Tam, "Use of Preferred Gender Pronouns Indicates Expanding Acceptance of Transgender People," *Washington Post,* Sept. 5, 2013, https://www.washingtonpost.com/lifestyle/style/use-of-preferred-gender-pronouns-indicates-expanding-acceptance-of-transgender-people/2013/09/05/25ffdb7e-1595-11e3-804b-d3a1a3a18f2c_story.html?utm_term=.a4e0b108849f.
7. Leslie Feinberg, *Stone Butch Blues* (Ithaca, NY: Firebrand Books, 1993), p. 213.
8. Kate Bornstein, *Gender Outlaw: On Men, Women and the Rest of Us* (New York and London: Routledge, 1994), p. 126.
9. Riki Anne Wilchins, *Read My Lips: Sexual Subversion and the End of Gender* (Ithaca, NY: Firebrand Books, 1993), p. 5.
10. Herbert A. Wisbey, Jr., *Pioneer Prophetess: Jemima Wilkinson, the Publick Universal Friend* (Ithaca, NY: Cornell Univ. Press, 1964), p. 25.
11. Abner Brownell, *Enthusiastical Errors, Transpired and Detected* (New London, CT, 1783; Early American Imprints, First Series, no. 17856).
12. Paul B. Moyer, *The Public Universal Friend: Jemima Wilkinson and Religious Enthusiasm in Revolutionary America* (Ithaca, NY: Cornell Univ. Press, 2015), p. 100.
13. Virginia Woolf, *Orlando: A Biography* (London, 1928; rpt. New York: Harcourt Brace, 1992), p. 138.
14. Virginia Woolf, *Orlando: The Original Holograph Draft,* transcribed and edited by Stuart Nelson Clarke (London: S. N. Clarke, 1993), p. 109.
15. Ben White, "Ex-GI Becomes Blonde Beauty," *New York Daily News,* Dec. 1, 1952, pp. 1, 3, 10.
16. "Nonbinary/GenderQueer Survey 2017." It's important to note that the preferences indicated in such surveys don't always reflect actual usage. https://docs.google.com/document/d/1Z_qOkiSol1fs8tLnTPfOg4HQtTXxvAVgzPqgX0tuXDo/edit, accessed Aug. 12, 2018.

17. Erika D. Smith, "'They' Is Here, So Get Used to It," *Danville News* (PA), Apr. 10, 2017, p. A5.

18. "More Genders on Tinder Are Rolling Out in the U.S., U.K. and Canada," Nov. 15, 2016, https://blog.gotinder.com/genders/; "Share Your Pronouns on Your OkCupid Profile," Sept. 10, 2018, https://theblog.okcupid.com/share-your -pronouns-on-your-okcupid-profile-16b307a227bb.

19. "How to Starfriends Alpha: Pronouns," https://strfrnds.tumblr.com/post /156950927612/how-to-starfriends-alpha-pronouns.

20. Gender Recognition Act of 2004, c. 7, schedule 5, pp. 30–32; Ralph Palmer, Lord Lucas, speaking to the House of Lords, June 25, 2018, https://hansard .parliament.uk/lords/2018-06-25/debates/A1C1FAD6-81A9-405D-B451 -20890306A6F1/LegislationGenderedPronouns.

21. Social Security Administration, "Changing Numident Data for Reasons Other Than Name Change," https://secure.ssa.gov/poms.nsf/lnx/0110212200.

22. U.S. Department of State, Form DS-11, "U.S. Passport Application," https:// eforms.state.gov/Forms/ds11.pdf.

23. Steve Kleinedler, @Skleinedler, tweet, Aug. 28, 2018, 10:41 p.m.

24. *Jones v. Bon Appetit Management Co.*, No. 1402-01454, Multnomah Circuit Court, dismissed July 23, 2014.

25. *Jameson v. U.S. Postal Service*, EEOC Appeal No. 0120130992 (May 21, 2013).

26. *Tamara Lusardi v. John H. McHugh, Secretary of the Army*, appeal no. EEOC Appeal No. 0120133395 (Mar. 27, 2015), https://www.eeoc.gov/ decisions/0120133395.txt.

27. *Anny May Stevens v. Max Williams et al.*, 05-CV-1790-ST, U.S. District Court, Oregon, decided Mar. 27, 2008.

28. *Giraldo v. California Department of Corrections and Rehabilitation*, 2007. No. A119046 California Court of Appeal, First District, Division 2.

29. *Diamond v. Owens, et al.*, 5:15-CV-00050, U.S. District Court, Middle District of Georgia, filed Feb. 19, 2015; dismissed, June 4, 2015; emphasis added.

30. Deborah Sontag, "Judge Denies Transgender Inmate's Request for Transfer," *New York Times*, Apr. 20, 2015, https://www.nytimes.com/2015/04/21/us/ judge-denies-ashley-diamonds-a-transgender-inmate-request-for-transfer.htm l?action=click&module=RelatedCoverage&pgtype=Article&region=Footer.

31. *United States v. PFC Bradley E. Manning (nka Chelsea E. Manning)*, Army 20130739, U.S. Army Court of Criminal Appeals, Mar. 4, 2015.

32. *Matal v. Tam* 582 U.S. _____ (2017). *Matal* invalidated a US law denying trademark status to products or entities with disparaging names. Holmes wrote his dissent in *United States v. Schwimmer* 279 US 644, 655 (1929).

33. *Oger v. Whatcott* (No. 7), 2019 BCHRT 58.

34. "UK Home Office: It's Not Just Offensive. It's an Offence." Nov. 1, 2018, https://www.bestadsontv.com/ad/98270/UK-Home-Office-Its-not-Just-Offensive-Its-an-Offence-1.

35. Toby Young, "No, of course 'misgendering' a trans person shouldn't be a crime," *The Telegraph*, March 23, 2019.

36. Catherine E. Lhamon and Vanita Gupta, "Dear Colleague Letter: Transgender Students. USDOJ Office of Civil Rights and USDOE Office of Civil Rights, May 13, 2016, https://www2.ed.gov/about/offices/list/ocr/letters/colleague-201605-title-ix-transgender.pdf.

37. Sandra Battle and T. E. Wheeler II, "Dear Colleague Letter on Transgender Students," Department of Education and Department of Justice, Feb. 22, 2017, https://www2.ed.gov/about/offices/list/ocr/letters/colleague-201702-title-ix.pdf.

38. Chicago Public Schools, "Guidelines Regarding the Support of Trans-gender and Gender Nonconforming Students," 2016, https://cps.edu/SiteCollectionDocuments/TL_TransGenderNonconformingStudents_Guidelines.pdf.

39. Trans Student Educational Resources, "Pronouns 101," http://www.transstudent.org/pronouns101/.

40. "Pronoun Dos and Don'ts," anonymous poster, The Station Theater, Urbana, IL, November 2018.

41. Ontario Human Rights Commission, "Questions and Answers about Gender Identity and Pronouns," http://www.ohrc.on.ca/en/questions-and-answers-about-gender-identity-and-pronouns.

42. Abigail Shrier, "The Transgender Language War," *Wall Street Journal*, Aug. 29, 2018, https://www.wsj.com/articles/the-transgender-language-war-1535582272.

43. In *West Virginia Board of Education v. Barnette*, 319 U.S. 624 (1943), the Supreme Court held that Jehovah's Witnesses may not be required to say the Pledge of Allegiance. That landmark decision established the First Amend-ment protection against being forced to say something that violates one's beliefs.

44. See, for example, the brief account by Prof. Anne Fausto-Sterling, "Why Sex Is Not Binary," *New York Times*, Oct. 25, 2018, https://www.nytimes.com/2018/10/25/opinion/sex-biology-binary.html.

45. In a well-publicized 2018 case, *Masterpiece Cakeshop v. Colorado Civil Rights Commission* (16-111, 2018), a baker claimed that a Colorado antidiscrimina-tion law requiring him to bake a wedding cake for a same-sex couple compelled speech that violated his constitutional right to practice his religion. The case

was sent back to the lower court on a technicality, and the question remains unsettled.

46. Samantha Schmidt, "United Becomes First US Airline to Offer Nonbinary Gender Booking Options—Including 'Mx,'" *Washington Post,* Mar. 22, 2019, https://www.washingtonpost.com/dc-md-va/2019/03/22/united-becomes -first-us-airline-offer-non-binary-gender-booking-options-including -mx/?utm_term=.2b96dbda091e.

47. Andrew R. Flores, Jody L. Herman, Gary J. Gates, and Taylor N. T. Brown, "How Many Adults Identify as Transgender in the United States?" Report of the Williams Institute, UCLA College of Law, June 2016, http://williamsinstitute.law .ucla.edu/wp-content/uploads/How-Many-Adults-Identify-as-Transgender -in-the-United-States.pdf.

CHAPTER 5 • THE MISSING WORD IS *THEY*

1. Lindley Murray, *English Grammar, Adapted to the Different Classes of Learners* (York, UK, 1795), p. 96; emphasis in the original. See also Ann Bodine, "Androcentrism in Prescriptive Grammar: Singular 'They', Sex-Indefinite 'He', and 'He or She,'" *Language in Society* 4 (1975): 129–46.

2. Lorraine Berry, "'They': The Singular Pronoun that Could Solve Sexism in English," *The Guardian,* May 5, 2016, https://www.theguardian.com/books/ booksblog/2016/may/05/they-the-singular-pronoun-that-could-solve -sexism-in-english.

3. Virginia Woolf, *A Room of One's Own* (Chichester, UK: John Wiley & Sons, [1929] 2015), p. 75; emphasis added. Woolf insists here that the politics of gender should be left off the page, but of course, even though she conflates the genders here, as she did in *Orlando,* Woolf's writing is all about the politics of gender.

4. Charles Dickens, *The Posthumous Papers of the Pickwick Club* (London, 1837; rpt. 1904), p. 294; emphasis added.

5. Mrs. Emma D. E. N. Southworth, *Eudora; Or, The False Princess, New York Ledger,* Sept. 28, 1861, p. 7.

6. Michael M. Grynbaum, "Anonymous Op-Ed in New York Times Causes a Stir Online and in the White House," *New York Times,* Sept. 4, 2018, https:// www.nytimes.com/2018/09/05/business/media/new-york-times-trump -anonymous.html; emphasis added.

7. "New Words," *New York Mercury and Weekly Journal of Commerce,* Jan. 31, 1839, p. 4.

8. *The Semi-Weekly Eagle* (Brattleboro, VT), Jan. 1, 1852, p. 3.

9. Richard Whately, "Anomalies in Language," Mar. 1862, in *Miscellaneous*

Remains from the Commonplace Book of Richard Whately, D.D., Late Archbishop of Dublin. Ed. Miss E. J. Whately (London: 1864), p. 219.

10. *Appletons' Journal,* Apr. 10, 1875 (vol. 13, no. 316), pp. 368–69.

11. "The New Pronoun," *New Hampshire Sentinel* (Keene), May 27, 1875, p. 1.

12. Richard Grant White, "Words and Their Uses," *The Galaxy,* Aug. 1868, pp. 241–44; emphasis added.

13. Frederick, "A Question of Syntax," *Boston Globe,* Nov. 19, 1887, p. 4.

14. "The New Pronoun," *Atlanta Constitution,* Feb. 25, 1885, p. 4.

15. "A Chicago Grammarian," *Atlanta Constitution,* Mar. 21, 1885, p. 4.

16. "The Epicene Pronoun," *Lincoln Republican* (Lincoln, KS), Nov. 15, 1888, p. 2.

17. *Boston Globe,* Aug. 7, 1884, p. 2.

18. J. E. Pratt, *The Critic,* Aug. 16, 1884, p. 80.

19. *New York Commercial Advertiser,* Aug. 7, 1884, p. 3.

20. *Chicago Tribune,* Apr. 24, 1886, p. 13.

21. "Whom Can We Trust?" *St. Louis Republic,* Jan. 5, 1889, p. 14; quoting the *New York Commercial Advertiser.*

22. Frederic H. Balfour, "Wanted—Another Word," *The Globe* (London), Apr. 12, 1890, p. 3.

23. Erasmus, *Weekly Irish Times,* May 1, 1897, p. 2.

24. Under "they," *New English Dictionary* (Oxford: Oxford Univ. Press, 1916).

25. James C. Fernald, *English Grammar Simplified,* 4th ed. (New York: Funk & Wagnalls, 1917), pp. 33, 54.

26. Frank H. Vizetelly, *How to Use English* (New York: Grossett and Dunlap; Funk & Wagnalls, 1932), p. 599.

27. Frank H. Vizetelly, "The Lexicographer's Easy Chair," *Literary Digest,* July 6, 1935 (120), p. 27 (Funk & Wagnalls published the journal). Vizetelly had clearly become a fan of simplified spelling as well as relaxed grammar.

28. Walter Curtis Nicholson, "Right Word in Right Place," *The Missoulian,* Jan. 16, 1939, p. 8.

29. Ursula K. Le Guin, *Steering the Craft* (Boston: Houghton Mifflin, 2015), p. 17. This book is a reprint of an earlier publication (Portland, OR: Eighth Mountain Press, 1998), which has a slightly different version of this passage.

30. "Super Bowl: Coca-Cola Represents 'Them' in Non-Binary Ad," hollywoodreporter.com, Feb. 4, 2018, https://www.hollywoodreporter.com/news/super-bowl-coca-cola-represents-binary-ad-1081767, retrieved Mar. 10, 2018. A full-page print ad repeated the diversity message, including the pronouns.

31. Alexander Bain, *A Higher English Grammar* (New York: Holt, 1879), p. 310. We'll see defenses of singular *they* by experts like Fred Newton Scott, Henry Sweet, and Otto Jespersen below.

32. "Contributors' Club," *Atlantic Monthly*, Feb. 1879 (vol. 43), p. 256.

33. Eliza Frances Andrews, "Some Grammatical Stumbling Blocks," *The Chautauquan: A Weekly Newsmagazine* (Meadville, PA), June 1896 (vol. 23, no. 3), pp. 339–43. Although progressive in her views on language, Andrews was also a white supremacist who wrote a memoir in which she insisted that before the Civil War, relatively few southerners owned slaves, and only a small percentage of those slave owners mistreated anyone. Andrews argued repeatedly that the liberated slaves had been better off before the war.

34. George Fox, *A Battle-Door for Teachers and Professors to Learn Singular & Plural* (London, 1660), p. 2. A *battle-door* is a textbook.

35. Anne Fisher, *A New Grammar, with Exercises in Bad English* (London: 1745; 3rd ed., 1753), p. 63.

36. James Anderson, "Grammatical Disquisitions," *The Bee*, Sept. 26, 1792, pp. 128–29.

37. "Grammar and the English Language," *Topeka Daily Capital*, Mar. 24, 1880, p. 2.

38. See, for example, Joe Pinsker, "The Problem with 'Hey Guys,'" *The Atlantic*, Aug. 23, 2018, https://www.theatlantic.com/family/archive/2018/08/guys-gender-neutral/568231/.

39. Julie Scelfo, "UVM Leads in Recognizing a Third Gender: Neutral," *Rutland Herald* (VT), Feb. 8, 2015, pp. A1, A4.

40. Alyson Krueger, "Bar or Bat Mitzvah? Hey, What About a Both Mitzvah?" *New York Times*, Mar. 27, 2019, https://www.nytimes.com/2019/03/27/style/gender-fluid-bar-batmitzvah.html; emphasis added.

41. *Cincinnati Enquirer*, Sept. 4, 1884, p. 4.

42. C. K. Maddox, "The New Pronoun," *Atlanta Constitution*, Sept. 26, 1884, p. 4.

43. Fred Newton Scott, "The Missing Pronoun," *The Current*, Jan. 17, 1885, pp. 43–44.

44. Otto Jespersen, *Progress in Language* (London: Sonnenschein, 1894), pp. 27–30.

45. Otto Jespersen, *Modern English Grammar on Historical Principles* (London: George Allen and Unwin, 1949), vol. 2, pp. 137–39, 495.

46. Thomas R. Lounsbury, "The Aristocracy of the Parts of Speech," *Harper's Monthly*, Feb. 1908 (116), pp. 373–79.

47. "We," *Nashville Daily American*, Feb. 28, 1886, p. 2.

48. An Epicene Pronoun," *Louisville Courier Journal*, May 10, 1900, p. 4.

49. "Devious English," *The Minneapolis Star-Tribune*, Oct. 29, 1911, p. 4.

50. Linda Critchell, "New Sex-Free Pronouns?" *Los Angeles Times*, Feb. 2, 1974, p. 32.

51. James McCrimmon, *Writing with a Purpose,* 7th ed. (Boston: Houghton Mifflin, 1980), p. 455.

52. James J. Kilpatrick, "No Neutral Pronoun for Us," *The Leaf-Chronicle* (Clarksville, TN), July 20, 1997, p. 5.

53. Theresa Novak, "Now Who Will Correct Us in Grammar and Words?" *Corvallis Gazette-Times,* Jan. 25, 2009, p. 26.

54. H. L. Mencken, "Needed Words," *The San Francisco Examiner,* Sept. 10, 1934, p. 17.

55. Henry W. Fowler, *A Dictionary of Modern English Usage* (Oxford: Clarendon Press, 1926 [1930]); under *they,* number 11; *they, them, their,* 1.

56. William Strunk, *Elements of Style* (New York: Harcourt Brace, 1920), pp. 57–58.

57. Sterling A. Leonard, *Doctrine of Correctness* (Chicago: National Council of Teachers of English, 1932), pp. xv, 104–6.

58. Casey Miller and Kate Swift, "Desexing the Language," *Ms. Magazine,* preview issue, Spring 1972; appearing as an insert in *New York Magazine,* Dec. 21, 1971, pp. 103–4.

59. Rudolph Flesch, *The ABC of Style: A Guide to Plain English* (New York, Harper and Row, 1964), p. 277.

60. Paul Roberts, *The Roberts English Series,* vol. 9 (New York: Harcourt, Brace and World, 1969), p. 49.

61. "Glossary: 'He,' " *Boston Globe,* Jan. 10, 1983, p. 14.

62. *Chicago Manual of Style,* 14th ed. (Chicago: Univ. of Chicago Press, 1993):76–7n.

63. *Chicago Manual of Style,* 16th ed. (Chicago: Univ. of Chicago Press, 2010): 5.227.

64. *Chicago Manual of Style Online,* 2017: 5.256 (http://www.chicagomanualofstyle .org/home.html).

65. *Chicago Manual of Style,* 17th ed. (Chicago: Univ. of Chicago Press, 2017): 5.48.

66. *The Associated Press Stylebook 2019* (New York: The Associated Press, 2019), p. 281.

67. Bryan A. Garner, *Garner's American Usage,* 3rd ed. (New York: Oxford Univ. Press, 2009), p. 179.

68. *American Heritage Book of English Usage* (New York: Houghton Mifflin Harcourt, 1996), p. 178.

69. *Merriam-Webster's Collegiate Dictionary,* 11th ed. (Springfield, MA: Merriam-Webster, 2003), under *they.*

70. Benjamin Dreyer, *Dreyer's English: An Utterly Correct Guide to Clarity and Style* (New York: Random House, 2019), pp. 93–95.

71. Modern Language Association Style Center, "What Pronoun Should I Use if I Do Not Know the Gender of the Person I'm Writing About?" Apr. 9, 2018, https://style.mla.org/pronoun-when-gender-is-unknown/.

72. Modern Language Association Style Center, "What Is the MLA's Approach to the Singular *They?*" Oct. 3, 2018, https://style.mla.org/singular-they/.

73. APA Style, "Singular 'They,'" https://apastyle.apa.org/style-grammar-guidelines/grammar/singular-they.

74. *Publication Manual of the American Psychological Association*, 7th ed. (Washington, DC: American Psychological Association, 2020): 5.5.

75. *The Oxford English Grammar* (Oxford: Oxford Univ. Press, 1996), pp. 19–20.

76. R. W. Burchfield, *The New Fowler's Dictionary of Modern English Usage* (Oxford: Oxford Univ. Press, 1996), p. 776.

77. Judy Pearsall, ed., *New Oxford Dictionary of English* (Oxford: Oxford Univ. Press, 1998).

78. *New Oxford American Dictionary*, 3rd ed. (New York: Oxford Univ. Press, 2010).

79. Pam Peters, ed., *The Cambridge Guide to English Usage* (Cambridge: Cambridge Univ. Press, 2004), p. 538.

80. Ben Yagoda, tweet. May 5, 2019. https://twitter.com/byagoda/status/1125070840423383041.

81. Ellen Hale, "Linguists Agree: English Language is Less Sexist," *Public Opinion* (Chambersburg, PA), Aug. 29, 1983, p. 2.

Index

WHAT'S YOUR PRONOUN?

Dennis Baron

WHAT'S YOUR PRONOUN?

Dennis Baron

FREQUENTLY ASKED QUESTIONS

What exactly are gender pronouns?

Gender pronouns are the pronouns we use to refer to people.

What are some examples of gender pronouns?

she, her, her/hers—Brett loves her cat and she wants one more.
he, him, his—Brett loves his cat and he wants one more.
they, them, their/theirs—Brett loves their cat and they want one more.
ze, hir, hir/hirs—Brett loves hir cat and ze wants one more.
xe, xem, xyr/xyrs—Brett loves xyr cat and xe wants one more.

What are gender-neutral pronouns?

Gender-neutral pronouns are pronouns that are gender-blind. They essentially ignore gender as irrelevant or needing to be hidden, or they include both genders (assuming only two) or all genders (assuming a more complex and nuanced view of human gender).

Singular *they* used for indefinites is a gender-neutral pronoun: "Everyone forgets their passwords."

What are binary and nonbinary pronouns?

Binary is a term that assumes that there are only two members of a given group or set, or two alternative states of being: *on* and *off* are binaries. Your computer is either *on* or it's *off*. *Dead* and *alive* are binaries: you're one or the other (or like Schrödinger's cat, you're both, but that is still a binary system). *Binary* in reference to gender refers to feminine and masculine. Some language systems have more than two grammatical genders—for example, masculine, feminine, and neuter.

He and *she* are binary pronouns: they assume a person is one or the other.

Nonbinary assumes a group, set, or system with more than two categories or states.

Nonbinary pronouns offer a more complex view of gender and are used to refer to people who do not fit the conventional or simplistic categories of male and female—for example, someone who is genderfluid or gender-nonconforming, or who is not comfortable with the designation of "male" or "female."

Singular *they* is a nonbinary pronoun when used to refer to a person who is nonbinary, trans, or gender-nonconforming: "Brett wants tomato on their burger."

What about pronouns like *zie* and *hir* and *per?*

Zie and *hir* and *per* are examples of nonbinary pronouns: "Brett wants tomato on hir burger."

If I want to share my pronouns, what are some ways of doing so?

If you're at an event, you could write your pronouns on a name tag under your name.

You could include your pronouns in your email signature and in your social media bios.

If you're introducing yourself to someone, you could say, "Hi, my name is Brett, and my pronouns are they/them."

If you're about to start a new class and you want the class to know what your pronouns are, you could email the teacher to ask if they will give students the option of sharing their pronouns.

If someone you know has been using the wrong pronouns for you, you could say, "I just wanted to let you know that my pronouns are actually xe/xem/xyr."

What do you do if you're referring to someone whose pronouns you don't know, as in, "The whistleblower wanted to be sure that _____ identity would be protected"?

The most common fill-in-the-blank solution, which people have been using for centuries, is singular *they*, now recommended by most major style guides. Some people don't like singular *they*, because they think *they* can only be plural. But in fact, singular *they* has always been common, especially in speech, even if the people using it aren't always aware that they're doing so.

Singular *they* is also useful if it's important that the person you're referring to remain anonymous. Maybe you're not shielding a whistleblower but just telling an embarrassing story. Or masking the identity of a patient, a client, even a criminal. Writers sometimes use singular *they* to disguise a character to heighten the effect when the character's true identity is revealed.

What about just saying *he*?

Style guides and grammar books used to recommend *he* when you don't know the gender of the person you're talking about, as in, "The writer should proofread his work," or "The student should make sure he checks to see when the essay is due." This use is called generic *he*. The problem with generic *he* is that it excludes a lot of people. Current style guides recommend you choose an alternative to generic *he*.

What about *he or she*?

Since using just *he* excludes so many people, from the 1970s through the early 2000s some of the "rule makers" recommended using *he or she*, as in, "Everyone should bring his or her lunch to the seminar." The problem is that *he or she* is cumbersome, even silly, especially if you repeat the pronouns several times. Also, it's binary: it's an attempt to be inclusive, but it still leaves too many people out.

What do you do if you're referring to someone who's present but you don't know their pronouns?

That depends. You can try offering your own pronouns, and you can also try asking someone what their pronouns are by saying, "What are your gender pronouns?" or "What pronouns do you use?" Asking for a person's pronouns shows that you're aware of the importance of pronouns and you want to be inclusive.

But some people may not want to be asked. They may think their pronouns are obvious, so why ask? They may not be ready to declare their pronouns. Don't ask if the question might put them on the spot or alienate them.

If you can't ask or you don't think you should ask for some reason, default to *they*. They'll correct you if you make a good faith effort but get it wrong.

Also—and this is important—pronouns are for everyone, so be sure that you aren't asking only those people you think may be trans or queer or nonbinary.

What if you use the wrong pronoun?

If you use the wrong pronoun, apologize quickly and correct yourself. Don't spend a long time on the apology or make a big deal out of it, because that can embarrass the person you're referring to and take attention away from the conversation. For example, you could say, "I told Brett that he—I'm sorry, I mean they—are going to be in charge of this year's cupcake sale."

Can you ask about someone's "preferred pronouns"?

Best not to say "preferred." Saying "preferred pronouns" implies that gender is a preference, when in reality, a person's gender is something innate and integral to their identity. Just ask "What are your pronouns?"—only remember, not everyone wants to answer this question.

What verb should you use with singular *they*?

Most people use the plural with singular *they*: "Brett told me that they are going to take the dog for a walk today"; "Everyone should bring their lunch to the seminar if they want to eat."

However, some people use the singular: *they is*. The singular verb is less common, so you should default to using the plural verb unless you are referring to a person who indicates otherwise. (The second person pronoun shows similar subject-verb agreement: singular *you* takes the plural of the verb—in standard English, *you are*. But some varieties of English use the singular, *you is*.)

Which is it: *themselves* or *themself*?

Usage varies: both *themselves* and *themself* are used.
"Everyone wants to do it themselves."
"Brett went for a walk by themselves."
"Everyone wants to do it themself."
"Brett went for a walk by themself."
Second person pronoun usage is more settled:
"You want to do this yourself." (singular)
"You want to do this yourselves." (plural)

Why is it important to use the "right" pronouns, the exact ones a person uses?

It's painful to be misgendered, and if you use the wrong pronouns for someone, they may feel that their identity is being attacked or questioned. It's important to respect a person's pronouns and make every effort to use them correctly.

Remember: you can't assume you know someone's gender or pronouns based on how they dress or what they look like. If you're unsure of someone's pronouns, you should ask. Use common sense, though; be aware that not everyone may feel comfortable sharing their pronouns, especially in a group setting.

And don't be surprised if someone uses one pronoun for work and another among friends. People are allowed more than one pronoun!

How do you keep from confusing people when using singular *they*?

Long answer: ambiguity is common in speech. If everything we said or signed was clear, people wouldn't have to ask questions.

We expect writing to be clear, because it's not always easy or even possible to ask questions. But some of the most important writing can be ambiguous. If writing was always clear, then literary critics wouldn't disagree about what Hamlet meant when he asked, "To be or not to be, that is the question." If the meaning of sacred texts was clear, people wouldn't argue over whose interpretation was right. If the meaning of laws and contracts was clear, lawyers and judges would have a lot more time for golf and social media.

Pronouns can be ambiguous as well. In modern English, *you* is sometimes singular, sometimes plural. This wasn't always the case. From the ninth through the seventeenth centuries, *thou* and *thee* were the singular second person pronouns, *ye* and *you* were the plural. But in the seventeenth century *you* started to be used as singular as well as plural. Opponents of this change argued that it was a recipe for ambiguity: people won't know if *you* refers to one person or to a group. But English speakers managed to tolerate ambiguous *you*: they developed new unambiguous second person plurals like *y'all*, *y'uns*, and *youse*, as well as *you guys*, which some people reject as sexist, and *you lot*, which tends to be more common in British English than US. And writers simply learned to check their work, to make sure that their prose indicated whether *you* was singular or plural.

Short answer: sometimes it's not clear whether *they* is singular or plural. In face-to-face communication, your audience can always ask you to clarify a pronoun's reference. But when you write you may need to take extra pains to ensure that your meaning is clear.

Example:

Brett wanted to buy their friend something from the new café, but they couldn't decide what to get.

Problem:

Their clearly refers to Brett, but *they* could refer to Brett or to Brett's friend or to both.

Possible solutions:

Brett wanted to buy their friend something from the new café, but Brett couldn't decide what to get.

Brett wanted to buy their friend something from the new café but couldn't decide what to get.

Brett wanted to buy their friend something from the new café, but it was hard to decide what to get.

Can someone make me use their pronouns?

First, let me state for the record that I am not a lawyer. I don't even play one on TV. So keep that in mind when you read these answers.

The long answer: the legal situation isn't entirely straightforward. Many countries protect some form of free speech. For example, Canada, the United Kingdom, and the European Union balance a person's right to say what they want against the right to be protected from harassment and discrimination. In the US, the First Amendment to the Constitution guarantees that the government won't limit your speech in certain important ways (including signing and writing). But the First Amendment says nothing about restrictions on speech that may be imposed by private employers or organizations, or by individuals who are not performing official (government) roles. US antidiscrimination laws, on the other hand, whether or not they say so plainly, may prohibit the intentional and repeated refusal to use someone's pronouns. You might wonder whether such laws conflict with First Amendment protections, but unless the laws are being applied in a government setting, they probably don't raise constitutional problems. That means a free-speech argument in an antidiscrimination case against a private employer—"You can't make me say your pronouns"—probably wouldn't be your first line of defense.

So consider this: you might not get sued for accidentally misusing someone's pronouns. But an intentional and repeated refusal to use a person's pronouns may create a hostile environment at work, or in school, and that could pose a problem for you that requires formal adjudication. Plus in social situations outside of school or work, the intentional misuse of pronouns may produce consequences for you that are, shall we say, suboptimal.

The short answer: the First Amendment gives you certain protections from the government telling you what you can and can't say, but the First Amendment is not the whole story, and it generally doesn't protect you from the consequences of your speech.